SAUDI BABYLON

By Mark Hollingsworth

The Press and Political Dissent: A Question of Censorship

Blacklist: The Inside Story of Political Vetting
– with Richard Norton-Taylor

The Economic League: The Silent McCarthyism
– with Charles Tremayne

MPs for Hire: The Secret World of Political Lobbying

A Bit on the Side: Politicians, Who Pays Them
– with Paul Halloran

The Ultimate Spin Doctor: The Life and Fast Times of Tim Bell

*Defending the Realm: MI5, the Shayler Affair
and the War on Terrorism* – with Nick Fielding

Torture, Corruption and Cover-Up
Inside the House of Saud

SAUDI
BABYLON

Mark Hollingsworth with Sandy Mitchell

MAINSTREAM
PUBLISHING
EDINBURGH AND LONDON

First published in Great Britain in 2005 by
MAINSTREAM PUBLISHING COMPANY
(EDINBURGH) LTD
7 Albany Street
Edinburgh EH1 3UG

ISBN 1 84018 961 4

A catalogue record for this book is available
from the British Library

Typeset in Caslon, Futura and ManzanitaBroad

Printed in Great Britain by
Antony Rowe Ltd, Chippenham, Wiltshire

CONTENTS

PREFACE

'As the Roman, in the days of old, held himself free from indignity, when he could say "*Civis Romanus sum*", so also a British subject, in whatever land he may be, shall feel confident that the watchful eye and the strong arm of England will protect him from injustice and wrong.'

Lord Palmerston, House of Commons, 25 June 1850

The Kingdom of Saudi Arabia is a country of remarkable paradoxes and contradictions. Any Western visitor to Riyadh is struck by its metropolitan, modern features, such as its flashy shopping malls dominated by familiar brands including Gucci, Lacoste, Next and Nike. Beneath a dazzling sun, the contemporary, palatial hotels and vast office buildings cast long shadows over motorways dominated by luxury cars and stretch limousines. And yet Saudis are ruled by strict Islamic customs. As the foreign correspondent Edward Pilkington noted during a visit in 2002, 'McDonald's is seemingly on every street corner and yet it closes its doors five times a day for prayers – making Saudi Arabia unique as a country where the most powerful franchise on earth bends its knees in front of an even stronger brand: Allah.'

There are women shrouded in their long black abayas, shopping with almost religious fervour at the chic Harvey Nichols store inside an elegant glass and steel building designed by the great British minimalist Sir Norman Foster. Then there are the men pouring into a mosque under an enormous neon sign advertising Sony. These everyday sights are as mystifying as they are disconcerting.

Most Saudis are conservative, devout Muslims. But behind the veil, some women, covered from head to toe in their abayas, flirt with a secret life where they discreetly try on provocative, erotic lingerie in the privacy of the opulent boutiques. On any late winter afternoon, meanwhile, drive an hour out into the desert and you might find young, restless men racing their Mercedes and SUVs. After passing the Bedouin shepherds and white-robed elders taking their afternoon prayers, the young Saudis congregate around fires, some drinking the strictly forbidden alcohol, or taking drugs while they listen to radios pounding out the latest Western music amongst the rolling, amber dunes of sand that otherwise are silent. They then race their cars wildly up and down the dunes, young boys hanging out of the windows, whooping and shouting.

This is Saudi Arabia today, ruled by a royal family that craves Western recognition, basks in the protection of American power and revels in the vices of the decadent West. And yet the Saudi royals rigidly and brutally govern the country like a medieval Islamic fiefdom. Despite its ostentatious wealth and the power of its oil, the insular Kingdom is highly secretive and unveils its mysteries only grudgingly.

This book is an attempt to unravel some of these mysteries and to understand the contradictions. The story centres around Sandy Mitchell, an anaesthetic technician at the Saudi Security Forces hospital in Riyadh who was imprisoned and tortured in a Saudi jail for nearly three years.

Sandy's dramatic personal experience highlights how the House of

Saud tried to deceive its own citizens and the rest of the world that Al-Qaeda was not a threat to its authority. Instead, Sandy and other Britons were targeted as expendable scapegoats. These intrepid Westerners – initially warmly welcomed by the Saudis for their professional expertise – were victims of a regime that refused to admit that Al-Qaeda insurgents were behind the devastating bombings in their own country. But they were also sacrificed by the British government on the altar of a foreign policy that appeased the House of Saud because of its oil wealth and strategic military value in the Gulf, not to mention its ongoing purchase of UK arms.

Sandy has emerged from his hell-on-earth experience a humble and forgiving man, but also determined to see that justice is done. It is highly unlikely that he would have survived his three-year ordeal without the tenacious support and selfless campaigning of his sister, Margaret Dunn. Fortunately, both of them kept detailed diaries and notes that have enabled me to reconstruct their dialogue in this book. During every telephone conversation and meeting, Margaret meticulously noted the comments of all the participants, notably Foreign Office and consular officials. I am most grateful to Sandy and Margaret for sharing their extensive private papers as well as their vivid memories – both horrific and fascinating – of this mysterious and dangerous country, Saudi Arabia.

The extraordinary suffering of Sandy Mitchell sheds new light on the hidden political, diplomatic and economic relationship between the House of Saud and the American and British governments. For those chapters I was assisted hugely by two excellent researchers. In Washington DC I was very fortunate to call on Will Ferroggiaro, former head of the Freedom of Information programme at the National Security Archive. His incisive interviews with Chas Freeman, former US ambassador in Saudi Arabia; Walter Slocombe, former undersecretary of state in the US Defence Department; and James Woolsey, former director of the CIA, were invaluable. Will is a researcher and writer on foreign affairs of the highest calibre. In London, I was equally lucky to retain Kate Quine for background research. Her meticulous accuracy and diligence were crucial and I cannot recommend her too highly. She also compiled the photographs.

Among the many people interviewed and consulted for this book, some understandably wish to remain anonymous, but I would particularly like to thank the following: Richard Fields, a lawyer specialising in terrorism and the Middle East at Dickstein, Shapiro, Morin and Oshinsky in New York City; Jason McCue, a senior partner at the London law firm, H2O; Tamsin Allen, a solicitor at Geoffrey Bindman and Partners; Peter Gardiner; the late Sir David Gore-Booth, former British ambassador in Saudi Arabia; Amy Lashinsky; David Leigh, Investigations Editor of *The Guardian*; John Lyons MP; Poppy Martin; and Christopher Thompson, the freelance journalist now in Harare, Zimbabwe. As with my previous books, I am especially indebted to Mary Ann Nicholas who, in addition to helping me in numerous ways, has enhanced the manuscript with her intellectual rigour and tightened the writing with her sharp analysis.

Most of this book was written in Florida at The Four Arts Library in Palm Beach, the West Palm Beach Public Library, and McKeen Towers Library, where the staff, especially Edith Pecan, provided inviting places to write. I also appreciate the staff at Type-It Services for their efficient and swift transcribing of interviews. At Mainstream, this manuscript would have never become a book without the efficiency and flexibility of Graeme Blaikie, editorial coordinator, or the forensic and perceptive eye of his colleague Kevin O'Brien, who expertly edited the manuscript.

Mark Hollingsworth
March 2005

ONE

THE SAUDI INQUISITION

'Based on 20 years as a diplomat, let me tell you that when governments tell you that they cannot speak out in public but are firm in private, they are lying. And even if they do say something in private, the host government will understand from the fact that it is not said in public that this is a formal protest which has no kind of serious intent behind it.'

Craig Murray, British ambassador to Uzbekistan, 8 November 2004

The prisoner is desperately trying to sleep. It is not easy when you are chained to the steel door of a filthy, damp, 5 ft x 8 ft cell with a television camera in the top left-hand corner observing your every move and fluorescent lights burning night and day. Chained to the top of the door by his right hand, he is forced to stand 24 hours a day and cannot reach his thin, foam mattress and plastic water bottle. Even when he goes to the insect-infected toilet – a hole in the floor along the passageway – he can barely sit because he is constantly in chains.

As he half-dozes, eyes heavy with exhaustion, his clothes soaked in blood, faeces and vomit, the prisoner can barely believe his situation. Perhaps it is a bad dream and he will wake from the nightmare. But the chain abruptly jolts him back to reality: it is the second day of his detainment and torture in the notorious Mabatha Interrogation Centre in Saudi Arabia. Known as 'The Confession Factory', Mabatha is not marked on any Saudi map and the ruling royal family like to keep its location secret. Driving south of Riyadh, it can be found past the Ministry of the Interior building. After the final underpass, you turn left and there is a GPS satellite-fixing mast. Further on you turn right to reach the main road and there it is behind an imposing light grey wall.[1]

Suddenly, the door opens and two Saudi guards burst in. 'Get up, get up,' they shout impatiently. Prodding him with a stick, they place a black hood over his head, lock handcuffs on both hands and snap leg irons on his ankles. The prisoner, Sandy Mitchell, a 44-year-old anaesthetic technician from Glasgow, frowns angrily as he notices his chains of torture are branded 'Made in the United Kingdom'.[2]

As he is dragged along the corridor, Sandy hears the screams of the other prisoners. Hauled into the interrogation room upstairs, the hood is removed and he is ordered to stand for the next 20 minutes. Then whack! Suddenly a punch to his stomach almost doubles him up in pain. As he drops to his knees, he is pulled up by his wrist chains and slammed against the wall, still blindfolded and with his handcuffs on. The punches pile in – to his face, groin and kidney. He raises his hands to protect his face, blood pours out of his left ear, but he just receives more blows to his body. Defenceless and helpless, he collapses to the floor. The punches stop.

After a few moments he is dragged up again and thrown against a wall. 'Tell us about the bombings,' one of them shouts, referring to two car explosions which had killed a fellow Briton, Christopher Rodway, and injured three others in Riyadh five weeks earlier, in November 2000.

'I know nothing about the bombings,' replies Sandy.

➤ 'Tell us about your family.'

'What about them?'

'Your wife and son. Were they involved?'

'Don't be fucking stupid,' says Sandy. 'My son is less than two years old and my wife hardly speaks English. What the hell are you talking . . .'

Whack! That earns him another severe beating before he passes out. Soon he is dragged up against the wall and his hood taken off. There he is confronted by his tormentors. One is Ibrahim, a Saudi intelligence officer who reports to the Ministry of the Interior, overseen by Prince Naif Bin Abdul Aziz, one of the most powerful princes in the Kingdom. His skin is pale by Arab standards, and he has light, curly hair with dark green eyes and a deep, intense stare, with a permanent five o'clock shadow. He is barely 5 ft 7 in., with pointed features, a slim build but physically strong, although he rarely inflicts violence unless the prisoner is in chains. Highly strung, he never smiles and makes no secret of his hatred for Westerners. He needs little excuse to fly into a violent rage.

His sidekick, Khaled, is the interpreter. He is taller, well-built, but, like many Saudis, prone to overweight. His top teeth are crowned but some of his teeth are brown and rotting. This does not help his attempts to play the 'good cop' in the interrogation. He appears frightened of Ibrahim, who is often on the verge of lashing out violently. Sandy does not trust Khaled, despite his comments about his prisoner being released, 'Enshallah' (God willing). Khaled tries to ingratiate himself by talking about the sexual misdeeds of Western women living in Saudi. But Sandy is not impressed. As his sister Margaret later remarked: 'His smile never quite reaches his eyes.'

Ibrahim shouts in Arabic at Khaled, who resumes the interrogation. 'We know you carried out the bombings. Confess.'

'You know that I had nothing to do with them,' replies Sandy. 'Look, why don't you talk to my alibi? I was at home with my family. Raf Schyvens [a Belgian trauma nurse] was giving first aid to the victims at the scene of the second bombing, and he called me at home. Why are you doing this?'

'Raf has already confessed,' counters Khaled. 'He said you and Bill [Sampson] carried out the bombings and he only helped you because he was scared of you. He said that you and Rodway were rivals in smuggling alcohol, so you killed him to get him out of the way.'

'Rubbish. I closed down my bar nearly two years ago when my son was born. All the bootleggers are already in jail, and they would have told you that I have not been involved in that business. If Raf said all that, then it was only because you beat him until he was broken.'

That earns him another assault: this time with a one-metre-long, wooden pickaxe handle. Despite the pain, Sandy tries not to scream, because it would give the interrogators a psychological victory. He can hear them chuckling in the background. But he cannot hold out for long. It is only when he can hardly breathe that they finally stop.

'We know you organised it and ordered them,' persists Khaled. 'Tell us, who told you officially to carry out these bombings?'

'What do you mean "officially"? Nobody told me to do anything.'

That produces more punches and kicks. Sandy is then stretched out on the floor face down. A huge Saudi comes into the room. He is at least 22 st. and looks more like a wrestler or a shotput thrower than a prison guard. He sits on Sandy's back while Ibrahim picks up the axe handle and beats the soles of his feet. Sandy screams in agony, his shouts muffled by the 22-st. man on top of him. He is near to passing out when the 'wrestler' gets up. Rolling over into a ball, Sandy gasps for air and screams again. Across the room, the wrestler and Ibrahim are smirking and it appears that they are taking pleasure from their violent power-trip. Sandy is furious. 'You sadistic bastards,' he thinks. 'You must know I am innocent. For years I have cared for Saudi families and this is how they reward me.'

Ibrahim and the wrestler leave the room and Khaled takes a gratuitous kick as Sandy lies on the floor. Retreating to the corner, he hears the screams of another prisoner, Bill Sampson, a friend and expatriate who is also being blamed for the terrorist bombings. Bill's torture goes on for hours as his body and head thud repeatedly against the wall. Part of Sandy wants to pray: 'Please God, let them stop.' But he knows that it will be his turn next.

After what seems like two hours, Ibrahim and Khaled return, grab Sandy by his hair and throw him against the wall. After a lot of Arabic shouting, Khaled interprets: 'Bill said that you ordered and carried out the bombings.'

Sandy knows that Bill would never implicate him, so he stays silent. He knows there is a political agenda: they are covering up for the recent resurgence of home-grown Islamic terrorists. But there is nothing he can do. Sandy is then forced to squat forward with a metal rod placed behind his knees and he is hoisted upside-down with his ankle chains attached to a bar, leaving his bare buttocks exposed. He is then lifted between two desks and Ibrahim lets rip with the axe handle into his buttocks and the soles of his feet.

'Confess,' he shouts, as the blows come down. 'Bill has already confessed.' Sandy knows that is a lie, because otherwise they would not be persisting with the beatings.

'What's the point of confessing to something that I didn't do? You would only come back and beat me into confessing to something else.'

This has no effect and his screams do not produce any sympathy. Sandy thinks that his only chance of survival is to hold out long enough for the British embassy to be informed, and then he'll soon be released.

But there is not much time to think as he stumbles to his knees. Kicks to his back and kidneys and beatings with sticks are then combined with continuous spitting. Soon he is saturated with their phlegm. It only stops because it is prayer time. He is ordered to stand against the wall on one leg. The interrogators then leave the room and wash before prayers. But the irony of worshipping Allah the 'merciful' has little impact on his persecutors. On their return the beatings continue for another hour.

There is only relief when they revisit Bill next door. The horrific screams and the sound of his body bouncing off the walls is heard with depressing regularity. Their next ploy is crude. 'Bill has confessed to having an affair with your wife,' Khaled tells Sandy.

'Bullshit. You are a pair of liars,' he replies angrily. He is then shown photographs of Westerners and officials at the British embassy. He knows some of them but when he does not recognise others, Khaled shouts 'liar' and the beatings resume.

At 8 a.m. Sandy is returned to his cell and is chained to the top of the door. He slumps forward and is desperate to sleep. But just as he is about to nod off, the guard hits him with a stick and he jerks awake. His only sanctuary is daydreaming and his mind wanders off to happier times. But they are short-lived as the reality of his nightmare confronts him. His thoughts turn to his wife, Noi, and two-year-old son, Matthew, and a family holiday on a Thai beach. 'What is happening to them?' he wonders, and his eyes fill up with tears. He silently cries and when the guard arrives to check, he hides his face. This produces another sharp poke in the ribs with the stick. But this time the daydreaming works and he enters another world – a past of family, prospects and adventure.

Alexander 'Sandy' Mitchell was born and raised in Glasgow. He was always interested in new adventures and travelling abroad. As a student, he was unusual in that he signed up as a part-time Territorial Army soldier to help finance his courses through college. He became a medic in the TA and later joined 21 SAS at the Duke of York's headquarters in Chelsea. 'It was not a cloak-and-dagger squad,' he later recalled. 'We were basically an airborne commando unit and we were trained as if we were operating in wartime behind enemy lines. Even for the medics, the training was realistic. I was sent to the casualty department of a busy London hospital. When I wasn't fighting off drunks abusing the staff, I was securing their wounds.'

Sandy became more experienced in dealing with trauma than most medics and was captivated by the military atmosphere, so he joined the Queen's 5th regiment. Within two years he was promoted to full corporal by Major Richard Holmes and also used as a radio operator, acting as the Major's shadow in the field.

In 1982, aged 25, Sandy was offered a job as an anaesthetic technician at the Military Hospital in Saudi Arabia. The irony was that he was hired by mistake. The management company, Allied Medical, confused him with a 'David Mitchell' who had far more experience. Based in the intensive care unit, he would fly out in helicopter ambulances and bring patients in from rural areas. Two years later he was transferred to Baghdad and worked in the Ibn Al-Bitar hospital, which specialised in treating wealthy Iraqis. One of them turned out to be Saddam Hussein's father-in-law, who had his toe amputated. Under Islamic law, the toe needed to be preserved and Sandy had the grisly task of taking it to the morgue. He was given a watch with a portrait of Saddam Hussein for his efforts.

Enthralled by life in the mysterious Arab world, Sandy then joined the Sultan of Oman's army in 1985 at the age of 30. The Sultan's Special Forces were trained by and modelled on the British, so Sandy felt at home. The Omanis are a generous and hospitable people and welcomed him with open arms. Based at the military garrison hospital in Seeb, and later in Salalah, close to the southern border with Yemen, Sandy thrived as a warrant officer.

But he had a restless spirit and in 1992 returned to Saudi Arabia as the chief anaesthetic technician at the Security Forces hospital in Riyadh. As the head nurse of the operating room, Cheryl Eichhammer, later recalled, Sandy was diligent, skilled and a hands-on manager. But it was a holiday in 1995 in Thailand that was the pivotal moment in Sandy's life. There he met a beautiful 21-year-old Thai girl called Noi. For Sandy it was love at first sight. He was captivated by her happy, uninhibited disposition and sense of humour. 'I would find myself studying her every move and when she caught me watching her, I would blush,' he reflected. 'I knew she was the one, or, as the Thais say, "Bupa Sunni Wah". [The one for this life and the next.]'

They married immediately in Thailand and the couple flew to

Riyadh to start their new life. But it was not an auspicious beginning. On their way back from the airport, there was a four-car pile-up and a crowd of Saudis began arguing about culpability. Leaving Noi in the back of the car, Sandy and his friend Ahmad, a doctor, grabbed their first-aid kit and climbed into a wrecked car which had trapped a young man of 20. His throat was cut open. Blood gushed all over them and the boy was taken to hospital. Sandy then walked back to his car. But when his new wife Noi saw her husband covered in blood, she was shocked and wanted to vomit. Later that day, the boy received surgery, in which Sandy participated. He was later discharged and his parents were overwhelmed with joy. Little did Noi know that more dramatic, and far worse, events were to happen in her and Sandy's life together.

Sandy and Noi settled into their new apartment in Riyadh near the Security Forces hospital. But his salary was relatively low and he now had a son to provide for. By the summer of 2000, he considered returning to the UK. But by this time he was a popular figure because of his use of 'wastah' – Arabic for 'to use your influence to help others'. Wastah is the grease that oils the wheels of Saudi life and Sandy was a master of it. Easy-going and jovial, he made friends with both expatriates and Saudis and relished the role of a Mr Fix-It.

As Sandy worked at the Security Forces hospital, he would often receive phone calls from policemen and their families who were trying to get treatment or appointments at short notice. Using his access, he helped them fast-track the system by speaking to the consultant directly. 'The waiting lists were a long and painful experience,' he recalled. 'In Arabic culture, if you help to save the life of an Arab, then they and their extended family are obligated to you for the rest of your life. It is considered a debt of honour.'

In return Sandy called in these debts when people were unfairly detained by the police and he visited them in jail. He was the man who people called when they ran into trouble. 'Because of my rapport with high-ranking officers, I could speed things up if someone was caught in a misdemeanour like drink-driving or speeding or get them off with a warning,' he later said. 'The Saudi police were very cooperative. They like being able to solve problems without going through the official channels.'[3]

Sandy was also well-connected at a higher level because he treated VIPs and children at the hospital. Occasionally he looked after Prince Naif, the interior minister, who would arrive quietly late at night with his four armed bodyguards and always wanted to be put to sleep while his teeth were polished. He was later sent some gold coins and a gold watch by the Prince. He also treated Prince Naif's son, deputy interior minister Prince Ahmed, and they would discuss the use of falcons in hunting.

Softly spoken and always willing to help, Sandy was highly regarded at the hospital. He was particularly adept at relaxing patients before operations and used a glove puppet to explain to children what he was about to do. And so, in October 2000, when Sandy told his employers that he wanted to resign, they were horrified. They immediately offered him a large new house at 28 Villa Compound and a rise in salary. He was delighted and vowed to stay in Saudi for the rest of his working life and then retire abroad.

That all changed two months later, one cool December morning – the kind that comes as a reprise from the relentless Saudi heat. As he was loading his car to go to work, his neighbour Steve came over and asked him, 'Have you heard about the latest car-bombing in Al-Khobar?'

'Another one?' replied Sandy. He already knew about two bombings a month earlier which had killed Christopher Rodway, a British engineer, and injured four others. His friend Raf Schyvens had stopped to give first aid to the victims and was later arrested. Nobody could understand why. He was a trauma nurse. He was obviously being set up. But why?

'Sandy, I know this is ridiculous,' Steve continued, 'but the police are telling us to be careful because they are not looking for Saudis or Arabs to arrest. They are looking to blame Westerners.'

As he drove to work, Sandy reflected on his neighbour's

comments. The problem was that the Saudi police knew that Islamic militants were responsible for the attacks. But the government and intelligence agencies refused to acknowledge the threat and clearly had a hidden agenda. Two days after the Rodway murder, an officer in the Interior Ministry told Sandy that his bosses were blaming Westerners but the police were dismissing the theories. As he drove through the busy traffic, Sandy considered the police reaction as bringing little comfort.

His friend Raf had been detained for two weeks and Sandy was disturbed because he was not being held in a local police station (his police contacts would have told him if he was). That meant he was being detained at an interrogation centre by intelligence officials, who were a law unto themselves.

At 7 a.m. on 17 December 2000 Sandy parked his 4 x 4 across the road from the hospital. Wearing his white coat and stethoscope, he began to think about the patients he was scheduled to see. He was so preoccupied that he did not hear two cars draw up beside him. All he saw was a flash of blue bodywork and suddenly he was thrown against his car and a hood was placed over his head and throat. Ankle chains and a set of handcuffs were snapped on and he was bundled into the car, which drove off at high speed through the city. 'Christ, what's happening?' thought Sandy. 'Kidnapping is unheard of in Saudi Arabia. It happened in Beirut, but never in Riyadh. What's going on?' During the high-speed journey, he was repeatedly punched and kicked in the face and abdomen. His groin was only half-protected by his handcuffs. His assailants yelped as the metal of the cuffs scratched their hands. Throughout the journey Sandy was in a state of disbelief. 'There has been a big mistake. The authorities will find out about this and rescue me for sure,' he thought.

Eventually the car screeched to a halt and Sandy was dragged into the Mabatha Interrogation Centre. Only when the hood was removed did he see the secret-police uniforms and some plain-clothed officers. They immediately stripped him of all his possessions, apart from his trousers, and marched him upstairs to an interview room and slammed the door shut. An hour later Ibrahim, Khaled and a third, unidentified Saudi entered the room. Khaled then asked him for what was to be the first of many times, 'What do you know about the bombings?'

'Nothing. Why should I?' replied Sandy. 'We both know that Westerners had nothing to do with them.'

That resulted in a slap in the face.

'Look, all I know is that you have arrested an American called Mike Sedlak.'

Mike Sedlak worked for the Vinnell Corporation, a US company that trained the Saudi National Guard.

'You know about the bombings.'

'No, I am innocent.'

Sandy's head was then banged against the wall. 'What do you want me to tell you?' he shouted in exasperation. 'That we are responsible for bombings that your own Al-Qaeda is carrying out?'

'Lie!' shouted Ibrahim.

'Before you leave this place you will either confess to these bombings or you will go insane from what we are going to do to you,' added Khaled. 'We are acting with the very highest authority and we can do anything we want. Do you understand? The very highest authority.'

Then the beatings started. The third, heavier Saudi held Sandy's chained hands and legs so the others could wade in. The only reason they stopped was because they got tired. 'Thank God they've stopped,' thought Sandy. 'Surely somebody has realised by now there has been a terrible mistake. I am a medic not a terrorist.'

Then an older man, with short-cropped grey hair and beard, came in and sat down. He stared at Sandy intently and paused. 'Sandy, can you hear me?' he started.

'Yes, I want to speak to my embassy and hospital.'

'You speak to nobody but me.'

'What do you want?'

'I want to know about the bombings.'

'Well, you are asking the wrong person.'

'You are going to tell me. Everybody tells me eventually.'

'I know nothing. Why would I kill innocent Westerners?'

'Oh, we'll get to that later. All you need to do is to tell us about the people who carried it out.'

'There is nothing that I can tell you.'

'You will cooperate. Do what's best for you and your family. Your government doesn't care about you. Why should they? You're expendable.'

The man got up and walked out. Khaled and Ibrahim returned. 'Are you ready to tell us anything?'

'Yes, I want to speak to my embassy and hospital.'

'You've been sacked. Nobody wants anything to do with you. You will soon find out that we are the only friends you have got.'

Sandy was raised up and the beatings resumed. He was then taken to his cell, where he was handcuffed to the top bar of the door. At 6 p.m. Sandy was returned to the torture chamber upstairs.

'OK, Sandy,' said Khaled. 'What I want you to do is to write down a list of anyone who can tell us about the bombings.'

'No, why should I do that? Because you tell me to? No, so you can go and arrest some other innocent people?'

'We are doing this by a process of elimination. Your name has been given to us by other people. We just cross-check their names and beat them also. I'll get you a list of names.'

Sandy looked at the list. They were mainly people he knew or who had been arrested for trivial court fines. It was a meaningless document.

Without warning he was taken downstairs and thrown into the back of a van, which sped away. As the vehicle slowed down, he realised that he was around the corner from his compound. 'We are going into your house,' said Khaled. 'If you do anything to alert your wife or neighbours about what is going on, we will arrest them. If there are any explosives there, we will arrest your family.'

'No problem,' thought Sandy. His only concern was that the secret police might plant evidence in his house. As Sandy was marched into the compound with the handcuffs still on, they were surrounded by some 30 policemen, some with dogs. When he was pushed through the front door, his wife Noi was sitting in front of the television in a T-shirt and shorts. As soon as she saw his chains and the two burly Saudi guards, he saw the terror in her eyes. As Sandy was thrown into a corner, he called out to Noi, 'Don't worry. It's just a big mistake. Everything will be OK.'

'Shut up,' said one of the officers.

They then ransacked the house: nothing was left untouched. They even emptied food on the carpet and opened up bottles of sauce. Some items, like valuable watches, jewellery and pocket computers, went into their pockets, notably a gift from Prince Naif, the interior minister and their ultimate boss. Next was the bedroom of their baby son Matthew, who was hastily picked up by Noi just seconds before the bed was torn apart. Everything was turned over and scattered onto the floor at random. Furniture was broken. Curtains were ripped off the walls. It was sheer vandalism. Then every personal item was thrown into rubbish bags. A horrified Noi rushed over to a neighbour's house clutching Matthew, fighting back the tears. Curled up in a corner, Sandy could only look on, helpless. Sniffer dogs were then brought in. Nothing was found. Noi was in a state of shock, but her abiding memory was of them dragging Sandy away in chains: 'I saw the hatred in the eyes of the Saudis. I feared for his life.'

By the time they returned to the Interrogation Centre, it was 3 a.m. Another beating. It was almost like a ritual. 'You are going to confess to this, Sandy. We know you did the bombings.'

'If you think I did it, where is your evidence?'

That just enraged his interrogator. He crunched the handcuff as tightly as possible. The pain in his wrist prevented him from sleeping and he stayed awake all day. All he could hear were the calls for prayer. Desperate and frightened, Sandy prayed too: 'God, how can you let this happen to me? The Saudi police know that the

Westerners had nothing to do with the bombings. Why are they blaming us?'

For the rest of the day, Sandy reflected on his life. He was no saint, but surely he had done nothing to deserve this barbarity and injustice, he thought.

At 5 p.m. on the third day of his detention, Sandy heard the dreaded rattling of the chains as the guards walked down the corridor. He knew what was coming. Once in the upstairs 'interview room', the guards decided to soften him up for the main event: by the time the intelligence officers arrived, Sandy had lost a tooth and broken two more, blood poured from his nose and he was covered in his own vomit. He was then suspended upside down with his legs hanging over a steel bar while Ibrahim battered him with an axe handle. Eventually, it stopped with the inevitable 'Bill said this' or 'Raf told us that.'

By this stage Sandy knew that time was running out. Everyone has a breaking point and one of them would confess. His thoughts turned to what he had read about the Spanish Inquisition, when poor souls were tortured and burned at the stake after they confessed to witchcraft. Ironically, sorcery was one of the crimes that still warranted the death sentence in Saudi Arabia. Many women, mostly Asian, are in Saudi jails after being flogged for 'confessing' to witchcraft.

Through the cell wall Sandy could hear the defiance of his friend Bill and his subsequent screams. But their resilience was getting weaker by the hour. The next day was a routine assault and battery combined with spitting. By now Sandy could not answer their claims because his head was spinning and he was passing out. The best he could manage was to mumble and slur an answer through his swollen mouth, parched throat and broken teeth. His head felt as though it would explode and eventually a doctor saw him and took his blood pressure. It was 170 over 120.

'Try to relax more,' said the doctor.

'But I am being tortured,' replied an astonished Sandy.

'Well, they all say that. I am not allowed to give you medication. You'll just have to cope the best you can.'

An hour later, at 6 p.m., another nightly ritual of grievous bodily harm was inflicted. 'Everyone else has admitted it and they will receive mercy from the King,' shouted an impatient Khaled. 'But because you are stupid, you will lose your head.'

The Saudi secret police then used their trump card. While Sandy was hanging upside down, vomiting what was left in his stomach, Khaled sidled up to him: 'We have the authority from the very highest level to obtain your confession. We can do anything. You have a wife here. She is Thai. We can do anything we want. Do you understand? Your embassy won't help you. Do you think they will lift a finger to help your wife? We will bring her in here and you will listen to her screams and it will be your fault because . . .'

'OK, OK. What do you want me to say?'

'We want the truth,' said Khaled with a rare smile. 'You carried out the bombings with Bill and Raf.'

'If that is what you want. Now can I call my embassy?'

That resulted in a frenzy of violence with the blood-covered axe handle until Sandy passed out. Hung up like a chicken by an iron bar behind his legs, Sandy's resistance was wilting as dawn broke. That day he was again denied sleep. He was now close to breaking point. He could not doze because the guards walked by every ten minutes. He silently prayed: 'Oh God. Please protect my wife and son from these sadistic bastards. Please let me die and put an end to this agony.'

An hour after sundown, the Saudis inflicted more lashings from the axe handle and sensed that he was broken. 'We have sent a car to collect your wife,' said Khaled as a sweating Ibrahim sat down. 'Perhaps you will cooperate when you hear her screams in the next room.'

'OK.'

'Who gave you the orders to carry out the bombing? We want the names of your controllers at the British embassy.'

As Sandy did not want to endanger the lives of anyone at the embassy, he fabricated two names in the hope that the government would be alerted.

'Duncan McDonald and Tom Brooks.'

'They are embassy officials, right?' shouted Khaled. 'They gave you the orders so we would think it was Islamic extremists.'

'Yes.'

Sandy was broken, humiliated and ashamed for falsely accusing his embassy of terrorist crimes. He was then placed in a chair. But his buttocks were hurting so much from the beatings that he could not sit down and kept slipping onto the floor.

Suddenly the atmosphere changed. One of the secret policemen brought Sandy some sweet tea. 'We know everything because we have broken your friend and we have an agent inside your embassy,' said Khaled. 'Now we will only beat you if you give us the wrong answers. Your wife will be safe as you cooperate. Right, so you did the bombings on behalf of your embassy. Who was your team? Who was with you?'

'I did it myself.'

'Liar! We know you have more intelligence cells operating in Saudi.'

The beatings resumed. Sandy collapsed in a heap and was slapped to keep him from nodding off. He resumed his death plea to God.

Just before sunrise, Khaled returned with a new version: 'You received your orders from McDonald and Brooks and they delivered the bombs later.'

'Yes,' replied Sandy, desperately hoping that the embassy would discover his plight and rescue him from this hell on earth.

On Christmas Day 2000, eight days after his arrest and his son's second birthday, Sandy reflected that he had confessed to being a spy, a terrorist and a killer. Driven mad from sleep deprivation, he was rambling incoherently to himself, hallucinating and conducting conversations with his mother, who had died six years earlier. She assured him that soon everyone would know that he was innocent.

His delusions were shattered when a guard ordered him to wash the blood and excrement off and use the toilet. Sandy began to try to rationalise his situation: why were we being tortured to implicate British diplomats in a terrorist act against a 'friendly state'? Could it be that Al-Qaeda has infiltrated the Ministry of the Interior to blame the Western infidels?

Later that day he was in despair and convinced himself that he would never see his young family again. When his meal arrived, he reached up and scraped out a one-and-a-half-inch screw from the wall. When he heard the guard coming, he quickly swallowed it with some food. He hoped that the screw would cause internal bleeding and end his life. 'At least if I die in custody,' he thought, 'they would not be able to use my false confession against the embassy officials and my friends.' He choked on the screw, but it had no lasting impact apart from stomach pains and cramps. It was a cry for help as much as a suicide attempt.

CLANG. The chains fell off Sandy with a loud crash and he collapsed to the floor. It was early the next morning and he was barely conscious as he was dragged outside into a waiting unmarked van. As they sped across the desert, Sandy kept passing out from fatigue, only to be woken up by the guards with slaps across his face. He had no idea where he was going until he saw a modern building made entirely of steel and stone. It was Al-Hiar prison, standing alone on the rocky landscape south-west of Riyadh, its walls rising starkly out of the desolate desert.

At first the air-conditioned prison seemed like a haven of civilisation compared to the Interrogation Centre. Sandy's hood and chains were removed and he was allowed to strip off his blood-stained ripped clothes for the first time in nine days. He was permitted a shower, which felt like paradise, and was told that he could sleep. When the governor, Colonel Said, arrived, he appeared distressed to see Sandy's body was completely black with bruises from the waist down and his feet were so swollen they looked deformed. 'What happened?' he asked.

'I've been tortured,' replied Sandy.

The doctor then inspected his body and immediately asked him to sign a statement which confirmed that his injuries only occurred before his arrival at Al-Hiar prison. As he was producing blood in his urine and his kidneys were severely bruised, the doctor told him to drink plenty of water. 'Great, if you can get the guards to give me some,' replied Sandy.

He was then escorted to his cell, which was an improvement on his previous accommodation. About 5 ft x 10 ft, it was clean, with a toilet and shower, a stool and a stone bed with a two-inch thick foam mattress and a blanket. A CCTV camera in the top left-hand corner kept him under 24-hour surveillance. As soon as the steel door closed, Sandy collapsed and slept for some 15 hours.

After a meal, a black Saudi introduced himself as the captain in charge of the wing. He was cordial and appeared embarrassed by what his fellow countrymen had done. 'Is there anything you need?' he asked.

'Something to read and access to my embassy,' replied Sandy.

'You cannot contact your embassy but I will get you a book.'

After the captain left, Sandy fell to his knees and prayed. He begged God for his private hell to end. He was interrupted by a guard who brought him a bottle of water and an English copy of the Qur'ān. 'Keep praying and God will help you,' whispered the officer. For the next three days he lay on the bed and read the Qur'ān. Although he felt abandoned, he took comfort from a story in which a boy called Yousef was betrayed by his brothers, sold into slavery and imprisoned for a crime that he did not commit. He spent many years in prison before the injustice was discovered. The boy was released and, as the Qur'ān described it, 'raised to a higher station in life' and forgave his brothers, who had abandoned him.

Sandy wondered if he could be as benevolent as Yousef. But as he lay in his cell, his only emotions were hatred and contempt for the torturers who were covering up for terrorists.

On the third day at Al-Hiar, the tranquillity was broken when he was blindfolded and chained and taken upstairs to an interview room. Waiting for him were his old friends Khaled and Ibrahim. 'OK, we know everything,' said Khaled. 'We know you were ordered to carry out the bombings by your embassy. We want the names. You have no idea how far we will go. You will beg us to stop.'

Ibrahim then produced a stick from under the desk and laid into Sandy. This time, Sandy managed not to scream. Khaled showed him photographs of all the diplomats at the British embassy in Riyadh and demanded their names. Sandy could not identify all of them, so Khaled kept pointing at the picture of Simon Macdonald, then the first secretary, who later became private secretary to Jack Straw and is now the British ambassador in Israel. 'Tell us about Macdonald,' he shouted. 'Why did he give you the order? We know you are a spy. We know that your embassy is trying to cause problems for our country, because we have an agent inside the building. You are trying to deceive us into thinking that Islamic militants are doing the bombings.'

'Well, they are responsible. Why would the British government kill their own people?'

'There is no Al-Qaeda working in the Kingdom,' screamed Khaled. 'It is the Westerners who are causing the trouble.'

After a further two days of beatings, Sandy's resistance faded as he fell into incoherent stupors. 'Think of your wife and son,' said Khaled. 'They are here. The British won't help a Thai woman. Do you really think the embassy will send troops in to rescue you? Think about your family.'

'OK, OK,' replied Sandy. He agreed that he was a low-level MI6 agent and ordered by Simon Macdonald to coordinate the atrocity. He was also forced to implicate Ian Wilson, then consul and now in Beijing, in the conspiracy. Sandy believed that both officials would be protected by diplomatic immunity. He also thought the allegation was so ridiculous that nobody would take it seriously anyway. And that other terrorist attacks would demonstrate that the Saudis had arrested the wrong people.

Over the next several days, Sandy was ordered to rehearse his 'confession' repeatedly: that he was part of an MI6 operation to destabilise Saudi Arabia and undermine its international credibility. The interrogations, combined with intermittent beatings, lasted 12–14 hours.

On returning to his cell, it was clear the guards were ashamed by the Saudi intelligence officers. 'Please do not judge the Saudi people by these officers. Keep praying,' said Colonel Said, the governor, a tall, slim, educated man who always wore traditional Saudi dress. His visits brought a tiny glimmer of hope and he arranged for the doctor to treat Sandy after every interrogation. But his power was limited. 'I cannot get involved,' he added. 'I have no control over Khaled and Ibrahim because they work for intelligence. My job is to run the prison. I am sorry.'

Meanwhile, Noi had been too frightened to tell the British embassy about her husband's plight. Two Saudi secret policemen regularly visited her to ransack the house and threaten her. 'If you leave the Kingdom, we can bring your son back and put you in prison,' said one. 'The British government will do nothing for you.' She felt that if she said anything, Sandy would be tortured. But the absence of knowledge was too much to bear and, on 6 January 2001, she informed the embassy. For nearly two weeks the Saudis refused to grant consular access, despite requests by the Foreign Office. Then, on 28 January 2001, Noi accompanied Gary Tible, the vice-consul, to the prison. When Sandy shuffled in, Tible, who knew him well, was shocked to see a haggard skeleton of a man who could barely lift his feet. It was a symbolic meeting because Sandy had been warned by Ibrahim: 'Don't complain. Deny your statement and we start all over again.' After ten minutes, during which Tible was not allowed to discuss the case, Noi came in with Matthew for a tearful reunion.

After several more beatings, Sandy was told that they needed a film of his confession which would purely be for Ministry of Interior records and not for outsiders. It would be shown to Prince Naif to appeal for clemency. The next day Sandy, Bill Sampson and Raf

Schyvens were escorted under heavy armed guard to an interview room in the prison which contained several video cameras. Sitting behind an oak desk, the Saudi flag to one side and several maps and photographs scattered in front of him, Sandy looked dazed, frightened and pale. He squinted at the TV autocue and hesitantly began his confession. Using stilted language in a monotone voice, he read nervously from a statement which was riddled with grammatical errors:

> I confirmly confess that I was ordered to carry out an explosion here in Riyadh which took place on Friday, 17 November 2000. The explosion was directed against Mr Christopher Rodway, who is a British nationality. I was assisted by Dr William Sampson. I placed the explosive device under the driver's seat of Christopher's car. William detonated the remote control, which caused the explosion. A second explosion was authorised and we carried out the order in a car which was similar to that of Christopher Rodway.

One by one, the men stared into the camera and read out identical phrases and details to describe their terrorist acts. Sandy even used a pointer stick on a map to show how he carried out these attacks, but did not say who gave the instructions or why. The recording took several hours, with numerous retakes as the men were told to read different versions of the statement.

The men were suspicious about the taping session and they were right. For, on the evening of Sunday, 4 February 2001, their confessions were broadcast on Saudi television. But as observers and relatives watched Sandy's heavily edited statement the next morning, they were sceptical as well as shocked. Sandy was reading from a prepared script and wore a drained expression of submission on his face and a zombie-like appearance. He seemed confused, unsure of himself and even drugged. 'I couldn't believe my ears,' recalled Margaret Dunn, his sister. 'This man was confessing to planting a bomb that killed another British man in Saudi Arabia and it was my brother.' She simply did not believe it. 'I saw him but he just didn't look like Sandy, who was a big man, physically and in personality.' She stared at the television set. 'Don't be daft,' said her husband, Phillip. 'Mitchell is a common enough name and look at him: it's not your Sandy.' It was only when she heard his middle names that she accepted the upsetting reality.

Immediately after the broadcast Prince Naif, the minister of the interior, announced on Saudi television that his department's investigation concluded that Sandy, Bill Sampson and Raf Schyvens were guilty. 'I would like to reiterate that no Saudi was involved in the bombings,' he said. 'Thanks to the almighty Allah and to the intensive efforts exerted by the security organs and, in particular, the intelligence administration, we have been able to discover the facts. We pray to the almighty Allah to protect our country and keep it away from all evils.' He claimed to know the motive, but was withholding details, pending more investigations. The Prince added that the men would be tried under sharia law, which stipulates execution for convicted murderers.

Languishing back in his cell, Sandy was not aware that his confession was headline news throughout the world. He reflected that he would have confessed to anything – murdering President Kennedy, being Lord Lucan or blowing up the Houses of Parliament. The frequent threats about torturing his wife and the relentless beatings were easily sufficient to break his resistance. The will to survive exceeded everything, except when the pain was so excruciating that suicide invaded his thoughts.

Three days after the broadcast, two solemn guards appear in Sandy's cell, handcuff him and place a dark blue velvet hood over his head. As he is led to his next interrogation, the corridors seem longer and it feels like an unfamiliar route. He can hear some guards talking and gathering. 'Something is wrong,' he thinks. Inside the room he waits for 20 minutes in an eerie silence. He is told to kneel down. Then it dawns on him. This is it. He is going to be executed. Anguished thoughts about his family and friends race through his mind as he kneels down, his head bowed. About ten minutes pass by and then 'thwack' – a sharp pain on the back of his neck and his darkness becomes blacker. He passes out. 'Am I dead?' he thinks. Then he hears Ibrahim shouting and laughing. No, it is a sick joke, and to make matters worse, he wakes up to find himself covered in his own vomit.

Ibrahim then takes out what appears to be a dismantled bomb from a plastic bag. It is disc-shaped and about ten inches in diameter – as opposed to the square device shaped like a brick which he described during his televised confession. There is also a metal tin and a nine-volt battery.

'Pick them up,' shouts Ibrahim.

'No way,' replies Sandy, knowing that his fingerprints would then be on an explosives device. Inevitably, this produces a frenzied bout of assault and battery and he handles the incriminating items. He has been framed and his only compensating thought is that no self-respecting judge would convict him. Ibrahim spits in his face and leaves the room but returns for more spitting and hitting.

After being beaten by Ibrahim, Sandy is returned to his cell in the early hours. At 10 a.m. a senior sergeant comes in and asks him to pray. He opens Sandy's copy of the Qur'ān and reads an extract to himself quietly in Arabic: 'Allah loves not the shouting of evil words, except by one who has been wronged. For they have the right to public redress.' The sergeant then leaves the page open, points to the section without saying a word and leaves the cell.

Sandy is amazed. Clearly, the sergeant had carefully selected the quotation. He watches him walking away, searching for any sign of sympathy, but he doesn't look back. Clearly, the senior official is sympathetic but equally helpless. The prisoner will need other sources of help to secure his release.

33

TWO

CAUGHT IN AL-QAEDA'S WAVE OF TERROR

'The Kingdom welcomes a visit by Amnesty International or others any time. We have nothing to hide or fear . . . They will find that the reality of our prisons and inmates does not conform with what is rumoured or said about them.'
Lt-General Ali Hussein Al-Harithi, general director of prisons in Saudi Arabia, *Arab News*, December 2001

In the House of Saud few members cast a longer and darker spectre than Prince Naif Bin Abdul Aziz, controller of the secret police and chief of general intelligence since 1 September 2001. Known as the 'Prince of Shadows', he is the pillar of the regime. The minister of the interior since 1977, he is arguably the second most powerful man in the Kingdom, behind Crown Prince Abdullah. Naif chairs the supreme committee on the Hajj, the pilgrimage to Mecca required of all Muslims, and oversees the notorious Commission for the

Promotion of Virtue and Prevention of Vice – in effect, the religious police. And he wields enormous influence as head of the Press Information Council, which licenses newspapers. Each month editors of all publications meet Naif and are told what is 'permissible and desirable'. A full brother of the King, his authority is so extensive that he is empowered to approve the exact words used by newspapers to describe other Middle East leaders.[1]

An effective, populist, if sinister, politician, Prince Naif is the authentic Saudi conservative nationalist who believes there are Christian and Jewish conspiracies against the Kingdom and deliberately panders to the fears and prejudices of the masses. One former diplomat described him as a combination of the evangelist Rev. Franklin Graham, the late right-wing US Senator Jesse Helms and the American radio commentator Rush Limbaugh. 'He is happy to appeal to the Saudi equivalent of a redneck vote,' said a former US ambassador in Saudi Arabia.

Not known personally as a pious man, Prince Naif's education was dominated by Muslim theology and he zealously defends Islamic puritanism. He encourages jihad (holy war) by presiding over the Saudi fund for the support of the Palestinian intifada and offers Al-Qaeda tacit support by barely acknowledging its existence. In one interview with an Arab magazine, Naif even absolved the Saudi hijackers of responsibility for 9/11. He stated that the Saudi operatives could not possibly 'have the capability to act in such a professional way' and mastermind an operation of such magnitude. Even Bin Laden was 'a tool of others'. Instead he maintained that it was an Israeli intelligence plot to destabilise the Kingdom. He argued that the attacks aroused so much hostility to Muslims that they must have been undertaken by enemies of Islam. 'We say that these people were either agents or ignorant,' he said.[2]

This statement, made over a year after 9/11, not only endorsed the radical clerics' conspiracy theory, but, more significantly, sent a message to Saudi Al-Qaeda operatives that the secret police would not track them down. Prince Naif could not bring himself to admit that Saudi Arabia was under threat by its own Islamic insurgents. 'He is in total denial,' the late Sir David Gore-Booth, former British ambassador to Saudi from 1993 until 1996, told the authors. 'He cannot – or does not want to – accept that Al-Qaeda is a real force in the Kingdom. Unless he wakes up to the fact that Bin Laden has a large pool of potential recruits among the disaffected youth and he is given legitimacy by the radical clerics, then the bombings will continue.'

It was in this atmosphere in the summer of 2000 that Bin Laden's fanatical network of activists were planning their bombing campaign. The frontline of their jihad was Saudi, the home to Islam's holiest shrines, and their aim was to frighten away the large number of expatriates on whom the oil economy depends. Bin Laden had already declared war on Saudi and its infidel ally the United States, and by 2000 was able to draw on thousands of disillusioned, unemployed graduates aged between 25 and 41. A Saudi intelligence survey, obtained by the *New York Times*, concluded that 95 per cent of them supported Al-Qaeda.

Bin Laden openly said that it was the 'duty' of Muslims to kill Americans and their allies – civilian or military. And his followers responded to the call. On 9 August 2000, a Saudi student fired on expatriates at a housing compound on the Khamis Mushayt airbase. Two months later, on 12 October 2000, seventeen servicemen on board the US warship *The Cole* were killed by Islamic suicide bombers in Yemen. At the same time, a bomb was thrown over the wall of the British embassy in the capital of Yemen, Sana.

A month later, on 17 November 2000, Christopher Rodway, a British hospital engineer, and his wife Jane pulled up in their American GMC 4 x 4 jeep at traffic lights in central Riyadh. Seconds later their car exploded, shattering the silence of the Muslim holy day of prayer. The bomb almost amputated Rodway's leg and, despite the best efforts of frantic fellow motorists, he died later that day. His wife Jane survived with minor injuries. Five days later, a second car bomb went off and injured two British defence workers

CAUGHT IN AL-QAEDA'S WAVE OF TERROR

and two nurses. They were driving down Riyadh's old airport road after 'chucking out time' at an improvised bar. And when a third explosion caused a British business executive to lose his eye in the eastern city of Khobar on 15 December 2000, pressure on the police intensified.

Terrified that instability would frighten away foreign investors and sensitive to Saudi's international image, Prince Naif decided to act. Two days later, Sandy Mitchell and his friend William Sampson were arrested, along with six other foreigners, for alcohol offences. That did not stop the terrorism and three more bombs were detonated, shattering the myth that the detentions had brought security. One of them ripped apart a telephone booth and car in a shopping mall in Riyadh and a note by Islamic militants was left at the scene.

This was the first clue to the culprits' identity. But evidence and warnings that the Al-Qaeda network were behind the attacks were suppressed, according to an investigation by *The Guardian*.[3] As Saudi opponents and Westerners were rounded up, the Ministry of the Interior received a letter warning that more bombings would follow unless the 'mujahideen youths' who had been arrested and tortured were released. In London, Dr Saad Al-Fagih, a prominent Saudi dissident and head of the Movement for Islamic Reform in Arabia, said, 'The government knows it was jihadi groups behind all these four attacks. They just do not dare to admit it . . . My sources clearly say that this is a cover-up. Prince Naif is obsessed with not allowing the Saudi regime to appear weak in the face of internal dissent. The easiest way to deflect attention from the fact that Saudi terrorists were behind these crimes is to blame the very people they were targeting: the Westerners.'[4]

Other well-connected Saudi dissidents, like Abdul Aziz Al-Khamis, director of the Human Rights Centre, say the random attacks were committed by small fundamentalist groups, affiliated to but not part of Al-Qaeda. 'They want to make a noise and embarrass the government but do not have the full firepower and logistics, so they choose smaller, softer, easier targets,' said another source, who asked not to be identified. 'There is an ideological war taking place in Saudi Arabia,' said Anjem Choudary, UK director of Al-Muhajiroun, a militant Islamic Iranian group. 'People are upset about Westerners coming to Islamic countries and those regimes that are, in effect, allowing them to drink alcohol, open pubs and discos, go on the beach. And so, of course, there will be Muslims who will take the law into their own hands, and if the Westerners are targeted, then they have only themselves to blame.'[5]

In total 14 Westerners were arrested for bombings that killed, blinded and maimed fellow expatriates. The House of Saud, desperate to deflect attention away from an Al-Qaeda-inspired rebellion, then set up an elaborate smokescreen. Prince Ahmed, deputy interior minister, denied there were fundamentalists in the Kingdom and added, 'These crimes have no political relevance.' He then claimed that Sandy Mitchell and co. had set off car bombs as part of a 'turf war' between feuding expatriate bootleggers, cashing in on the lucrative illegal alcohol trade.

But in linking the crimes to an underground drinking racket between rival factions, the Saudi royal family only drew attention to one of its best kept secrets – how its princes and Westerners enjoy an illegal, decadent lifestyle.

On the surface, Saudi Arabia is a devout, conservative, strict Islamic state. But underneath there is a secret underbelly of alcohol, drugs, illicit sex and private clubs. Wealthy members of the House of Saud enjoy hosting parties where vice is never far away. 'I've gone to some parties where things were getting pretty frisky,' recalled Hugh Moran, a former US ambassador to Saudi Arabia and one of the few who refused to cultivate business interests there. 'On one occasion I began to smell something in the air and someone said, "Yes, Mr Ambassador, you know what that is," and it was hash and then people were being thrown into the pool, so I said, "This is the time to get the hell out of here. This is no place for American diplomats to be seen."'[6]

Arab prostitutes would also be present at these parties. In 2000 a list of Saudi princes who hired call-girls was obtained by an official in the Interior Ministry. When Prince Naif, who is obsessed by sex and regularly consults doctors about a cure for his impotence, according to former CIA officer Robert Baer[7], was informed about the document, he called the subordinate. He told the official to withhold the 'client list' from the police and not to release it under any circumstances.[8]

However, it is alcohol, strictly forbidden under sharia law and punishable by flogging and jail, that is most available. There is even a royal drinking den called 'The Kingdom Compound'. The royal family are heavily involved in alcohol smuggling, mainly from neighbouring Bahrain and Dubai on their private jets, according to dissident sources. Most of the merchandise is hidden in an anonymous container with a label declaring ownership. The booze is brand-named and expensive: a bottle of malt whisky costs more than $200. In 2001 Customs officials in Bahrain searched by mistake the cargo of a plane belonging to a Saudi prince that was about to leave for Riyadh. They found 200 cases of whisky, worth about $300,000. Under the rules of Gulf etiquette, Customs should not have pried. Apologies followed and the plane was allowed to take off.[9]

For those princes who seek vice abroad, the liquor is brought out by the flight attendants as soon as the aircraft leaves Saudi airspace. So much Johnnie Walker Black Label whisky was drunk during one flight to Paris that they ran out. Once in Europe, the royals are notorious for their outrageous behaviour which, if Islamic law were applied, would result in public flogging or a healthy stint in jail. 'They would be totally wild,' said Steve Sillianoodis, who worked for the House of Saud for 30 years. 'They would get drunk and then flirt or grope someone else's girlfriend and, of course, this would create a commotion. The police then arrived and they would pay off the police and the club, so everyone went home happy and they would not press charges . . . It was part of my job to pay off the media to keep them quiet . . . Some people got killed because of their bad [drink] driving, but they never showed any remorse.'[10]

Alcohol is available at all levels of Saudi society as long as it is discreet. A convoy of some 25 cars often drives out to the desert late at night and parks in a group. Bonfires are then lit and the group, mainly younger Saudis, sit around drinking. Those with a taste for the strong stuff will imbibe 'sedeeqi' (Arabic for 'my friend'), a home-made concoction of sugar-water and yeast which is distilled and purified like vodka. Escaping a jail term for getting caught depends on status. If a Saudi is found guilty of drink-driving, it will be kept quiet. If a Filipino is found drinking, he or she will be publicly flogged.

Despite the law, the government allows foreign embassies to import a quota of legal alcohol. But, for Westerners outside the diplomatic circle and unwilling to pay the exorbitant prices of the bootleggers, a thriving cottage industry of underground clubs and home-brewed beer, wine and spirits has emerged. Sensitive to the stifling heat and heavily restricted social life of their employees, companies have set up their own bars. British Aerospace has eight compounds and each one has a huge long bar with a restaurant and club, surrounded by a 15-ft wall. The bar at Cable and Wireless is called 'White Elephant' and the profits are sent to the UK for the charity Dogs for the Blind. And Boeing has set up two pubs.

The expat drinking scene is tolerated by the Saudi authorities, who view it as a regrettable consequence of the country's reliance on foreign labour. Alcohol is not officially condoned but a modest bribe is sufficient to persuade the local police commander to look the other way. For Sandy Mitchell – gregarious, sociable and an active user of wastah – the drinking scene was his outlet to alleviate the tedium of Saudi life. He set up his own pub, the Celtic Corner, a small-scale bar on a compound of 15 houses in Riyadh. It became a social refuge for expats who wanted a quiet beer after work, a game of darts or a sneaky bacon sandwich, away from the prying eyes of the religious police. Home-brew and imported gin and whisky – smuggled in the false bottoms of lorries or the holds of oil tankers – and sedeeqi were the order of the day.

Sandy, and his co-manager Les Walker, had to play a careful game. Occasionally they were raided and for a few weeks their clientele would stay at home. Their phones were tapped by the security services and so they placed their orders in code and club members carried fake identity cards. Sandy was known as 'Kipper', his nickname at the Empire Club.[11] As long as the illicit drinking was confined to the compounds, the police turned a blind eye provided they were paid off. But it was far from the bootlegging gangs of Chicago during the prohibition period of the 1920s.

A feature of the expat drinking scene was the camaraderie and bonhomie of the bar managers. Their motive was not commercial. After all, they were already on tax-free high salaries. It was to escape the unmitigated boredom of life in Saudi outside work. There were no cinemas or theatres and very few restaurants. Drinking coffee in a hotel lounge was about the most exciting pastime for a Westerner. The pubs, decked out in an English style, were a welcome respite and there was a friendly, cooperative bond between them. As long as the bosses were careful, it was a comfortable life. In 1998 that was shattered when the Empire Club, the largest and most profitable drinking club, was raided by the mutawwa, the religious police. The House of Saud was under increasing pressure after Al-Qaeda bombed US embassies in Kenya and Tanzania. Mindful of growing fundamentalism and always willing to appease the clerics, the authorities were no longer lenient on anti-Islamic behaviour.

The co-manager of the Empire Club, Mary O'Nions, a former assistant nursing director, was jailed for three months in horrific conditions. Sandy lobbied the British embassy on her behalf and arranged for women friends to visit her in prison regularly. They brought her food and toiletries. When she was released, he retrieved her passport from contacts in the governor's office and helped her to leave the country. Her husband, Gary O'Nions, 55, was the other co-manager. He was on holiday during the raid, but returned using a new name. Fearful of arrest, he decided to flee. Sandy taught him desert survival techniques and Gary was driven to the border town of Al-Khobar. After spending several weeks in training, he walked, by night, the 35 km across the desert to Dubai. Six months later Gary returned and opened more bars in Riyadh but was arrested a year later and served two years in a Saudi jail.[12]

With the Al-Qaeda threat looming, the relaxed attitude to expat drinking was gone. When his son Matthew was born on 25 December 1998, Sandy resigned from running the Celtic Corner, although he occasionally used it as a customer. He knew that he would be too busy looking after his child.

For the expats running the bars, the notion that Sandy and his friends murdered other British citizens as a way of removing the competition was risible. Firstly, his 'victim', Christopher Rodway, had never met Sandy and was not involved in the business in any way. Secondly, the 'turf war' among the managers did not exist. In fact, quite the opposite, because they helped each other obtain supplies. 'We had a waiting list of thousands, so we really welcomed other people starting clubs,' said Mary O'Nions. 'All our members were also members of other clubs. There was no hostility or rivalry . . . You could not afford a turf war, because you might need to borrow a bottle of whisky from another club.'[13] Gary O'Nions agreed: 'It was a myth. The bars operated on the basis of cooperation, not conflict.'[14]

However, assassinating a rival bootlegger using C4 plastic explosives like a gangster was the official version of events given by the authorities for Sandy's detention. As the bombings against Westerners continued for months after his arrest, Prince Naif sounded like the Iraqi minister of information during the 2004 Gulf War who denied that Baghdad was under threat as the US tanks entered the city. 'There are no terrorist attacks against foreigners in our country,' he announced. 'What is happening is score-settling and feuds between groups competing in illegal trade and immoral issues.'[15]

In any case, Sandy could not have committed the atrocities.

The police claimed that he was driving behind Rodway's jeep and detonated it by remote control. But on the day in question, 17 November 2000, his car was being repaired in the GMC dealership in Riyadh, as the invoice and his Visa credit card receipts demonstrate. As they were moving house within a few days, Sandy and his family spent that day shopping and at home. Testimony from his neighbour Steve and the CCTV footage from the mall, which the Saudis refused to inspect, would prove this incontrovertibly. There was no forensic evidence or examination of the bomb device. No fingerprints were taken. There were no witnesses. The televised confessions, in English with an Arabic voice-over, were transparently implausible and the product of extensive torture and intimidation. A criminal psychologist, Ian Stephen, who was the expert adviser on the TV series *Cracker*, concluded after watching the confessions: 'They look as if they're reading something. They look apprehensive and afraid to make any kind of comments which are contrary to what they've agreed with their captors. If he's been the subject of lengthy questioning, stress, loss of sleep and with a lot of threats put to him, then he's going to say, "I will say what you want me to say. Please get me out of this. I can't cope with this any more." . . . The whole body language suggests to me that this is a man who has just gone in there and said, "I did it."'[16]

Within days of Sandy's and Bill Sampson's arrest, Prince Naif publicly declared that they would be subject to sharia law and not be given preferential treatment. 'We cannot accept interference by anybody in matters like this or treat one person differently from others, regardless of nationality, although each country can follow up the interests of its citizens,' he said.[17]

But Naif did not follow his own laws within a few days of Sandy's arrest. In 1983 he had issued a new executive order which 'forbids arrest or detention of anyone unless there is ample evidence calling for his arrest and stipulates that investigation should be completed within three days of detention.'[18] In Sandy's case, no evidence was offered and it was six weeks before he saw a consul from the British embassy, who was not allowed to discuss his case or treatment – a clear breach of international law.

Back in the UK, Margaret Dunn's head was pounding and she felt isolated and sick. She needed to be strong but this was a new experience and she felt out of her depth. She received immediate support and advice from Stephen Jakobi, head of Fair Trials Abroad. But she knew that only government influence could help her brother. The day after the TV confession she drove down to London and met Gary Powell, a police officer from the Anti-Terrorist Squad who was assigned as the Family Liaison Officer. 'If there are things that I cannot tell you, then I will say so,' he told her. 'But I will not lie to you.'

Surprised by the implied secrecy and caution of his remarks, Margaret consulted the experienced Jakobi. There were immediate concerns which she then put to Powell: 'Has anyone from the embassy seen Sandy's confession? Why are the Saudis allowed to block access from the embassy, which is illegal? Why has the government not issued a statement? How far is the Foreign Office prepared to go to secure his release?' Powell did not respond.

The next day brought news: a British consul had seen Sandy for 15 minutes on Sunday, 4 February 2001, just before the confessions were broadcast. He had clean clothes on and 'appeared relaxed'. But Saudi guards were present and the consul was told that he could not discuss the case or treatment in prison. If he did so, the meeting would be stopped immediately and it could jeopardise future access.

In London Margaret rang David Sharp, an official in the Middle East consular division, who told her, 'The government has started negotiations with Prince Naif, but we are concerned that any media coverage will put those discussions under strain. It is very delicate dealing with the Saudis and we are best placed on how to deal with the situation. The government will not publicly condemn the Saudis, but we are very active behind the scenes.'

Ten days had gone by and nothing was happening. Then Prince

Charles made an unexpected intervention. During a week-long private visit to Saudi, he discussed the plight of the beleaguered detainees with Crown Prince Abdullah, the de facto ruler because of King Fahd's stroke. Prince Charles arrived on 10 February 2001 and was escorted to Prince Abdullah's desert palace at Rawdat Khuraim, on the outskirts of Riyadh. That morning the two heirs apparent reviewed international events and Prince Charles raised the issue of consular access to Sandy and his absence of legal rights. Abdullah listened politely and nodded without commenting.

A reception and lunch was then held in Prince Charles's honour, attended by senior Saudi ministers, notably Prince Naif and Prince Saud, the foreign minister, and British diplomats. As a guest of Prince Abdullah, Charles attended a series of joint Saudi–British sports and welfare programmes, sponsored by BAE Systems, which sells weapons to the Kingdom. He also met businessmen and government officials to discuss a centennial fund which would finance small enterprises. This would be overseen by the Saudi Arabian Monetary Agency with technical assistance and advice from BAE Systems and the Prince of Wales Foundation.

Prince Charles also launched a joint exhibition of his paintings with his old friend Prince Khaled Al-Faisal, governor of Asir Province. Billed as 'Painting and Patronage', the event was sponsored by Shell and BAE Systems and promoted by two UK public relations firms – Sheeran Lock and Eligo International. The launch at Al-Faisaliyah Hall in Riyadh on 15 February was attended by Crown Prince Abdullah, who hosted a royal banquet that evening.

A key member of the House of Saud, Prince Khaled is the eldest son of the late King Faisal. He is in charge of sport and culture and has been assiduous in developing relations with the UK. In 1999 he set up the Saudi British Society, of which Prince Charles is co-chairman. While it purports to promote cultural exchange, its members tend to be businessmen and lawyers. But it is their interest in painting which binds their friendship. Prince Charles has visited Asir Province for many years for painting holidays, where he indulges in watercolours, while Prince Faisal prefers oil.

In 2003 embarrassment loomed when Prince Faisal presented Charles with a rare Rolex Daytona watch valued at more than £3,000. After his private secretary, Michael Fawcett, organised an exhibition of his paintings in Saudi, Prince Charles gave him the watch. This breached court rules and an official inquiry was launched after it was discovered that Fawcett was selling on many of the official presents. Of the 2,304 gifts the Prince accepted between 1999 and 2001, only 903 were recorded on the 'gifts received' form.[19]

Fascinated by the history and mystique of the House of Saud, Prince Charles retains close ties with its members, but appears oblivious to the diplomatic minefield in which he steps. In June 2001, he was introduced by Prince Khaled to Bakr Bin Laden, the eldest brother of one Osama, in London and is reported to have said, 'So, what is your brother up to these days?'[20] Four months later, on 13 October 2001, just four weeks after 9/11, Prince Charles hosted a dinner at Highgrove, his Gloucestershire country house, to support the Oxford Centre of Islamic Studies, where the Bin Laden family funds a fellowship programme. Bakr Bin Laden, who disowned his wayward brother in 1994, was one of the guests.[21]

Perhaps Prince Charles's most serious diplomatic faux pas was hosting a lunch in London in October 2002 in honour of the outgoing Saudi ambassador to the UK, Dr Ghazi Al-Gosaibi. As Dr Gosaibi – now the minister for water – was being recalled in disgrace for writing a poem which praised suicide bombers, the Prince of Wales's judgement was called into question. He has also become friendly with Dr Gosaibi's successor, Prince Turki Al-Faisal, who was accused in a lawsuit by the 9/11 families of funding and supporting Bin Laden in the past. Prince Turki strongly denied the claims and he is no longer a defendant in the case, although this is subject to appeal.

Prince Charles's relationships with prominent House of Saud members have created serious problems and obstacles to UK agencies investigating claims of Saudi financing of international terrorism, according to Special Branch sources. The delicacy and sensitivity of Prince Charles's friendships was raised during a meeting at New Scotland Yard in April 2003. Families of the victims of 9/11 had filed a lawsuit accusing some members of the House of Saud, notably defence minister Prince Sultan and the new UK ambassador, Prince Turki, of supporting Al-Qaeda in the past. Their lawyers were in Europe investigating allegations that senior Saudi royals had backed Islamic charities, run by the government, who funded the 9/11 hijackers.

The meeting at New Scotland Yard was attended by detective chief inspector Stephen Ratcliffe, the Special Branch officer in charge of tracking terrorism financing, Peter Clarke, national director of countering terrorist funding, Robert Randall, a police liaison officer, and lawyers for the families of the 9/11 victims. Alan Gerson, a lawyer for the 9/11 relatives, outlined their case and said that the Saudi royal family were put on notice in 1999 by US National Security Council (NSC) officials in Riyadh that funds for Al-Qaeda came from Saudi. 'There were similar warnings to the Saudis in London as well,' said Ratcliffe, 'although some of our regulatory agencies were not always up to scratch in tracing the money.'

'Well, have the UK authorities uncovered anything to show that charities run by some members of the Saudi royal family were channelling money to the terrorists?' asked Gerson.

Ratcliffe looked hesitant and a little sheepish. 'Our ability to investigate the Saudis is very limited,' he said. He then paused, looked across at a photograph of Prince Charles on the wall, raised his eyebrows and smiled knowingly without saying a word. 'He did not say anything but the message was crystal clear when he looked at the picture,' said a police officer who was present. 'It was Prince Charles's special relationship with the Saudis which was a problem. He gave no other reason why they were restricted.'

The House of Saud was unmoved by the Prince of Wales's discreet lobbying. It was now up to the government. On 20 February 2001,

Margaret met several consuls at the Foreign Office. 'We have to be very careful not to insult or upset the Saudis, because we must keep the dialogue going,' said James Watt, head consular. 'There are very specific ways in which they have to be handled. They have to save face with the world and their people.' He added that the death penalty was a real threat, and concluded, 'Westerners can be found guilty, imprisoned for many years and, when the interest dies down, they are sent back to their own countries. That is what they are hoping for in this case.'

Leaving the Foreign Office, Margaret was stunned and shattered by the complacency. On the surface she kept calm but inside she wanted to grab them by the shoulders and shake them. 'This is my brother you are talking about!' she silently screamed to herself.

By now some newspapers had picked up the story. Margaret accepted the Foreign Office line that publicity might damage private negotiations. So she was surprised to hear Gary Powell's private view when he called: 'Actually, media interest might force the Saudis' hand, because they won't like negative publicity. It might damage their international business interests. We may get better access. I know it sounds cold and calculating when we are talking about your brother's life, but that's how they look at things.'

Despite repeated requests, not least by Prince Charles, the Saudis continued to refuse consular access to Sandy. On 28 February, Noi had seen him in prison for 15 minutes and he looked sick and disorientated. He talked almost incoherently, as if he was on medication. 'Don't say anything to anyone,' he told her nervously.

No charges or trial date had been lodged. It was not until 13 March 2001 that Ken Neill, the vice-consular at the embassy, saw Sandy in an interview room at the police headquarters in Riyadh. Again, he was prohibited from discussing the case and his questions were vetted in advance. Perched on the edge of a sofa with his hands in his pockets and looking at the floor, Sandy replied 'Fine' when asked how he was. When asked if he wanted to send a message to his family, he said, 'No.' How are you sleeping? 'OK' was the bland response.

Clearly heavily medicated or frightened, Sandy only showed emotion twice during the seven-minute interview, according to the consular report. When he was told that his family sent their love, he got upset. And when he was informed about the media reporting, he became agitated and on edge. 'Has my name been mentioned?' he asked nervously. 'I don't want any press coverage.' He then became very distressed and left the room.

That night Gary Powell rang Margaret with an account of the meeting. 'The Saudis are calling all the shots and we are letting them get away with it,' she replied angrily. 'Our government seem to be more bothered about arms deals and oil than people.'

'They are doing all they can at this time,' he replied. 'It is a case of waiting, but it can be very difficult to get a straight answer from diplomats. They are always hedging their bets.'

'How long will this carry on for?'

'They won't cause an incident over this. There will be political discussions at the very top.'

Margaret agreed to keep quiet, accepting that it could protect Sandy from further torture and allow the diplomatic experts to continue their negotiations. But she could not help thinking that there was a hidden agenda and that silence was more convenient than a robust approach.

It was another month before consular officials were allowed to see Sandy – another breach of the Vienna convention, which the Saudis had signed. The British ambassador in Riyadh, Sir Derek Plumbly, and Baroness Scotland, the Foreign Office minister, both complained, but it was not having much impact. The Interior Ministry replied that they needed to 'complete their investigations before access could be granted'.

But by April 2001 the Saudis were breaching their own sharia law, which states that the arrested individual must be charged within three months. Under diplomatic pressure, they promised to complete their inquiries, file charges by the end of the month and Sandy would be allowed lawyers.

Nothing happened and, on 1 May, the Foreign Office consulted an expert on sharia law who said that it depended on which member of the royal family was dealing with the case. 'It will be difficult to predict because each prince has a different view and level of tolerance,' he said. 'The charge will be either "murder" or "action against the state". It would be better if it is murder because you can negotiate that with the victim's family, Saudis and blood money [compensation]. There will be no jury; just one presiding judge.'

Unlike Western law, which seeks to protect public order but also guarantees the rights of the individual, the sole mission of sharia is to protect the social order. As Sandra Mackey, who lived in Saudi for many years, put it, 'Since the goal in the treatment of any person who violates the rules [under sharia] is never rehabilitation but the defence of Islamic society, the idea of justice is inseparable from punishment. Therefore, punishment becomes organically related to the social order.'[22]

Prosecuting a Westerner under sharia is thus political and Foreign Office policy is to swiftly hide behind that veil. 'There is nothing we can do to speed things along,' Gillian Wilson, a vice-consul, told Margaret. 'These matters are complicated because we are dealing with sharia law. It is totally in the Saudis' hands.'

But it was now nearly six months since Sandy's arrest and no progress had been made. 'We have done everything asked of us,' replied Margaret. 'Don't talk to the press; don't say anything to anyone; but really we are no nearer release than at the beginning. Perhaps it's time to talk publicly.'

'That wouldn't do any good,' replied Wilson.

'Well, I am sure the Saudis would love us to keep quiet and let it all disappear.'

After three months of requests, Margaret finally received her visa and on 2 June 2001 she was being driven through the three large sets of gates to Al-Hiar prison to see her brother. She noticed that some of the guards were in uniform, and some wore the traditional white robes with Arab headdress. The interview room was spacious and surrounded by white sofas with a glass table in the middle. Khaled told Margaret and Noi that they would only have 15 minutes and if they discussed the case, their visit would be terminated. 'Sandy is not a bad man but he made a mistake,' he said. 'Everyone wants this to end soon, so he can go home, Enshallah.'

Sandy was then brought into the room, crying and looking rake-thin. They embraced tearfully. 'I am sorry for all the trouble this has caused you,' he whispered. Looking around the room terrified, he kept holding up his trousers with a waistband because he had lost three stones. He asked Margaret to tell his family how he much he loved them. The time flew and all Sandy could say was that he was in solitary and spent his days praying and thinking. When it was time to leave he held Margaret and whispered in her ear, 'I just want this to be over. Please don't talk to the press, because it will be very bad for me, much worse than before.'

Margaret and Noi were then driven to see the British ambassador, Sir Derek Plumbly, in his house on the grounds of the embassy.

'I believe that Sandy was tortured into making that confession,' said Margaret.

'I realise that it looks as though nothing is being done to bring this to an end, but meetings are being held at the highest level,' said Sir Derek. 'It really is in Sandy's best interests for everything to be dealt with quietly. The Saudis want to end this but they cannot be seen to back down. When it comes to court, the embassy will arrange a lawyer for you.'

The next evening Noi, Matthew and Margaret flew out of Riyadh airport. Noi could only take clothes and photographs with her and had to leave her son's toys behind. It was a nerve-racking departure as they felt the Saudis would summon them back at any time and no one would know until it was too late. As they flew over the desert, Margaret looked out the window and cried quietly, consumed by guilt. On arriving at Manchester airport, two Special Branch officers met them and escorted them through customs. The main priority was to avoid any waiting journalists.

Frustrated by how the Saudis were calling the shots, Margaret was unsure what to do next. She felt that the world should know that her brother had been tortured and was held in solitary confinement with no books or letters to read, just long, empty, mindless days which would drive him crazy. 'Maybe that is what's happening,' she reflected. 'Maybe the Saudis want him to go mad. After all, who will believe a mad man?!'

But she kept her counsel and instead vented her anger on consular officials. She was not a political animal, but it was hard to ignore the influence of Britain selling lucrative military hardware like the BAE Eurofighter aircraft to Saudi during the negotiations.

'Business contracts are not and will not bear any relevance to Sandy's situation,' Gillian Wilson said.

'Like hell!' thought Margaret.

Meanwhile, Sir Derek Plumbly had been working diligently to lobby senior Saudi princes. Meetings were cancelled at the last minute and he was being stonewalled. Eventually, on 18 July 2001, Sir Derek met Prince Saud, the foreign minister, and said how disappointed he was about the delay. He pointed out that the government promised that their investigation would be complete by 31 March 2001, and Sandy was still in solitary confinement after seven months. 'The lack of information is also not acceptable,' he said. Prince Saud looked embarrassed and very uncomfortable and agreed that it was a long time. 'I am sorry but I have no authority in this matter,' he replied. 'I am afraid that you should talk to the Ministry of the Interior.'

It was another three weeks before Sir Derek could speak to the deputy interior minister, Prince Ahmed, by telephone. They agreed to meet three days later. 'I would like to discuss the case with Sandy,' said Sir Derek.

'No, that will not be possible. No discussions at this time.'

The meeting proceeded on 11 August 2001, but little was resolved. Prince Ahmed, son of Prince Naif, was tight-lipped and said the case 'would come to court', but he would not commit to a timetable. A week later an exasperated Sir Derek met Crown Prince Abdullah and pressed him on the lack of legal representation. He replied that that was a decision for Prince Naif. He was non-committal but again refused unrestricted consular access to Sandy.

Privately, Foreign Office officials admitted that the stalling tactics were because the Saudis knew that Al-Qaeda had been responsible for the bombings. Dissidents like Dr Saad Al-Fagih in London agreed but added a more sinister explanation: his inside sources told him that the legal case against Sandy was a sham. Instead, he was being used as a political bargaining chip by the Saudis to persuade the British government to clamp down on troublesome dissidents in London.

For Margaret and the other relatives of men held in Saudi, the secrecy and delays were painful. On the morning of 11 September 2001, they attended a meeting at the Foreign Office with Baroness Amos, the minister responsible for the Middle East. 'Privately, we are taking a hard line and at the highest level,' she said as they sat around a large boardroom table. 'We cannot be seen to be backing the Saudis into a corner or they could take a stand to save face within their own country and make an example of this case.' She added that the government had evidence that the men had been tortured but refused to say who had provided the proof and how.

It was an emotionally charged meeting and some relatives were very angry. The brother of James Cottle, who was being held and tortured into confessing to his involvement in the Khobar bombings in January 2001, was very blunt and agitated at what he saw as the supine approach of the Foreign Office. Cottle's former wife, Mary Martini, was also unhappy. 'Will they be executed?' she asked.

'We cannot rule that out,' replied Baroness Amos.

It was a startling comment and there were some intakes of breath. But then the meeting had to be cut short at 2.15 p.m. when a civil servant whispered some far more dramatic news in the minister's ear and she was recalled to her office: terrorists had flown hijacked planes into the World Trade Center in New York City and the Pentagon in Washington DC.

THREE

A SECRET DEATH SENTENCE

'If a sinner comes to you with any news, ascertain the truth. Lest you harm people unwittingly and afterwards, become full of repentance for what you have done.'

Verse 6, Page 1589, 'The Inner Apartment', The Qur'ān

When Sandy Mitchell shuffled into the interview room of Al-Hiar prison on 12 September 2001, he was visibly shaking and very nervous. Looking around anxiously, he was gaunt and tense. His memory was faulty and his voice trailed off incoherently. He told his visitor, consular official Ken Neill, that he was still in solitary confinement. 'I am allowed 15 minutes of exercise a day and I try and walk around the cell,' he said. 'But I have no idea whether it is night or day, except when I look through a small skylight.' An onlooking Saudi police officer, Ahmed, interrupted hastily: 'Do you know what you are being charged with?'

Sandy began shaking even more and appeared extremely frightened.

'Yes or no?' commanded the officer.

'Yes.'

The meeting was then ended abruptly. As they were about to leave, Neill took his arm and noticed how thin he was. But it was the 'shaking to the bone' that was the recurrent memory for the vice-consul, and dominated his report.

A month later Neill returned and Sandy was again terrified – like a frightened child who had lost his parents. He had lost even more weight and he constantly clutched the top of his trousers, holding them up. 'What do you think about appointing a lawyer?' asked the vice-consul. A shivering Sandy looked at Ahmed, who said, 'You don't need a lawyer.'

But Neill pressed on and said that two Saudi law firms had offered to represent him. One recommended that he plead guilty and negotiate a brief jail sentence. The other suggested maintaining his innocence and cast doubt on the veracity of the confessions.

Sandy opted for the latter option and on 6 November 2001, he met Salah Al-Hejailan, a well-connected lawyer based in Riyadh, and his colleague Ahmed Twajary. It was nearly 11 months to the day since his arrest and imprisonment. The Saudi guards were not present, but Sandy, Bill and Raf still whispered their answers, frightened that the room was bugged or videotaped. They described how their confessions were obtained through extensive torture. Hejailan replied that under sharia law a conviction for murder meant that they would be executed. 'But we are appealing and the Saudi legal system allows for a series of appeals,' he said.

Sandy was shocked. He told his new lawyer that he had never been properly tried in the first place and described his bizarre court appearance. Early one morning, about six weeks earlier, a different set of guards, more edgy than the others, appeared and told him to shower quickly. He was given clean, Western clothes but Sandy was perplexed. 'Where am I going?' he asked.

'Has nobody told you about today?' replied the guard apprehensively.

'No.'

'The investigators should have told you about today,' said an irritated sergeant as he held the leg-irons and handcuffs.

Suddenly the thought that he was about to be executed raced through his brain. 'It has already been decided. It is only a matter of time,' he recalled the interrogators bragging. He raced to the toilet and threw up. After a brief prayer, the handcuffs and irons were snapped on and he was taken to an interview room, where Khaled was waiting for him. 'What is going on?' asked Sandy.

'You are a killer. What do you think?' he replied.

Sandy was blindfolded and pushed into a van for what he believed was his final journey. Nervous, he tried to strike up a conversation.

'No talking,' shouted the guard.

As the van stopped and the doors opened, he pulled off his blindfold and noticed that he was outside the Palace of Justice where the beheadings take place. The guards started shouting orders. Fearing the worst but with nothing to lose, Sandy snapped back, 'Oh, piss off. What are you going to do – kill me twice?'

But Sandy was led straight into the Palace of Justice through a side door into a room where Khaled was again waiting. Finally, he was told what was happening: this was his day in court.

'When you go in, all you must do is confirm your statement [confession],' said Khaled. 'If you say anything else, you will be sent back to the [interrogation] centre and the beatings will start all over again. Remember, we broke you before and we can do it again.'

On entering the court, Sandy was confronted by three bearded judges sat at a high table peering down at him. Looking like three mutawwas (religious police), the judges glared at him with withering looks of hatred and contempt. Ibrahim then read out his confession in Arabic, which was simultaneously translated. The torturer was also the state prosecutor. When asked if he had made the statement, Sandy replied, 'Yes, but under duress.'

'Do you confirm your statement confessing to this crime?' shouted one of the judges. 'Yes or no?'

'I was being abused and . . .'

'Just answer the question – yes or no, yes or no?'

Under threat of torture, he had no choice and concurred, expecting a lawyer to represent him later in the hearing. But he was not even asked to testify or plead. The judges then delivered the death sentence in Arabic.

'Would you like to ask for mercy from the court?' he concluded.

Sandy looked at the hatred in the eyes of the judge. 'Forget it' was all he could muster, resigned to his fate but somewhat mystified by the proceedings. It was a secret summary hearing and had lasted barely ten minutes. As he was led outside and bundled into the waiting van, he thought it was a preliminary hearing, but that was it. 'I did not realise that this was my trial,' he said. 'I didn't even realise that I'd been convicted, let alone sentenced to death. It was too much to take in.'

The British embassy was never informed about this court hearing and only discovered it happened eight months later. 'We have never been given any official notification about the outcome of the (Saudi) judicial process,' Gail Jenkinson, a Foreign Office official, later admitted. But the Saudis were now treating British diplomats and the lawyers like indulged employees. Even the agreed one-month consular visits were not adhered to and private access, mandatory under international law, was constantly denied. The lawyers had to terminate meetings at the prison because of interference by the 'mabaheth' (secret police) officers. During one session an officer chimed in with, 'Did you assemble the bomb yourself or was it already assembled?'

Back home, Margaret was increasingly frustrated. 'Why is this being allowed to happen?' she asked Gillian Wilson. 'Why is no one pulling rank and going the distance?' But she loyally cooperated with the Foreign Office policy and refused to talk to the press. 'There is no way that I am going to talk to the media,' she told Stephen Jakobi, head of Fair Trials Abroad, on Saturday, 26 January 2002, as *The Guardian* prepared an article. 'It could jeopardise everything. We have to live with the knowledge that what we do or say may make things worse. We've got to give the Foreign Office time to work something out.'

The next day the insidious nature of the Saudi state was revealed when Margaret telephoned Ken Neill in Riyadh and left a message giving her home number. When he called back he asked her about the different number and added, 'This is an open line and so I cannot talk to you frankly.' The clear implication was that British embassy phones were tapped by the Saudi regime, which was a close ally. This was reinforced later in the year when Neill telephoned Gail Jenkinson. 'This is an open line, so I will be very guarded in what I say and can only talk in general terms.' And on a third occasion, Neill told Margaret that he would not call her from the embassy, because he was not confident that the phones were secure and believed that they were 'being monitored'.

Meanwhile, Sandy's lawyers had been asking to see 'all the evidence' against him and interview the prosecuting officer. This was promised by the Interior Ministry for 25 January 2002, but never materialised. Much to Foreign Office irritation, Hejailan, who has contacts in the Saudi royal family, started briefing the media. But it did not create the seismic damage they predicted. He astutely told BBC's *Newsnight* that the Saudi legal system was fair and just and that he was confident that due process would show there was no evidence against his clients.

Despite several tempting offers, Margaret cooperated with the FO line. During a meeting on 4 February 2002 with Baroness Amos she asked, 'At what point will we know that this strategy of keeping quiet and not forcing the issue with the Saudis will work? We don't want to be sitting here in 12 months' time thinking about what we should have done when the men have been sentenced to several years in jail.'

The minister replied, 'We will not be in this position in 12 months' time. We are achieving a lot of ground by diplomatic means.'

Margaret later told Gillian Wilson, 'I am putting all my trust in you. I just hope you are right.'

The dilemmas of negotiating with the Saudis at prison level was outlined by vice-consul Ken Neill to Margaret: 'It can be so frustrating dealing with the Saudis. You have to decide in a second "Do I make a fuss, shout, raise the temperature, create an incident or do I try and reason and do the least damage?" It's a hard call to make. In my experience, if you push too hard with the Saudis, they do the exact opposite of what you want.'

For the Saudis, time is not a precious commodity. Deadlines missed, meetings cancelled, promises broken, legal rulings delayed: none of this matters in a country where, culturally, life moves at its own pace. Even in high-profile, politically sensitive cases, the wheels of justice move slowly. On 27 February 2002, when asked about Sandy's case, Prince Naif said, 'It is now before the judiciary,' and declined to elaborate. On the surface, it appeared as though a trial was imminent. But in fact his comment just meant that legal procedures were being followed.[1]

The House of Saud and the British government may have adopted a cautious, relaxed strategy. But, for someone being tortured and then jailed for the past 14 months for a murder that he did not commit, time was extremely valuable. For Sandy, life in prison had not changed that much. He was still in solitary confinement. But his visits from embassy staff were now more regular and less restrictive. Before every meeting, he would be blindfolded and chained in his cell and taken to an underground tunnel where he was driven on a golf cart to the interview room. Just before the visit his shackles would be removed, always with the warning 'Don't talk about your treatment here.'

Silence was his constant companion, and he spent most of his time daydreaming and endlessly replaying events leading up to the bombings. Depression inevitably set in and one day he just stopped eating for a week. It was not a hunger strike. He just lost the will to live. Occasionally, a friendly guard would drop by and they would discuss Islam and read stories from the Qur'ān.

'People like Ibrahim are not true Muslims,' said a black Saudi with the rank of captain.

Sandy could not bring himself to forgive Ibrahim. It was only his serious heart condition that stopped the torture. Every week Ibrahim and Khaled paid a visit and tried to persuade him to implicate other Westerners for recent bombings. But Sandy just stared at them without saying a word, much to their intense frustration. The secret police turned their attention to Raf Schyvens, the Belgian inmate who was also tortured. One day Sandy was taken to an interview room to find Raf sitting at the table with Ibrahim and Khaled looking on. 'Sandy, I want to see my children again,' he said, crying and with a look of shame on his face. 'Please tell them anything they want, because I can't take this any more.'

One night the eerie silence was broken by a loud commotion from across the corridor. It was Bill Sampson ripping his cell apart. He had been tortured just as savagely as Sandy and he'd lost it. For the next few hours he fought the guards in what sounded like a pitched battle.

The consequences of torture were ever-present. Sandy had been hospitalised three times with heart problems after Ibrahim's interrogations. Each time he was chained to the hospital bed and the nurses were prohibited from talking to him. When they came into his room, the guards would hastily cover his injured face. On one occasion he was treated in the emergency department for serious heart irregularities and given beta-blockers. After the third hospital trip, the governor was concerned that Sandy would die in his prison and arranged for the doctor to inspect him after every interrogation.

Waiting to be executed was, of course, the worst aspect of all. He had been sentenced secretly in October 2001, and he knew that appeals were in motion. He also knew that sharia law allowed him to avoid the death penalty if relatives of the victim accepted 'blood money' in compensation, but Prince Naif suggested that this might not be applicable. 'Under our system, there are the rights of the families of the dead man and those injured, and then there is the public right, which is up to the government,' he said.[2]

A SECRET DEATH SENTENCE

The death sentence handed to Sandy was the most brutal and extreme punishment under sharia law: crucifixion. Known as 'Al-Hadi', it involves being tied and affixed to an X-shaped wooden cross and then partially beheaded by sword. The body is left to rot in public for a few days to serve as an example to any potential transgressors. The last person to be executed in this way had robbed pilgrims on their way to Mecca. The execution would take place on Justice Square, a triangular area in central Riyadh defined by the governor's office and the main mosque. It is next to the Palace of Justice, so that judges and princes have a clear view of the proceedings below. Known by Westerners as 'Chop-Chop Square', it serves as a parking lot for the mosque most of the time. But almost every Friday hundreds gather to see beheading for a variety of offences – drug-smuggling, witchcraft, adultery, sodomy, highway robbery, sabotage, apostasy (renunciation of Islam) and 'corruption on earth'.

Sandy's lawyers assured him that while he had been sentenced to Al-Hadi, it would not happen. But it was little compensation to someone sitting alone on death row with minimal access to the outside world.

That anxiety-filled isolation ended in March 2002, when the door to his cell opened and in walked Les Walker, the old friend who had run the Celtic Corner with him. Les, a 49-year-old grandfather, had been arrested for bombing a phone box with a remote-control device. Like Sandy, he had been told, 'We are the government. We can do what we want.' Then the ten-hour torture sessions started: beatings, sleep deprivation and being suspended upside down for long periods. And when that did not work: threats of decapitation and raping his wife unless he confessed.

'They wanted us to say that the British government ordered us to place the bombs and gave us all confessions to sign which named British diplomats,' he said later. 'I never signed the confession because it wasn't true.'[3]

Sandy was shocked to see a frail-looking Les but delighted to see a familiar and friendly face. For the first 24 hours they talked non-stop about their experiences, which were almost identical, and why the Saudis decided to frame them. Shaken and troubled, it took a few weeks for Les to recover his confidence and sense of humour. A quick-witted Scouser, he enjoyed winding Sandy up with jokes and outrageous opinions. As they reassured and bolstered each other's resolve, humour was their best means of survival and sanity. Les created an imaginary dog called Sid (named after his real pet who had died two years earlier) and took him on imaginary walks during exercise watched by bemused guards. He also remarked to Sandy – just loud enough for the guards to overhear – that they should dig an underground escape tunnel. Despite the fact that the prison was built of solid concrete, the guards took this seriously and occasionally turned over their cell. 'The thought of us digging through concrete with plastic spoons was amusing to us but not to our guards,' said Sandy.

One day a third prisoner, James Lee[4], joined them. Known as 'Jimmy the Leg', he had been sharing a cell with Raf Schyvens. Jimmy said that Raf was not physically tortured, but he had listened to Sandy's and Bill's screams and that was enough to break him. Raf agreed to say that Sandy was the bomber and was riddled with guilt. He tried to retract his confession several times but his Saudi lawyer and the Belgian ambassador persuaded him not to do so. 'He was just not strong enough to stand up to them,' said Jimmy. It was an observation, not a criticism.

Every month Jimmy's fiancée, Gillian, who stayed in Riyadh at some risk to herself, brought in a package of books, games and jigsaw puzzles. They spent hours playing Scrabble, with Les cheating blatantly, using the Welsh words he knew. Jimmy outdid him in this, though, being a bone fide Welshman himself.

As they all had lost about 30 kg in weight, the three prisoners started an exercise programme. 'If they are going to execute me, then I want to look good on the big day,' quipped Jimmy blackly.

Prison life was improving. Sandy and the others were even allowed to watch television from time to time. Until then, he had been kept completely in the dark about events in the outside world. He hadn't even known about 9/11 until many months after the event. When a visiting British embassy official had first mentioned it to him, he did not know what he was talking about. It was only some time around the spring of 2002, when Ibrahim started shouting about how the Saudis had nothing to do with it and it was another plot by the Western world to bring the Saudis into disrepute, that he fully realised what had happened.

Then, on the morning of 20 June 2002, another attack against Westerners took place in Saudi. A newsflash appeared on Saudi television: a British expatriate called Simon Ventess was killed after his car exploded. The inmates' immediate reaction was that it helped their case. But they were wrong. Two days later the guards came in with their chains. As a fearful Sandy was led away with no explanation, he told his friends, 'I may not see you again.'

Les immediately defused the tension: 'Don't lose your head!'

Sandy could not help but laugh at his remark.

As he was marched to the Interrogation Centre, Sandy was more prepared to meet his persecutors this time. Ibrahim was there waiting impatiently and appeared less confident than in the past. 'This bomb [which killed Ventess] was identical to the one that killed Rodway,' he said via Khaled. 'There must be another Western cell working in Riyadh. Your embassy has got another team to do this to show the world that our case against you is false.'

'No, it just proves that you have arrested the wrong people,' replied Sandy.

'Shut up,' shouted Ibrahim. 'Your embassy has other intelligence operations in Saudi.'

For the next two weeks they tried to break Sandy and persuade him to implicate British diplomats in the atrocity. They also tried to extract names of other Westerners that he knew in order to blame them. But this time they could not use physical torture – only psychological. It did not work and he was returned to his cell.

A British expatriate called Glen Ballard, a friend of Sandy, was then arrested for the murder of Ventess and tortured into stating that he was a low-level MI6 agent. Two months later, on 29 September 2002, another car-bombing in Riyadh killed another Westerner. This time the guards took Jimmy Lee from the cell for interrogation. The fact that his fiancée had stayed in Riyadh was his vulnerable spot. Ibrahim tormented Jimmy with the threat that if he did not implicate other Westerners, Gillian would be raped and then arrested. It was too much to bear and he gave them a statement naming other Westerners. He later signed a clemency letter to King Fahd which admitted his guilt and said that he had been led astray by his lawyers. It was a real blow to the others, but they did not blame him. 'Everyone has a breaking point,' said Sandy.

'It was the only way I was going to get out of there,' said Jimmy later.

As the terrorist acts continued, the indiscriminate arrests of ordinary working-class British expats was becoming almost farcical. Since Sandy's detention, seven more bombs had exploded in Saudi. Even the guards and prison officers were openly telling the inmates that they knew it was Al-Qaeda and not the Westerners. But Prince Naif could not admit that he had lost control of security of the country and the expats were soft targets.

For the relatives it was an immensely frustrating experience. In April 2002, their lawyer Hejailan reported to Margaret that he had met with the chief justice and the public prosecutor and 'agreed on a specific time-frame and procedure for the defence of the detainees'. Margaret took this to mean that a trial was imminent. In fact, the families did not know that Sandy had already been tried and sentenced to death secretly without a defence. Under sharia law, a confession is the only requirement for conviction. It is very rare that a defendant is allowed a lawyer, let alone the chance to retract their confession. Usually, there is only a judge, the mabaheth officers and the accused. Once the thumb-print of the defendant has been placed on the document, the judicial process is complete.

In Sandy's case the legal situation was arbitrary, unclear and based on retracting his confession at an appeal hearing. But the Saudis were anxious that the court would be closed to the media, to prevent the lawyers from pleading that his confession was obtained by coercion and intimidation. They began to restrict Hejailan's access to Sandy and adopted delaying tactics.

Despite the unbearably slow pace, the families were looking forward to the trial. Then, on 23 April 2002, came the bombshell. Gillian Wilson rang Margaret with some definitive official news: Sandy had already been tried, found guilty and sentenced to death. The Supreme Court of Saudi Arabia then ratified the ruling as 'fair'. Margaret was stunned, but there was more: Sandy had not even known that he had been convicted. 'He will be allowed to appeal, though,' she concluded.

Infuriated and upset, Margaret called Wilson back that afternoon. She reminded her of assurances by Baroness Amos that there would be a new trial regardless of any past court hearing or decision. 'It doesn't look like that will happen now,' said Wilson.

'Why not?' replied Margaret. 'What about your assurances? How can we trust anything you say?'

'What alternative do we have? We must keep talking.'

The next day Baroness Amos called Margaret via a 10 Downing Street switchboard. She was very apologetic about the 'trial' debacle but had confidence in the person they were using as an intermediary in the diplomatic channel to the Saudis. The minister then became very mysterious, almost conspiratorial, and said there was a communication breakdown: 'The other party feels that we cannot speak freely on his line. He was not sure who was listening in and so it was not advisable to talk in detail. It's very important that our negotiations do not become public.'

What the Foreign Office appeared unable to grasp was that the Saudi judicial process was not in line with conventions and procedures accepted and expected in the West. This was self-evident when the lawyers finally saw the court papers. Incredibly, it was unclear what Sandy had been found guilty of. Equally bemusing was that the Saudi lawyers were not unduly worried! 'This is bizarre,' said Margaret. 'If no one is clear what Sandy was convicted of, then how can we appeal?'

The reality is that the legal system was almost totally controlled by political factors and power struggles inside the House of Saud. 'There is a lot of politics in the way this whole issue has been conducted,' acknowledged Wilson. 'We are working our way towards a pardon but they cannot be granted until we have lodged the appeal. We believe that once the appeal has been heard, the King will grant pardons in November [Ramadan time, when hundreds of prisoners are pardoned], so that the Saudi state does not lose face with its own people.'

Finally, on 24 July 2002, the appeal was presented before the Supreme Judicial Council, based on the retraction of their confessions, which were obtained under torture. It also argued that the statements should not have been used as evidence because the men were not legally represented and did not know they were on trial.

While they waited for the verdict, a serious obstacle was put up by the Belgian Foreign Ministry. Hejailan disclosed that Raf Schyvens had upheld his confession on the advice of the Belgian embassy in Riyadh and was, in effect, a prosecuting witness against Sandy and Bill. It was a real setback. 'The Belgian ambassador is contributing negatively by not antagonising the Saudi authorities in the hope of securing a royal pardon,' said Sandy's lawyer. 'We must put pressure on the Belgian government and voice our disapproval. Raf must not be allowed to save his own situation at the cost of Sandy and the others.'

But the Foreign Office disagreed. 'It is not a good idea to write to the Belgian embassy,' said Wilson. 'It's unreasonable to expect the government to put pressure on Raf to change his plea.'

The initial feedback from the Supreme Council was favourable, said the lawyers. But Hejailan often raised hopes about imminent release based, to some extent, on wishful thinking. 'I promise the men will be home soon,' he told a relative. It was his colleague Michael O'Kane who delivered the brutal reality on the appeal decision on 11 September 2002: 'It could take a year.'

Inside the Saudi royal family there was some anxiety about the case, according to Foreign Office sources. Crown Prince Abdullah was becoming impatient and uneasy. 'Nothing can be done until the case is in my hands,' he admitted in a rare moment of candour. But Prince Naif, who had spent much of the summer in Geneva, was intransigent and even authorised a private statement by the head of mabaheth to deny that the men had been tortured.

'Forcing confessions might exist, but if it does it's rare,' said the director of the secret police. 'There are reports of people being tortured by electric shocks, finger nails being removed and things of this nature, but I swear to Allah that I have not seen any of this.'

Prince Turki Al-Faisal, the Saudi ambassador in London and former head of intelligence, was more circumspect. 'Torture is forbidden in the Kingdom,' he told *Channel 4 News*. 'If there has been torture practised against them [Sandy and Bill], then whoever has done that will be punished . . . I don't think anybody can guarantee – whether in the Kingdom or in any country – that mistreatment of prisoners may or may not have occurred.'[5]

Hejailan believed that the feared and unpopular Prince Naif was the most vulnerable to criticism in the House of Saud. He was an apologist for Islamic militancy and the repressive and intolerant religious police. Furthermore, he was, at best, in denial about Al-Qaeda insurgents in Saudi. Pressure needed to be put on Naif to hand over the case to Abdullah, who would be more pragmatic and conciliatory. But it always came back to 'saving face'. 'This is all domestic politics,' said Hejailan. 'He [Naif] does not want this to end. He does not want to admit publicly that he has made a mistake. What is said publicly and what is said away from the public glare by the authorities is entirely different.'

As a member of the Saudi Establishment, Hejailan also believed that after 18 months the British policy of quiet diplomacy had demonstrably failed. His assessment was that a higher profile would increase the pressure and produce results. He recommended that the relatives criticise Prince Naif through the press by pointing out that he had issued a directive in 1985 stating that confessions cannot be obtained by force. 'Tell the newspapers,' he told Yvonne Wardle, whose father was Les Walker. 'Listen, Madam, you do as I tell you. It will help them get home soon.'

Margaret remained loyal to the Foreign Office policy of polite diplomacy at the highest level. But her patience was wearing thin. Gail Jenkinson, the new FO official responsible for the case, admitted that Prince Naif was the problem. He was blocking everything, including – still – access to Sandy by his lawyers and embassy officials and refusing to meet the British ambassador, Sir Derek Plumbly, who was lobbying hard. Until Crown Prince Abdullah could secure control, resolution was potentially a very long way away. Later that night, 28 October 2002, Margaret angrily noted in her diary: 'How the hell can we bring this to an end?'

For over a year the Foreign Office had assured Margaret that access to consul officials and lawyers – the most elementary right under international law – would be guaranteed. But in November 2002, the mabaheth started cancelling meetings for lawyers and consuls at the last minute. 'They said that they were too busy,' said Jenkinson. 'There is very little we can do.' Not good enough, said Margaret. 'Why does no one go back to these people in high authority and ask what the hell is going on? We should not let this go on without a great deal of fuss.'

The next day Neill telephoned Margaret from his private home number. Venting her frustration, she reminded him that unfettered access to the prisoners had been promised by ministers several months ago. 'Why doesn't anyone kick up a fuss?' she said. Neill was sympathetic but with sighs of weary resignation.

It was now clear to Margaret that only a political deal would release her brother. A decision on the appeal could take months, if not years. Once the judicial process had concluded, the two prime ministers could cut a deal. 'When is Tony Blair going to take a more active role in this?' she asked Jenkinson on 4 November 2002.

'He is sending an envoy and writing a letter,' she replied.

'He has already done that, so what else?'

Jenkinson was vague but then added, 'Crown Prince Abdullah has always said that nothing can be done until the case is in his hands. He is the one we are banking on. We don't want to offend him by pushing too hard, but we don't want to let things drag on by not pushing hard enough. The Saudis feel they must save face. That is what is holding things up, and they are now scurrying around like rats.'

A month later the lack of options and lateral thinking was apparent. 'What else can we do to bring this to an end?' asked Jenkinson. 'Withdraw trade? That is not an option. It is highly unlikely the government will consider that. We all know they are innocent. But what else can we do?'

'Well, I don't know,' replied Margaret. 'But something else needs to be done. It is cruel to give the men false hope.'

As Christmas Day 2002 approached, Margaret was increasingly angry. Every week she was told, 'Pressure is being applied at the very highest level and this is a top priority.' But what did that mean? It was too vague and she was never told what the 'pressure' involved. 'It is not enough,' she told a meeting of senior FO civil servants. 'What is your strategy? Do you have an alternative plan?' To Margaret's ears, their response was *Yes, Minister* waffle. She felt betrayed.

An unexpected bonus occurred on 30 December 2002, when the phone rang and an Arab voice asked, 'Is this Mrs Margaret Dunn?' After a pause, she heard Sandy's voice. She did not know whether to laugh or cry.

'I am not allowed to talk about the case,' he said.

'Don't worry,' she replied. 'I won't mention it at all.'

After Sandy spoke to a delighted Noi, who had moved in with Margaret after returning to the UK, Margaret said that she was flying out to see him in about two weeks. It was only a five-minute conversation but Margaret was in a daze. She called Jenkinson, who was also amazed. The embassy knew nothing about it.

On 19 January 2003, Margaret and Yvonne Wardle flew by Air France to Saudi via Paris. At Charles de Gaulle airport they were confronted with a foretaste of the impending culture clash when they mixed with a crowd of Asian Muslim women who were covered from head to toe in black robes. On arrival, Margaret also wore a long, black abaya coat, despite the stifling heat, making her feel anonymous and vulnerable. The next morning they sat down to breakfast with Hejailan at his house in Riyadh. Her stomach churning with anxiety, Margaret was impatient to know what was happening, but the servants kept serving her food that she did not want. After an update, Hejailan asked her to sign a press statement which thanked the Saudi government for allowing the visit to take place. 'I don't feel like thanking the Saudi authorities at this stage,' said an irritated Margaret. 'I would feel like a hypocrite and it would stick in my throat.'

Hejailan looked unhappy. 'OK, we can talk about it later,' he said and then delivered the bad news: 'This is not the right time in Saudi Arabia for the men to be released. There are new factors that need to be squared away. It looked favourable in December. But now we have James Lee confessing again, the possibility of a war with Iraq and you must remember that Saudi people are aware that there are innocent Saudi men being held in Guantanamo Bay without trial. There are many stories circulating about their treatment. They may be fact or fiction but the Saudis hear them and believe them, and therefore it makes it very difficult to justify the release of the British men held here.'

'Is there any leverage we can use with the Saudis held in Guantanamo Bay?' asked Margaret. 'Surely the Americans will be releasing some of them, the ones they feel are not that important?'

'There is no way the Americans will help with any deal,' interjected Michael O'Kane, a colleague of Hejailan. 'But if the

Americans released the Saudis who have little value, it may have a beneficial effect for us.'

Margaret raised the case of Mike Sedlak, an American who was the first suspect in the bombing of Christopher Rodway in November 2000. After explosives were 'found' at his home a week later, he was detained and the *Arab News* published a statement declaring his guilt. But the US embassy intervened and secured his release and he quickly left Saudi. He has never been heard of since. 'What a contrast to Sandy's case,' thought Margaret. 'If the Americans can expedite the acquittal of their innocent citizens, why not the British?'

After a discussion about 'blood money', Hejailan gathered some wrapped gifts and a dictionary for the men. Margaret and Yvonne were then driven to Al-Hiar prison, about 45 minutes out of Riyadh. They were greeted by six guards armed with machine guns who appeared rather casual: the backs of their boots were cut out and the laces untied. The guards stared at the two women with mean, cold eyes, full of hate, and waved them through.

As they entered the waiting room, Margaret was greeted by Khaled, the interrogator, like a long-lost friend, which made her feel very uncomfortable. After some small talk and serving coffee and orange juice, Khaled asked, 'Is there anything I can do?'

'Yes, you can let Sandy come home with me,' replied Margaret. This was translated to his colleague Ibrahim, who pretended that he could not speak English.

'If I did that, then I would be put where Sandy is sitting now – in jail,' Khaled said.

'When I saw you 18 months ago, you promised that this would soon be over and said "Enshallah."'

Khaled looked uneasy, averted his eyes, opened his hands wide and mumbled something but his words faded away. After accepting the presents and photographs, he agreed to two meetings with the men. Margaret was then taken into an interview room accompanied by Khaled and Ibrahim and sat in exactly the same place as she had 18 months previously. Then Sandy walked in. Looking pale, his face was red and his hands had some strange marks on them. Margaret also noticed his skin was clammy when they hugged.

'I am innocent,' he whispered in her ear.

'I know,' she replied. 'But you need to stay strong.'

While they were talking about family matters, Khaled was translating to Ibrahim. Trying to keep her voice calm, Margaret spoke in semi-code about tactics and the campaign. Sandy picked up on the clues and responded in kind. 'Do whatever you need to do to get us home,' he said quietly. 'Push the government harder and use the press if you need to.'

Margaret had brought some letters and books from Noi but they needed to be vetted by the secret police first for any 'classified information'. She asked if she could send him a video of his family, but Sandy said that tapes would be too upsetting and it was better to stick to pictures. She also met an emotional Les Walker, who whispered, 'If it was not for Sandy, I would not have survived.'

It was a strained meeting of 30 minutes. Sandy tried to make jokes but the underlying tension prevented it from being a relaxed atmosphere. It was a very quiet drive back to the city. Yvonne's meeting with her father, Les Walker, had been equally upsetting. As they sat in the car, Margaret turned her head towards the desert so no one could see her tears.

On returning to the embassy, they met Jan Banks, a consular official. 'How did it go?' she asked. Margaret and Yvonne explained how they went through the charade of exchanging pleasantries with the guards in the waiting room of the prison. They were then ushered into the huge, windowless interview room where they noticed that one of the lights had a tiny camera, and the Saudis always wanted them to sit opposite that particular spot. While they were describing this bizarre scenario, the women were astonished to see Banks suddenly press a finger to her lips and point to the air-conditioning unit behind her chair and on the ceiling. She was clearly indicating that she thought they were being listened to. She said that she fully expected that the interview room at the prison was bugged and videotaped. She did not seem too surprised but the women were shocked to discover that British diplomats believed their own embassy was also under secret surveillance by the Saudis. 'The next time you see the men, please tell them that they are being supported from every quarter,' said Banks.

Two days later Margaret and Yvonne returned to Al-Hiar prison. This time Margaret made a point of sitting where Khaled and Ibrahim were positioned at the previous meeting. Khaled looked a little dumbstruck and hovered behind her. While they waited, he brought in some sweet mint tea and orange juice, but an emotionally charged Margaret was in no mood for pleasantries. When he began telling her what she could or could not talk about, she interrupted: 'I am here for my brother. Everyone else can do their job.'

'Why are you so sad and upset?' he asked.

'Sandy should not be here,' she replied angrily. 'He is innocent. What did you do to make him confess to something that he didn't do? God is not keeping him in this place.'

After she finished, Margaret was scared that he would prevent her from seeing her brother. To her astonishment, the man who – unknown to Margaret – had been a ready accomplice in the torture sessions became even more accommodating. 'I also want this to be over,' he smiled thinly.

Five minutes later Sandy came in, wearing the tracksuit bottoms and polo shirt that they had brought from the UK. He seemed stronger and said that he had come off the anti-depressant medication, because he could feel himself craving it. But he continued with the Warfarin because it reduced the risk of blood clots which caused strokes or heart attacks.

The atmosphere turned tense when Margaret asked if Khaled and Ibrahim were the main guardians of the men. 'We are not based at the prison,' said Khaled. 'We only come here if we need to talk to the men, which isn't too often now.' Smiling, he then looked straight at Sandy and said, 'Would you like us to come and talk to you often?'

Sandy looked away nervously and tried to make light of it. 'No, no,' he said. 'The guards here are OK.'

It was time to go and Margaret cried a little. She walked over to the mirror where she thought the video camera was recording them, looked right into it and wiped away a tear. Looking on, Khaled appeared very uncomfortable. 'Good!' thought Margaret as she was led away.

The next day Margaret and Yvonne had lunch with Ken Neill, the consul, in his back garden. Over samosas, sandwiches and coffee, they discussed the situation. 'The Saudis know they have made a mistake,' he said. 'The problem is how they get out of it.' At 4.15 p.m. they met Sir Derek Plumbly at the embassy, who reaffirmed that view: 'It's a big headache for the Saudis. They want it to end. But it must be done in such a way that they don't lose face.'

It was a much more emotional visit for the two women than the last one. At 7.30 a.m. on Saturday, 25 January 2003, Margaret woke up crying. The next prison visit was not until 12.30 p.m., so it would be a long morning. She sat in the garden alone and cried, with the tears splashing on the pavement. It was best to cry now, she thought, rather than in front of Sandy and Khaled.

After a long wait at the prison gates, Margaret met Khaled in the waiting area while the guards stared at her intently. 'Are you feeling better today?' he enquired.

'No, I am heartbroken, sad and angry that Sandy and the others are still here,' she replied.

Khaled said nothing except that some of the men's letters had to be stopped because they had written about the case. He was interrupted by Sandy entering the room. Wearing the same clothes, Sandy said that they were now allowed to buy a video every few weeks. 'We asked for *In the Name of the Father* [about an Irishman who was wrongly jailed for an IRA terrorist bombing] but it was not allowed,' he said. 'I think the similarities are too close.'

It was a more relaxed meeting. Sandy said that he was keeping a close eye on his cellmate Les and that they looked out for each other.

Their room was monitored by CCTV and there was a panic button for emergencies. He told macabre jokes about beheadings and Margaret described how she joked with Khaled about breaking into the prison if the visit did not occur that day. Sandy laughed and said, 'I wouldn't put it past you.' He then turned to Khaled: 'It's a good job you let her visit. She would have caused a riot. Imagine the headline: "Mad Scottish Woman Storms Prison to Rescue Brother".' Khaled just smiled.

On returning to their house, allocated to them at the embassy, they met Sir Derek Plumbly. He was waiting with some news: the lawyers had just told him that the Supreme Court had rejected the appeal and upheld the conviction. Amazingly, the embassy had not been told officially and, if it was left to the Saudis, may never have been informed.

During their final prison visit on Sunday, 26 January 2003, Khaled told Margaret not to whisper anything to her brother. 'You must be clear when you speak,' he said.

But she managed to slip in a quiet remark: 'There is high-level pressure to get you out of here. Keep your chin up.' When it was time to leave, Margaret joked, 'No, I am not going anywhere. I am staying here and will claim squatter's rights until they are released.'

Khaled looked nervous but Sandy just laughed and gave her a big bear hug. He held her tight and whispered, 'Don't you cry in front of these bastards.'

Margaret held it together until she got outside and kicked the wall. Telling Khaled that she was outside for some air, she pulled her scarf around her face and sobbed uncontrollably. A consular official joined her. 'Are you OK?' he asked.

'No,' she said, struggling to keep her chin up. He then put his arm around her shoulder until she pulled herself together.

During the journey back to the embassy the driver stopped the car on the desert road and the consular official got out to have a cigarette. He then motioned Margaret and Yvonne to join him. 'Let's go for a walk to stretch our legs,' he said. It was a strange request, considering the heat in the desert. But he did not want the driver to overhear what he was about to tell them. 'If you repeat or quote what I am going to say, I will deny it,' he said. 'But the truth is that the embassy and the ambassador have done everything we can. The big push now has to come from London. The government has to go the extra distance. You need to make them do more. Go to your MPs, use the media. Whatever it takes. The Saudis just do whatever they like regardless and we do nothing to stop them. They are making a laughing stock of us [the British government] and like fools we do very little to stop them.'

It was a shocking admission and contradicted what ministers, Foreign Office officials and consuls had been telling the families for the past two years: that quiet, respectful, tactful diplomacy would secure the release of the prisoners. They had been told that an aggressive, assertive, public lobbying campaign would be counter-productive and a disaster. Now one of their own colleagues in Riyadh was confiding what they suspected all along: discreet, passive diplomacy alone did not work.

As a startled Margaret was driven back to Riyadh, she reflected on the advice. For two years she had obediently kept quiet and let the 'experts' bring her brother home safe and sound. Now she was told by an insider that the government's strategy had failed. It was the catalyst she needed to go public. But she was curious about the implication in his remarks that Saudi Arabia was a special case and there was a hidden agenda. Why is it that the Saudis can 'do whatever they like regardless and we do nothing to stop them'? Why does the West allow only this country to torture innocent British citizens and jail them for years without charge? And why did the Saudi royal family allow extreme Islamic terrorists to fester like a disease in their own kingdom until it was too late and resulted in catastrophic consequences?

FOUR

SLEEPING WITH THE ENEMY

'You steal our wealth and oil at paltry prices because of your international influence and military threats. This theft is indeed the biggest theft ever witnessed by mankind in the history of the world.'
Osama Bin Laden, 'Letter to the American People', 1998

'Getting Riyadh to divorce itself from radical Wahhabism will be as great a task as getting the Soviet Union to renounce Communism.'
Michael Scott Doran, *Foreign Affairs*, January/February 2004

On 12 September 2001, less than 24 hours after the hijacked planes crashed into the World Trade Center and the Pentagon, the Saudi royal family authorised the distribution of nine million barrels of oil to the United States over the following two weeks. By keeping prices low, this ensured that America only experienced a slight inflation increase and stabilised its economy amidst the most devastating terrorist atrocity in its history.

It was an awesome display of the House of Saud's power. For it has repeatedly wielded its surplus oil capacity as a political weapon, notably during the 1991 Gulf War when it produced an extra five million barrels a day. The Saudis also keep an estimated 500 billion dollars on deposit in US banks and another 450 billion or so in the stock market. If they were to suddenly withdraw all their investments, it would have a catastrophic impact on the American economy and, in turn, other Western states. And no country is more dependent on cheap, plentiful Saudi oil than the United States.[1]

As long as Saudi remains the world's dominant, low-cost producer, it retains a pivotal influence on oil prices – raising them by cutting output, lowering them by suddenly turning on the taps. It can, if it chooses, destabilise non-OPEC (the Organization of the Petroleum Exporting Countries) producers by excess production, which will force their prices down to single digits. And, if it is so inclined, Saudi can replace interrupted supplies from Iraq by making its three-million-barrels-a-day excess capacity available to prevent a post-war recession-causing price hike. 'If Saudi oil production were to vanish, the price of oil in general would shoot through the ceiling, destroying the American economy along with everybody else's,' said Kenneth Pollack, the former CIA analyst.[2]

In this way, Saudi Arabia, or, importantly, anyone who controls the country's resources, has a significant leverage over the rest of the world. America duly remains anxious to prevent a potentially hostile state from gaining control over the region and then using that power to blackmail the world.

But the United States' concerns in Saudi are not merely confined to cheap oil and its continuing distribution. Saudi is also of prime strategic value to the West, as Walter Slocombe, undersecretary of defence for policy between 1994 and 2001, underlines: 'Access to Saudi bases was very helpful, but it wasn't essential,' he said. 'What was essential was Saudi support for [US] access to Gulf bases, with the arguable exception of Qatar, maybe Bahrain and now Kuwait. After the 1991 war, none of the Gulf states were likely to do anything much with us militarily unless the Saudis wanted it to be done . . . So we needed Saudi political support.

'We also needed more direct cooperation from the Saudis. Though most of the actual US combat missions were flown out of bases in other Gulf states, we needed to have permission to fly over the Kingdom and to do the air-to-air refuelling either in their airspace or from tankers based in the Kingdom . . . So if we wanted to be able to use military force in the Gulf, we needed Saudi cooperation.'

Saudi acquiescence is vital for US strategic interests and military ambitions. The wars against Afghanistan in late 2001 and Iraq in 2003 were launched from bases in Saudi and smaller Gulf states and were dependent on unencumbered use of their airspace. 'This was at the sufferance of the Saudis rather than with their enthusiastic backing, because the US is now pursuing an agenda in Iraq and conceivably in Iran which the Saudis do not approve,' said Chas Freeman, US ambassador in Riyadh from 1989 until 1992.

'If the United States was denied access to the Persian Gulf, its ability to influence events in many other key regions of the world would be greatly diminished,' said Kenneth Pollack.[3]

That gives the Saudi royal family real power and influence when they walk into the White House and 10 Downing Street. While it needs the revenues to fund the profligate and extravagant lifestyles of its 6,000 princes, the House of Saud is quite prepared to forego enormous profits in tight oil markets and subjugate its country to US interests in the Gulf. In return, the USA and the UK protect the Kingdom from Islamic insurgents and neighbouring states, sell them weapons at inflated prices to produce kickbacks for its senior princes, support their negotiations with the IMF and World Bank, overlook their complicity in supporting terrorism and, according to former senior CIA officers I spoke to, turn a blind eye when confronted with human-rights abuses.

This Faustian pact has been insured by Saudi cash and oil. For decades the House of Saud has heavily financed US foreign policy, notably $32 million to the Contra rebels against the Socialist

Nicaraguan government, $4 billion for the mujahideen and other guerrilla forces to remove the Soviet Union from Afghanistan throughout the 1980s and another $17 billion to the US itself during the 1991 Gulf War. 'Saudi was traditionally a financier and partner of American foreign policy regionally and globally,' said Chas Freeman, the former US ambassador. 'Since the end of the Gulf War, which essentially bankrupted the Kingdom, they no longer have that role.'

The House of Saud is built on a fragile, paradoxical foundation: while it depends on the secular, materialist West for its security and wealth, it relies on the fundamentalist Wahhabi support for internal stability. This uneasy alliance ended in catastrophe: allowing extreme Islamic elements to exert influence in Saudi society and schools enabled Al-Qaeda to thrive and resulted in 9/11.

The roots of Saudi's pacts with both religious and military forces can be traced back to 1744, when a hardened tribal warrior called Mohammed Al-Saud joined forces with an austere Muslim preacher called Mohammed Abdul Wahhab. Determined to preserve his brand of pure Islam in the heart of the Arabian desert, Wahhab needed the power of Al-Saud's sword. It was the first military–religious alliance. But over the next 150 years of tribal warfare, Saudi descended into warring tribes and rival fiefdoms, overrun by bandits and highwaymen. It was not until 1902, when Abdul Aziz Ibn Saud, a great-grandson of the family chieftain, seized Riyadh with an army of barely 200 warriors and a raiding party of 40 men that the Kingdom took shape.

Intent on restoring the family dynasty, Ibn Saud wanted to transform the country into a modern state rather than allow it to wilt into a forgotten desert wasteland and a collection of tribes arguing over grazing or water rights. But to conquer the whole Arabian peninsula he needed the fighting skills of the Bedouin tribe, known as the Ikhwan. A puritanical fundamentalist sect, the Ikhwan believed that only they applied the true Islamic faith – all others were infidels.

The fanatical Ikhwan troops were unstoppable. But the one tribe who rebelled against the invading Saudi–Ikhwan forces was in Asir, a southern, remote, mountainous area near Yemen. Singularly defined by their tribal culture, Asir people were descendents of a Surfi holy man called Ahmed Ibn Idris, who was revered as a saint. In 1922 Ibn Saud sent 6,000 troops to punish the Asiris for their resistance. Their incorporation into the Saudi state was achieved mainly by buying off the tribal sheikhs and arranged marriages between the Al-Saud clan and their women.

One Asir tribe, the million-strong Al-Ghamdis, is by far the most significant, because most of the 9/11 Saudi hijackers came from that area. At least four of them were Al-Ghamdis, and the cave in Afghanistan where the 9/11 operation was plotted was called 'Al-Ghamdi house'. The man visiting Osama Bin Laden in the video during which he reflects on the 'victory' of 9/11 was called Sheikh Al-Ghamdi. Many of them were eager recruits to Bin Laden because he shares their Yemen roots. They also resent being ruled by a royal family that they believe is corrupt and does not enforce Islam with sufficient rigour and authority.[4]

By 1926 the Ikhwan armies had conquered all the provinces along with Mecca, the holiest site of Islam. They then wanted to raid and annex neighbouring states and create a Muslim Empire. But Ibn Saud, determined to introduce the new technological advances of the West, opposed them. It was the first clash between Islam and the modern approach that dominates Saudi to this very day. The dispute was solved by Ibn Saud, now known as King Abdul Aziz, appealing to the religious establishment, known as the Ulama. In effect, he told them: you must choose between me and the Ikhwan. After scrutinising the Qur'ān, they concluded that the Ikhwan were wrong to rebel against the King's authority.[5]

But the Ikhwan were subdued rather than crushed and continued to exert influence. They accused the King of collaborating with an 'infidel power': Great Britain. Wahhabi doctrine banned all connections with the 'kufar' (infidels) – a true Muslim could not employ them, seek their advice or be friends with them. But King Abdul Aziz needed their cash to finance modernisation and for himself. At the time his kingdom's only revenue was income from pilgrims to the holy places at Mecca and Medina, caravan traffic and fishing in the Gulf. And so, in 1915, the King allowed the Najd area to become a British quasi-protectorate. In return he was paid a monthly 'subsidy' from the British Indian government. He also forfeited his right 'to grant concessions . . . to the subjects of any foreign power without the consent of the British government'.[6]

The King tried to hide his financial dependence on London, explaining to his followers that he was only collecting 'jizya' from the infidel British – the tax that the conquered non-Muslims who lived in Islamic states traditionally paid. But the British knew that the Wahhabi influence was too strong and once Ibn Saud annexed the Hijaz, where the holy sites were based, Saudi could not remain a colony like Kuwait or Bahrain. To make the holy land part of the British Empire would also alienate Muslims worldwide. As a result, in 1927 Britain recognised its independence.

King Abdul Aziz was now free to realise his vision of a contemporary Saudi state. But he never overlooked the core value of Islam, particularly Wahhabism, to his cause. Years later, in a meeting with the British minister in Jeddah, F.H.W. Stonehewer-Bird, the King explained why Islam was the unifying force of Saudi society: 'The Arabs have two characteristics – Islam and "Arabiyah" [Arabism] . . . But to be an Arab is not enough. There are still too many primitive and ignorant people among the Arabs for them to form themselves into a great, united nation. There remains their Islam: that is something capable of a basis on which to found a nation. If it be true Islam [that is] uncorrupted by ignorance and innovation.'[7]

Based on this religious mandate, in 1932 King Abdul Aziz was able to combine the tribes into a single realm and named it after his family: Saudi Arabia. But maintaining the unity of this vast, isolated, impenetrable desert was troublesome. Building marital and religious alliances was the solution. The King promptly married a daughter of every tribal chief that he had conquered and fathered 44 sons by 22 wives (exclusive of the concubines and young girls constantly offered to him as gestures of hospitality). This created the dynasty of the House of Saud, whereby every Saudi prince is descended from the founding father. As King Abdul Aziz still needed the military might of the purist Islamic tribes, he also married a daughter of a prominent Wahhabi chieftain.

The Wahhabis have been umbilically connected to the Saudi state ever since. In return for their support, King Abdul agreed a pact: their clerics would be in charge of enforcing laws on personal morality, law and culture, while the royal family would run the government, the economy and foreign policy. In the mid-1930s Saudi was still a primitive country. The King ruled like a benevolent despot. When his impoverished subjects needed money, they would plead their case before him. If he believed it was a deserving cause, the King would retrieve a bag of coins from his car and hand it over. The national treasury was still being hauled around in a tin trunk. Revenue from taxes on livestock, food and trade were stashed in the case. When the King needed to spend some money, he simply wrote out a chit to the recipient, which his finance minister would pay out from the trunk.[8]

The discovery of oil in 1938 exposed the fragile, uneasy partnership with the Wahhabis. The black gold was discovered by accident: one day the King was complaining about the lack of water to an American philanthropist and during the search they discovered oil by chance. The only way to exploit the benefits was to invite foreign companies into the country. This was immediately challenged by the Wahhabi clerics, known as Imams, who were already unhappy that the King was straying from the Islamic path. According to Prince Talal Bin Abdul Aziz, the King summoned the Imams to Riyadh and told them: 'Listen, do not interfere in the affairs of the state. I hold you in high esteem, but be warned: if you meddle, I will cut you down. We cannot have two ruling powers. It will only be divisive and cause disorder. Have your say, give your advice, issue your fatwa, but through me. There can only be one ruler, as I am the state.'[9]

It was not long before the oil prospectors came calling. The King did not care which country secured the coveted concession. His priority was: show me the money. The Americans were the first to hand over the cash – $170,000 in gold – and Aramco, the Arabian American oil company was formed: purely with the aim of prospecting and selling the oil of Saudi Arabia. The shareholders were America's four largest oil corporations. There were no Saudis. A typical contract was agreed with Standard Oil of California, which granted them 'the exclusive right, for a period of 60 years, to explore, prospect, drill for, extract, treat, manufacture, deal with, carry away and export' oil in an area of 40,000 square miles – twice the size of France. In return, the company promised to immediately lend the Saudi government £30,000 gold or its equivalent, an 'annual rental' of £5,000 gold, an advance royalty of £50,000 gold and an identical payment once oil was discovered in commercial quantities, plus ongoing royalties. Within four months of signing the deal, Standard Oil's geologists were in the Kingdom.[10]

During the Second World War, Saudi oil assumed great importance as other sources of petroleum were cut off when Japan occupied Burma and Indonesia – two critical producers. After never extracting more than 5.1 million barrels annually through its first six years, Aramco ramped up to 21.3 million barrels a year by 1945. Saudi oil was vital to the Allied war machine. But President Roosevelt hungrily eyed the strategic value of the vast Saudi reserves for the post-war years. First he needed to marginalise Britain as the dominating force in the Middle East. On 8 February 1943, Standard Oil wrote to the secretary of the interior, Harold Ickes, encouraging the Roosevelt administration to counter British influence and seduce Saudi by bringing the Kingdom under the umbrella of American lend-lease assistance. Ten days later the USA declared Saudi was a state of vital interest and extended financial aid that eventually amounted to $100 million.[11]

However, the fragile Saudi economy was struggling. The war curtailed the Kingdom's trade with the rest of the world. The aid money was slow in arriving and even slower in trickling down to the people, partly because of an antiquated transport system whereby some food went by camel. In January 1945, in a top-secret memorandum to Dean Acheson, then assistant undersecretary of state, Wallace Murray, head of the Office of Near Eastern and African Affairs, noted that the government should 'consider what positive steps it must take immediately in order to afford adequate protection to this [Saudi] interest'. He added:

> If the Saudi Arabian economy should break down and political disintegration ensue, there is a danger that either Great Britain or Soviet Russia would attempt to move into Saudi Arabia to preserve order and thus prevent the other from doing so. Such a development in a country strategically located and rich in oil as is Saudi Arabia might well constitute a *causa belli* threatening the peace of the world.[12]

The top priority of American foreign policy, Murray argued, should be to safeguard and develop 'the vast oil resources of Saudi Arabia, now in American hands under a concession held by American nationals'. As former senior CIA officer Robert Baer argues in his book *Sleeping With the Devil*:

> By filling Europe's post-war oil appetite with Saudi oil – instead of oil from Venezuela, Mexico and the Caribbean basin – the United States could preserve its region's resources and maintain a reserve it could fall back on in times of military emergency.[13]

In the meantime the US was locked in a power struggle with Great Britain for the right to build military airfields and flight privileges for its planes en route to the Pacific. Since 1940 Great Britain had pumped nearly $40 million into Saudi to maintain stability and its own influence. So far American aid had been about $13 million, with another $13.4 million in oil royalties from Aramco. And so the State Department recommended another $57 million in aid over the next five years. But it was exploiting the oil reserves that made Saudi the prize, as a letter, stamped top secret by US Navy secretary James Forrestal, confirmed: 'The prestige and hence the influence of the United States is in part related to the wealth of the government and its nationals in terms of oil resources, foreign as well as domestic.'[14]

In the courtship to secure 'The Prize', Great Britain was handicapped by its long imperial past. King Abdul Aziz had fought hard to assemble his kingdom. He was not interested in abdicating control to a nation with a track record of interference in the Middle East. Renowned for its isolationist foreign policy, the USA seemed a safer bet for a backward new country. But as the Second World War drew to a close, the King was unsure which suitor to favour. In a letter delivered to the American minister at Jeddah for transmittal to President Roosevelt, King Abdul Aziz and his ministers were coy in their deliberations:

> When the King sees the great nation of America content to have its economic activity in Arabia reduced and defined by its ally Britain, America in turn will surely understand that Saudi Arabia may be excused if it yields to the same constraint from the same source – not merely to please an ally, but to survive. Without arms or resources, Saudi Arabia must not reject the hand that measures its food and drink.[15]

It was time for the King to meet the President. On his way back from the Yalta conference in February 1945, Roosevelt sent a coded telegram to Abdul Aziz asking for a secret meeting. The King agreed and brought his customary entourage of his sons, advisers and tribal chieftains. They met on the deck of the *Quincy* ship. Their physiques did not match their political stature: Roosevelt was a small man in a wheelchair, afflicted with polio, while Abdul Aziz, although much taller, was stricken with trachoma, did not see well and walked with a cane. But they got on well and exchanged jokes about the President's wheelchair.

High on the agenda was the delicate issue of Palestine. 'Your Majesty,' said the President. 'I'd like your thoughts on a problem that I am facing back home. A lot of my constituents are pressurising me to recognise the Jewish homeland in Palestine.'

The King replied: 'What Hitler did to the Jews was a terrible thing. It really was the worst thing that man could do to man. But I don't understand why you would take land away from us, the Arabs, and give it to the Jews. We didn't do anything to the Jews. If you want to give them something, why don't you give them the best part of Germany?'

Roosevelt's response was canny: 'I promise that I will not make any decision until I first consult with you and the Jewish side. Both sides have to be consulted in order to reach a decision.'[16]

King Abdul Aziz was happy with this commitment. But he was more concerned with the security of his kingdom and that lay at the heart of the US–Saudi relationship. The President agreed to construct a military base in Dhahran and provide military training. In return the King guaranteed that the US would always have secure access to Saudi oil at cheap prices.

The two heads of state exchanged letters confirming their mutual commitments. But Roosevelt died a week later and was replaced by Harry Truman. Anxious that the promise on Palestine would be upheld, Prince Faisal, the King's second son, consulted George Marshall, the US secretary of state, who reassured him. There was talk of a trusteeship under the United Nations charter. But when the partition plan was announced, the United States was the first to back it. The Saudis were outraged and felt betrayed and Palestine became the one source of tension in their relationship.

But, for the King, encirclement from neighbouring states was his primary fear, notably the Hashemites, backed by Great Britain.

When, in March 1950, America's assistant secretary of state, George McGhee, visited Riyadh, King Abdul Aziz said why he thought the British opposed him: the oil concession. 'He [the King] felt that with the Hashemites in Iraq and Jordan and the British in Kuwait and the Gulf states that he was encircled,' said Hermann Eilts, US ambassador to Saudi from 1965 until 1970, in an interview for the BBC3 documentary *House of Saud*. 'There were hostile elements around the country coveting its riches and counting upon its internal weakness and limited ability to defend itself, and so it needed an outside protector. So he looked to us [the USA] and this particular security track became stronger and stronger over the years.'[17]

When King Abdul Aziz died in 1953 aged 73, he had restored the kingdom of his ancestors, despite its survival being dependent on a non-Muslim superpower. He had anointed his eldest son, Prince Saud, who had fought with him in battle and was close to the tribes, as his successor. It was a smooth transition. But the new King was a disaster. Ostensibly polite and pleasant, he was corrupt, profligate, chaotic and hypocritical. He was obsessed by money and loved the trappings of being King – the sycophancy and the deference of the court. But he had no understanding of finance. 'It was total chaos,' recalled William A. Stoltzfus Jr, US ambassador to Kuwait from 1971 to 1976. 'Anyone who wanted to dip into the till did so. If he [the King] ran out of the privy purse, he dug into the general purse.'[18] And if cash-flow was tight, King Saud could always count on his American friends at Aramco, who would happily hand over an advance on oil royalties.

Like many royal Muslims, King Saud also indulged in the infidel's brew. One day he decided to fly out to the desert and stay at Aramco's guest house and do some hunting. But when the plane landed, Aramco executives noticed large cases of whisky and hard liquor being unloaded and later placed under the King's bed. 'We were shocked because he was head of the Temperance League,' recalled Mike M. Ameen, vice-president of Aramco from 1971 until 1975. 'During his stay we could see that they were drinking the stuff neat and straight in those little tea glasses or miniature beer jugs. It was kept very quiet.'[19]

During King Saud's reign the Cold War was at its most intense. This reinforced the US–Saudi alliance because they shared a common enemy: Godless imperialist Communism. 'We had a common interest, which was very strongly held, based on survival of our national independence and values,' said former US ambassador Chas Freeman. 'It made our interests indistinguishable and meant that other issues like Israel's handling of the Palestinians, which were emotional on both sides, could be subsumed and set to one side for [later] resolution and were less important.'

In the 1950s President Nasser was the Soviet Union's main ally in the Middle East. When the Egyptian president delivered his rabid, revolutionary rhetoric, denouncing the despotic monarchies, it caused consternation in Riyadh and Washington DC. In 1955 Nasser's message took root in the Kingdom, leading to a coup attempt by Saudi army officers against the House of Saud. King Saud hastily mobilised his tribal army and turned for protection to the United States, who were desperate to protect the oil fields from Nasser's nationalising tendencies and prevent the Soviet Union from setting up more satellite states.[20]

In February 1957 this resulted in King Saud being invited to America on a state visit. Arriving at New York airport with a retinue of 80 courtiers, the King was met by President Eisenhower, which was very unusual. Knowing King Saud's propensity for pomp and ceremony, he was given the full honours as if he was an old diplomatic friend. But the real purpose of the trip was to renew the lease on the Dhahran airbase. The King wanted the money for his own nefarious activities and the US needed Dhahran as a strategic asset against the Soviets and to protect their oil fields. 'My father negotiated the agreement,' said Hassan Yusif Yassan, 'and he was very sensitive to not calling it a base. It was a transact place for the Americans to take fuelling.'[21] The deal gave the US the right to fly in military aircraft without permission and for free use of the airfield.

The rent money for the airbase was then pocketed by the King, who spent much of it on luxury trips to Cannes and St Tropez. For the House of Saud, the problem was not just that their ruler was stealing from the public purse, but that government finances were in chaos. Like a Western corporate raider of the 1990s, King Saud saw no distinction between the official treasury and his personal income. Government salaries were not paid. Anarchy reigned and bankruptcy loomed. The family quarrelled. But everyone agreed; the King needed to be removed. To take such a drastic, serious, dangerous step, the 20-odd Al-Saud brothers needed the support of the bedrock of Saudi society: the religious leaders, collectively known as the Ulama.

In November 1964, the Ulama issued a fatwa sanctioning the abdication and King Saud was quietly asked to leave the country. Ravaged by hard drinking and royal excess, he spent his last years exiled in Greece. Like Leon Trotsky in the Soviet Union, King Saud was then airbrushed from history. Dignitaries who visited the royal palaces after his death noticed pictures of Abdul Aziz and later kings, but Saud was nowhere to be seen. It was as if he never existed.

~ The new ruler, King Faisal, was confronted with serious challenges. Despite the oil revenues, his kingdom was still a destitute, primitive sandbox with few roads, schools and hospitals. He wanted to build a new infrastructure. But he was faced with the familiar perennial problem: how to improve living conditions without incurring the wrath of the rigid puritanism of the Ulama and Wahhabis. With deft diplomacy, King Faisal won over the clerics because he knew as much about Islam as they did and was able to interpret the Qur'ān to demonstrate that modernisation was not a sin against Allah.

Negotiating with the religious scholars and their enforcers was a constant struggle. The King succeeded in introducing girls' schools. But broadcasting television was viewed as Satan's medium and led to violent demonstrations. In 1965 one group, led by a nephew of King Faisal called Prince Khaled Ibn Musad, tried to bring down and destroy the television tower in Dhahran. After a firefight, Prince Khaled was shot dead. The King refused to take action against the police officer and that decision would later have tragic consequences.

The Wahhabis' relentless efforts to enforce their purified version of Islam within Saudi society was, ironically, helped by Israel. On 5 June 1967, Israel launched a pre-emptive strike on Egypt, Syria and Jordan and decisively defeated all three nations in just six days. It was the most humiliating defeat the Arabs had ever suffered. But for Muslims it was the loss of Jerusalem and the Dome of the Rock, the third holiest site, that hurt the most.

At first, ordinary Arabs reacted by pouring into the streets in outrage. But then their religious leaders told them that they had been let down by their own governments – most of the defence budget had ended up in the pockets of greedy, corrupt rulers who had betrayed Islam. The Wahhabis argued that a much larger Arab force had been humbled by Israel – a tiny state, but one based on religious fundamentalist cohesion. A return to true Islamic principles was the solution to defeating the infidels. This message was received with increasing fervour in the mosques of Saudi. Anxious to preserve its status and privileges, the House of Saud used its petrodollars to build mosques and religious schools where a new generation could be taught this militant interpretation of Islam: hostility to Western materialism and values, the unflinching imposition of Wahhabi law and death to infidel states.

After the 1967 debacle, there was a backlash against American interests in the Middle East because of its weapons sales to Israel. Arabs accused the Saudis of being mere appendages of the USA: 'You do not even control your own oil' was the mocking refrain. It was only then that the Saudis woke up to the fact that oil could be used as a political weapon. For the next six years King Faisal warned the Americans: find a solution to the Palestine–Israel conflict or international relations will deteriorate.

The US State Department reacted complacently and so, in October 1973, Egyptian and Syrian forces launched a surprise attack on Israel. The Americans responded by airlifting equipment to Israel while the war raged on. Outraged and remembering America's betrayal in 1947 over the partition of Palestine, King Faisal lost patience. He finally pulled the lever and withdrew huge quantities of oil from the global market. The sudden shortage increased the price by 400 per cent and sent the world economy into recession.

King Faisal had made his point and now the Americans took him seriously. President Nixon sent Henry Kissinger, then secretary of state, on an urgent mission to lift the oil embargo. Kissinger had to walk down a very long room to greet the King, an austere-looking man with very sharp features who never smiled or joked. But diplomacy did not work and after five months of the boycott the US economy was hurting, so more drastic measures were being planned inside the Pentagon. Publicly, Kissinger said the US may consider direct intervention. Recently declassified top-secret MI6 documents reveal that this was more than an empty threat: Britain and America were on the verge of invading Saudi and taking over the oil fields.

In Britain the Foreign Office was even considering buying a letter written by the prophet Mohammed so that it could be given to Saudi as a sweetener to improve its access to the oil fields. Secret declassified documents show that the kudos of presenting to the King such a significant historical artefact was appealing in Whitehall. But one civil servant disagreed. He said that if the letter proved genuine, the cost would be 'astronomical' and the Saudis might view it as a bribe. And Anthony Parsons, then a senior Foreign Office official, had other concerns: 'Would King Faisal . . . be insulted to receive so holy a Muslim relic from the hands of the infidels?'

The idea had been floated by the auction house Sothebys, which had been offered the letter by its owner, the widow of King Faisal II of Iraq, who had been overthrown in 1958. After subjecting the letter, written to Emperor Heraclitus, to authentication tests, Sothebys suggested to the Foreign Office that they buy it privately. But the Foreign Office declined. According to *The Art* newspaper, which disclosed the documents, the letter was finally sold through private channels to a mystery buyer.[22]

The King was not impressed by the Western plotting. According to one of his sons, Prince Amr Al-Faisal, his answer was: 'We come from the desert. We have been living on camel milk and dates and we can easily go back and live in the desert.'[23]

In public, the two nations were at loggerheads and the embargo was threatening the Pentagon's ability to prosecute the war in Vietnam. But, behind closed doors, according to new evidence obtained by the BBC3 *House of Saud* documentary, King Faisal secretly gave permission for Aramco to breach the boycott. Two Aramco executives told King Faisal that they desperately needed the oil to fight worldwide Communism and it was a national emergency. An irritated King, sympathetic to the crusade against Godless Marxism, reluctantly agreed: 'God will help you, but don't get caught.' After that the supply of oil was less of a problem.[24]

However, before he could reap the diplomatic benefits of the embargo, the King's past caught up with him. On 25 March 1975 he was shot dead by one of his nephews, Prince Faisal Ibn Musad, while greeting the Kuwait oil minister. The Wahhabi ghost had returned to haunt the House of Saud – for the assassin was the brother of Prince Khaled Ibn Musad, who had been killed by a police officer ten years earlier during an Islamic protest against the introduction of television.

Succession in the Saudi royal family is usually smooth and predetermined. But the next in line, Mohammed Bin Abdul Aziz, was viewed as another Prince Saud – too susceptible to money, women and hard liquor. And so the family chose Prince Khaled, a full brother of Faisal. Softly spoken, introverted and calm, King Khaled was not a political animal. He preferred to talk about the desert and his hawks and left matters of state to his brother, Crown Prince Fahd.

The late 1970s saw Riyadh transformed from a desert backwater to a sprawling metropolitan area of four million people. Funded by petrodollars, the rest of the country was also converted in a breathtaking development programme – villages into cities, desert paths into motorways and camels into Cadillacs (gold ones for the princes). It was boom time in Saudi. Western contractors poured in and were allowed to bring their own labour. As a result, the expatriate community became substantial (today there are 6 million foreign workers in a total population of 21 million).

But this importation of Westerners, with their decadent, materialistic culture, deeply offended the Wahhabis. They were angered by the infusion of infidel values and the fast modernisation and urbanisation of their country. In November 1979 this simmering resentment boiled over when 117 Islamic fundamentalists hijacked the Grand Mosque in Mecca. As the cleric walked to the microphone to begin the dawn prayer, he was pushed aside and the ringleader announced that a new Messiah, Juhaiman Al-Oteibi, was present and allegiance should be pledged to him. Hundreds of pilgrims were then held hostage by the armed insurgents, many of them religious students, who barricaded themselves inside the mosque. As they fired shots, shock waves flooded through the House of Saud. For Muslims, this was the holiest place on earth. The authorities could not just send in the tanks.

Once again the Ulama rescued the royal family. Quoting from verses in the Qur'ān, they issued a fatwa that allowed the government to retaliate with violence. Troops then launched a frontal assault against the main gates. But the open ground of the Grand Mosque was floodlit and they were cut down by snipers. After six days the insurgents were forced down from the upper galleries and retreated underneath the mosque into a network of store rooms and tunnels.

For the next two weeks the battle raged on and the royal family was in despair as to how to end the siege. Some Saudi officers were even refusing to obey orders. They turned to the French Secret Service, the DGSE (Direction Générale de la Sécurité Extérieure), for assistance. 'I talked to the director of the [French] intelligence service,' said Prince Turki Al-Faisal, then head of Saudi intelligence and now ambassador in London. 'I told him that we needed gas canisters and equipment and we needed people to train our officers to use them and he agreed right away. That was the end of their participation.'[25]

After nearly three weeks, the religious rebellion ended with a bloody finale. Final casualties included 255 dead, 127 of them Saudi troops, and 63 of the surviving insurgents were secretly tried and publicly beheaded. Privately, the House of Saud was shaken. But publicly, it refused to accept that the siege marked the birth of a violent Islamic opposition movement.

In fact, the revolt crystallised the growing influence of the fundamentalists. Its leader, Juhaiman Al-Oteibi, was a direct descendant of the Ikhwan warriors who had rebelled against the Saudi founder. He attacked the official clerical establishment as 'sheiks with degrees, ranks and social pursuits'. Echoing Bin Laden, he claimed that the royal family had forfeited the allegiance of the Kingdom's Muslims because they were misappropriating the oil revenues and consorting with the infidel Westerners. They deserved to be overthrown.

The royal family had already been rattled by the Islamic revolution in Iran which had toppled the regal Shah of Iran ten months earlier, with Ayatollah Khomeini denouncing the corrupt monarchies of the Middle East. Threatened and fearful, they threw money at the problem, according to a former senior US intelligence official in an interview for this book: 'What really happened in the Kingdom was that the royal family simultaneously got very frightened and very rich. They went from $2 billion a year from oil sales in 1970 to $20 billion in 1980 and heading way up. They cut an implicit deal with the Wahhabis: "Here is all the money in the world that you could ever want and you leave the royal family alone and not call attention to some of our lifestyles and financial irregularities." The Saudi Establishment accepted a Faustian bargain, buying protection for itself by financing the spread of Wahhabi hatred around the world.'

Hoping to co-opt the Islamists, the House of Saud handed over education, the judiciary and cultural affairs to the Wahhabi clerics. It was a policy of appeasement: they spent a fortune expanding and modernising the holy shrines at Mecca and Modena. They also built more schools and universities with the curriculum dominated by an extreme, literal version of Islam. As one businessman later reflected, 'Having killed Al-Oteibi, the regime implemented his entire agenda.'[26] The total cost from 1980 until 2000 was estimated at a cool $75 billion.

The Wahhabis relished their new role as the voice and enforcer of this purist Islam – no music in any media, no women on television and stores closed during prayer times. Ironically, this was done by modern technology. The religious police, the mutawwa, used closed-circuit television cameras to monitor women's attendance at universities and the behaviour of young people in shopping malls – just in case they strayed from the stern rigidity of Wahhabism.

By the mid-1980s these new schools had produced a generation of graduates who had been indoctrinated by this violent and totalitarian interpretation of Islam which preached death to Westerners. Unfortunately, while many students were conversant in Islamic theology, few were engineers and so were not easily absorbed into the economy. Many of them were unemployable and disaffected. For the jihad generals, they were ideal recruits as spiritual warriors. And they were ready to die for their beliefs.

The Saudi royal family failed to see the danger. Instead, they actively encouraged about 10,000 of their young Muslims to go to Afghanistan to wage jihad against the atheist Communists at the request of the US government. Armed with American weapons and funded by the CIA, the Arab–Afghan mujahideen militia, led by one Osama Bin Laden, drove the Soviet Red Army back to Moscow. It was a remarkable victory. But using fanatical young Muslims as a bedrock against Godless Marxists did not solve the underlying problem of a growing number of jihadists disillusioned with the House of Saud. At the heart of their grievance was the royal family's relationship with the United States.

On 2 August 1990, the Iraqi invasion of Kuwait was greeted with shock and disbelief in Riyadh. As Saddam Hussein's tanks rolled towards the Saudi border, their reaction was one of betrayal. For the past 10 years King Fahd, who succeeded Khaled in 1982, had supported Iraq in its war against Iran and paid out an estimated $50 billion to keep Saddam Hussein, a fellow Sunni, in power. Now that counted for nothing and their small, untrained army of 70,000 and National Guard of another 70,000 was faced with 1.2 million battle-hardened Iraqi troops. Catastrophe loomed.

With Saddam's forces on his border, King Fahd knew that only the Americans, who were anxious to secure the oil fields, could save his regime. Yet again the Ulama's blessing was required before allowing non-Muslim troops into the Kingdom. This was granted but it resulted in loud rumblings of radical Islamic dissent. King Fahd and the senior princes wanted more time to establish their customary and elaborate consensus. It was only when Dick Cheney, then US defence secretary, and Chas Freeman met King Fahd on his own and showed him the satellite photographs of Iraqi soldiers patrolling 25 km inside his country that he agreed. The only issue was whether the US would produce a substantial response or merely send unarmed aircraft as President Carter once did in the late 1970s. Dick Cheney told him the US would deploy 220,000 troops. 'That is a serious response,' replied the King. 'Please instruct them to come.'

As US soldiers marched into Saudi Arabia, radical Muslims were infuriated not just because their rulers had allied themselves with God's enemies. There was a more earthly, economic grievance. For the past 30 years the government had spent billions of dollars on expanding and modernising its armed forces. Where was the Saudi army? The problem was that the majority of the defence budget went on training, spare parts, maintenance, future upgrades and ground support equipment for aircraft rather than operational weapons. This was partly because extracting kickbacks on infrastructure deals was easier. 'How could we justify spending so much money on an army that could not be used in a real combat situation?' said Dr Madawi Al-Rasheed. 'And this brought to the forefront the problem of corruption and the commissions paid on military contracts.'[27]

In fact, the need for foreign forces was unavoidable because Iraq had vastly more men of military age than Saudi. But moderate dissidents still argued that fraud and incompetence by senior royals provided a propaganda weapon to the radical Islamic cause: if the Kingdom had had an army and air force effective enough to resist Iraq, then the hated American troops would not have been required.

But survival was the only priority for the House of Saud in 1990–91. Despite falling oil revenues, it spent about $17 billion in cash on 'Operation Desert Shield' and also imported huge amounts of aviation fuel for the thousands of American air strikes against Iraq. Estimates vary but the total bill, including all ancillary services, was close to $40 billion, according to a former US senior diplomat. The Kingdom was secure but broke.

For the militant Muslims, victory against secular Iraq was welcome. But they expected the US forces to return home. So, when 5,000 American GIs and the military airbases remained, with not even a conditional agreement, there was an outcry in the mosques. Before the Gulf War the US was wise enough to understand the political sensitivities and avoid an open physical presence. Now Washington DC crossed the psychological barrier and failed to appreciate the danger, and worse – as Saudi dissident Dr Saad Al-Fagih pointed out – 'The Saudi government was never brave enough to remind them.'[28]

In Riyadh, the US ambassador Chas Freeman did understand the threat. He realised that the perception of the Americans' presence was like a volcano waiting to erupt. Soon after the Gulf War, he sent a series of telegrams to the State Department arguing in forthright and often robust language that, if left unattended, the issue would intensify anti-US hostility in Saudi. His views were rejected. 'The American forces were present with a wink and a nod from the Saudis,' recalled Freeman. 'And yet the Saudis continued to pay for all their food, housing, jet fuel and military activity for what could be described as supporting "Operation Southern Watch" [monitoring of the no-fly zone in south Iraq] which itself was not authorised by the UN but invented by some creative Anglo-American diplomacy as an appropriate measure . . . The money spent was clearly seen by the Saudi public as coming out of its pocket without any clear justification for it . . . Then there was the social and religious friction [caused by the American camps].'

The combination of the financial burden, cultural tension, military presence and religious sensitivity induced intense anger among ordinary Saudis. It was the perfect recruitment drive for proponents of jihad. As Al-Qaeda's founding statement in February 1998 proclaimed:

> For over seven years the United States has been occupying the lands of Islam in the holiest of places, the Arabian peninsula, plundering its riches, dictating to its rulers, humiliating its people, terrorising its neighbours and turning its bases in the Peninsula into a spearhead through which to fight the neighbouring Muslim peoples.

It was an open declaration of war on America. In August 1998, the US responded by placing a $5 million bounty on Bin Laden's head. What both the American government and the Saudi rulers completely underestimated, however, was the popularity that Al-Qaeda would engender by tapping into widespread resentment throughout the Arab world, and the grave, global implications of this. In the 1990s the US and UK intelligence establishments became complacent and went 'asleep at the wheel', according to James Woolsey, director of the CIA from February 1993 until January 1995. 'We more or less partied through the 1990s,' he told the authors. 'The 1990s were like the roaring 1920s when we had won the First World War and made the world safe for democracy. The stock market is up. It's time to party. And we did the same thing after the Cold War. It was a Great Gatsby world and the 1990s was a rerun.'

Meanwhile, Bin Laden was quietly recruiting his jihad warriors. Al-Qaeda was an international network but found fertile fundraising ground in the Kingdom where religious extremism flourished. As a 2003 US bipartisan taskforce commissioned by the Council on Foreign Relations, comprising former senior CIA directors, ex-senior NSC and Treasury officials and a former FBI director, concluded: 'For years, individuals and charities based in Saudi Arabia have been the most important source of funds for Al-Qaeda. And for years Saudi officials have turned a blind eye to the problem. This is hardly surprising since Saudi Arabia possesses the greatest concentration of wealth in the region. Saudi nationals and charities were previously the most important sources of funds for the "mujahideen". Saudi nationals have always constituted a disproportionate percentage of Al-Qaeda's own membership. And Al-Qaeda's political message has long focussed on issues of particular interest to Saudi nationals, especially those who are disenchanted with their own government.'[29]

During his testimony to Congress in June 2003, David Aufhauser, the senior US official responsible for tracking terrorist financing and general counsel for the US Treasury department, said that Saudi was 'the epicentre' of terrorist funding in general and Al-Qaeda in particular. He added that the Kingdom's multibillion-dollar spending spree on Wahhabi propaganda 'is a combustible compound when mixed with religious teachings in thousands of "madrasses" [Islamic religious schools] that condemn pluralism and mark non-believers as enemies'.[30]

A CIA memo, dated 2 August 2002, concluded that there is 'incontrovertible evidence that there is support for these terrorists within the Saudi government'. And if more evidence was needed, a United Nations Security Council report stated that between 1993 and 2003 Saudis contributed a total of $500 million directly to Al-Qaeda.

When asked by the PBS (Public Broadcasting Service) programme *Frontline* about his country bankrolling terrorists, Prince Bandar, the Saudi ambassador to the US, replied: 'We have a religious tax that is dictated by our religion that is compulsory but not enforceable . . . God blessed us with a lot of wealth and so it is supposed to go the poor. We take care of almost all our people. That doesn't mean everybody, but almost all. So we send it to Afghanistan, Bosnia and Senegal, anywhere in the world, but as charities . . . I am not saying that somebody will not use the goodwill of these charities and recycle that money and send it for a bad cause. I am not denying it. I am saying we have never been confronted with such a possibility without taking a look at it and, if it was true, we stopped it.'

When asked if those funds were disbursed to Osama Bin Laden, the Saudi ambassador admitted, 'Not to Bin Laden, but to organisations that were just as bad as Bin Laden, from other countries: some Egyptian organisations. Once it came to our attention, we stopped it.'[31]

What Prince Bandar declined to mention is that many Saudi charities are an integral part of the government and overseen, regulated and controlled by senior ministers, notably Prince Naif. They are not voluntary, detached and unaccountable, and so, according to US and UK intelligence officials, the government must have known that cash was channelled to suicide-bombers rather than alms to the destitute. Chas Freeman denies this but accepts that 'a significant number' of charities were penetrated in the early 1990s – like a Trotskyist entrist operation during the Cold War. 'Their [charity] local offices throughout the world had been infiltrated by Al-Qaeda, which found them to be a very convenient and effective form of cover,' he said.

Far from the links being historical, Islamic charities remained a heavy contributor to terrorist cells. This was discovered by Robert Jordan, US ambassador to Saudi from 2001 until 2003. 'We learned early in my tenure, in the first quarter of 2002, that a number of Saudi charities were actually out of control,' he recalled. 'They had millions and millions of dollars and were using it in what we might call evangelical activities in failed states like Bosnia and Albania which had a kind of vacuum. These [Saudi] Muslim charities would proselytise there and increase the number of Muslims, but sadly, they would also allow radicals – in some cases actual cell members – to use their facilities and abundant resources.'[32]

When Jordan took his findings to Crown Prince Abdullah in late 2002, he cautiously agreed that something needed to be done and authorised a joint US–Saudi intelligence investigation. But the US intelligence officers were very reluctant to share much information with their counterparts because of Al-Qaeda penetration of Saudi agencies, notably the National Guard. 'We wanted to protect sources and methods,' said Jordan. 'We also wanted to be sure how much we could trust the Saudis.'[33]

Their enquiries discovered that the charities remained a problem long after 9/11, notably Al-Haramain ('The Call'). This was the charity of choice for Saudi Muslims, who were obliged to donate money to the poor. Billions of riyals were raised. But most of the cash went overseas to set up Al-Haramain branches in Bosnia, Albania, Chechnya and Africa. 'Al-Haramain was encouraged to clean up its shop,' said Jordan. 'They told us they had closed their offices. But then these offices were springing back up down the street in another location, maybe under a fictitious name, within a few days of closing the first office. It was like crabgrass sprouting back up again . . . And yet we saw some progress and Al-Haramain has been taken down.'[34]

In his interview with PBS's *Frontline*, the former US ambassador also disclosed, 'There are well-connected Saudi princes contributing to the charities, but we have not yet received any reliable intelligence information that they knowingly contributed to any kind of terrorist activity.' But evidence of Saudi support for terrorism is not hard to find. In January 2001, a press release from the embassy in London boasted how the 'Saudi Committee for Support of the Al-Quds Intifada', chaired and administered by Prince Naif, the interior minister, has distributed $33 million to 'deserving Palestinians', including 'the families of 2,281 prisoners and 358 martyrs'. The 'martyrs', of course, were suicide-bombers, each of whose families received about $3,500 from the fund. Another statement quoted the Saudi finance minister confirming a $50 million contribution to a pan-Arab fund designed to 'educate the sons of martyrs'. In Saudi, newspaper advertisements even solicit funds for Palestinian terrorists, openly supplying the designated bank-account numbers. It is estimated that 50 per cent of the income for Hamas, the Islamic group that targets Israel, comes from the Kingdom.[35]

However, at the peak of this bankrolling of terror, and as the loudspeakers in the mosques blared out messages of hate to the infidels, US intelligence agencies appeared to be snoozing, or at least taking long naps. Robert Baer believes it was more deliberate. 'Washington wore blinkers,' he said.[36] In 1997, just before leaving the CIA, Baer checked what information the Agency had on the Saudis and was shocked by his discovery. 'We had nothing. No intelligence,' he recalled. 'It was almost as if Saudi Arabia was not the source of terrorism because we didn't want it to be.'

The FBI in particular was strangely reluctant to consider incriminating evidence implicating the Saudis. In 1994, soon after defecting from Saudi Arabia with 13,000 internal government documents, the former Saudi diplomat at the United Nations, Mohammed Al-Khilewi, took extracts of his archive to a meeting at his lawyer's office with two FBI agents and an assistant US attorney. He claimed to have evidence of corruption, human-rights abuses and financial support for terrorists, notably how the Saudis funded and provided logistical support to Hamas. 'We gave them a sampling of the documents and put them on the table,' recalled Michael Wildes, Al-Khilewi's lawyer. 'But the agents refused to accept them.'[37]

A similar encounter occurred in 1999 during a meeting of the US Counter-Terrorism Security Group in the White House, attended by National Security Council officials and two FBI agents. The NSC had discovered evidence of a fundraising visit to the USA in the early 1990s by Ayman Zawahiri, long considered to be Osama Bin Laden's deputy.

'I can't believe it,' an NSC official told the FBI agents. 'Did you know about that?'

They answered with wary nods.

'Well, if he was here, someone was handling his travel, arranging his meetings and giving him money,' said the official. 'Do you know who these people are? Do you have them covered?'

'Yeah, yeah, we know,' replied the surly agents. 'Don't worry about it. We got it covered.'

The NSC later learned that one of Zawahiri's American hosts had been Ali Mohammed, a US army sergeant who was already in jail while their conversation with the FBI agents took place. But the FBI did not pursue that connection, according to Benjamin and Simon, and rejected offers of new authorisation to monitor activity in militant mosques.[38]

The FBI was not alone in its reluctance to take Al-Qaeda sufficiently seriously. In 1999 William Wechsler, then chairman of a government inter-agency group tasked to disrupt Al-Qaeda's financial network, visited the Kingdom with Richard Newcomb, director of the Office of Foreign Assets Control. Their mission was to warn intelligence officials about Saudi funding of Al-Qaeda and demand that it stop. They were granted a respectful audience, but little was done to counter the threat.[39] A similar visit occurred in the early 1990s, when a senior MI6 director issued a similar warning. 'By not moving quickly and forcefully enough to combat the terrorist infrastructure on its own soil, the Saudi government has allowed the terrorists and their supporters to gain strength and influence steadily among their own population,' Wechsler later noted. As the 9/11 Commission later found, the House of Saud 'turned a blind eye' to the government-run charities channelling funds to the terrorists.

London and Washington DC were woken from their collective slumber with a loud bang on the morning of 13 November 1995 when a powerful car bomb shook Riyadh. The target was the communications HQ and training facility of the Saudi National Guard, administered by US personnel. The building also housed employees of a private security firm, BDM, chaired by Frank Carlucci, the former US defence secretary. The vehicle containing the bomb was in the facility's car park, which was open to the general public, and timed to detonate at 11.30 a.m. as staff left for their lunch-breaks. Destroying the front of the building, the blast killed seven people – five American military advisers, an Indian and a Filipino – and injured forty-two. It was clearly designed to draw attention to and undermine the American military presence.

Two obscure Islamic groups claimed credit but in the immediate aftermath it was unclear who was responsible. The Saudis blamed 'outsiders', the British implicated Iraq, the Americans suggested Iran. In fact, it was indigenous insurgents led by Al-Qaeda, as Prince Turki Al-Faisal, then director of intelligence, admitted privately to the Egyptian authorities.[40] Dozens of suspects were promptly arrested. On 31 May 1996, four of them were executed, although it is likely they were tortured into confessing in front of video cameras, according to Mohammed Al-Khilewi. Amnesty International agreed and accused the Saudi authorities of using the bombing to terminate political opponents.

As five Americans had died, the FBI requested an interview with the four terrorists before they were beheaded. The Saudis refused point-blank. And when the US ambassador, Raymond E. Mabus Jr, protested and requested clarification about the 'investigation', he was smeared. 'Saudi intelligence sent agents, disguised as religious police, to publicly embarrass his [the ambassador's] wife by humiliating her on several occasions,' said Mohammed Al-Khilewi, who resigned from the Saudi government in 1994. 'They forced her to cover her head and prevented her from wearing slacks in public. One time they threatened to lash her with a bamboo stick on her buttocks. The State Department responded not with alarm about protecting Uncle Sam's representative in Riyadh but with soothing words about quietly cooling down the situation.'[41]

Barely seven months later the Americans were given another wake-up call. On 25 June 1996, 19 US military personnel were killed and 364 American and other nationals were injured when a car bomb exploded at the Khobar Towers apartment complex near the Dhahran airbase. Once again the FBI wanted to investigate. But when its director Louis Freeh arrived in Saudi Arabia, he was treated with contempt. His counterpart, Prince Naif, minister of the interior, stayed on his yacht anchored off the coast in the Red Sea, near Jeddah. Instead, Freeh met with two low-ranking officials in the Saudi internal security service who knew nothing about Khobar. He was completely stonewalled. According to Al-Khilewi, Prince Naif and his officials deliberately buried any evidence and kept it from the Americans.

The reason, of course, was that the bombers were Saudi Islamic insurgents. The US State Department said nothing and in 1999 declared that the Saudi police were still investigating the Khobar atrocity. Not only was this untrue, but that year Prince Naif released from prison two clerics who had issued fatwas to kill Americans. One of them, Safar Al-Hawali, was a devotee of Osama Bin Laden.

Eventually, on 21 June 2001, 13 Saudis and a Lebanese were indicted by a US Federal Grand Jury for planning and implementing the Khobar bombing. The defendants were members of the Saudi Hizballah group. The indictment caught Prince Naif by surprise. He confirmed that 11 of them were imprisoned in Saudi Arabia and would be tried under sharia law. When asked if any of the suspects would be sent to the USA for trial, he replied, 'No, never, impossible. We have nothing whatsoever to do with the US court and we are not concerned with what is going to be decided by the US. The Americans never informed us or coordinated with us on this issue.'[42] Prince Bandar blamed the debacle on a turf war between rival intelligence agencies: 'Security services are very jealous at what they do. And our people at the end of the investigation have to go to the sharia religious court and they must make sure that the information is not contaminated by foreign influence. If the accused says "I challenge this evidence because foreigners gave it", then we lose the case and that guy goes free. So there was a method in that madness. There was also a national security matter. There are things that you [the USA] know but don't tell us. There are things that we know that we may not tell you . . . When it [the case] was all done, we shared what was necessary with you [the FBI].'[43]

Faced with the rising surge of indigenous terrorism, the House of Saud reacted in characteristic style: they tried to pay off the insurgents. 'They have a different way of dealing with all threats, including terrorism, which is that everybody has a price,' said Walter Slocombe. 'It is usually cheaper to pay the price than to fight wars – a proposition which, if not carried to too great an extreme and however morally repugnant, is probably true.'

After the bombings in Riyadh and Khobar Towers in 1995 and 1996, the Saudis feared that Osama Bin Laden, who had just relocated to Afghanistan from Sudan, was planning a full-scale revolution. It was time to cut a deal. In June 1998, Prince Turki Al-Faisal, then head of Saudi intelligence, flew in his private jet to Kandahar airbase in Afghanistan for a secret meeting with Mullah Omar, the Taliban leader, to negotiate the extradition of Bin Laden. 'I told him [Omar] that if they value their relationship with Saudi Arabia, it was better to deliver Bin Laden,' recalled Prince Turki, who strongly denies there was a financial deal.[44] But a sworn affidavit by the Taliban's intelligence chief, Mullah Kakshar, tells a different story. He states that Prince Turki agreed to arrange for wealthy Saudi businessmen to transfer funds to Al-Qaeda in return for their guarantee not to attack the Kingdom. According to Kakshar's testimony given to lawyers acting for relatives of the 9/11 victims, oil and financial assistance to the Taliban were also promised. The donations to Al-Qaeda were facilitated and a few weeks later 400 brand-new pick-up vehicles had arrived in Kandahar.

Prince Turki claims that the Taliban agreed in principle to hand over Bin Laden. But then, in August 1998, US Tomahawk missiles bombed Al-Qaeda camps in Afghanistan and Sudan in retaliation for the attacks on the US embassies in Kenya and Tanzania. 'It was what I would call a feel-good military campaign – firing million-dollar missiles at $10,000 tents and generally reacting spastically in an effort to demonstrate to the public that he [President Clinton] was doing something,' said Chas Freeman. 'For one of the targets we had to pay compensation to the owner of a pharmaceutical factory in Sudan who in fact was a Saudi national. It was identified by [US] intelligence as a biological weapons factory. It was not. What we did with that military campaign was to demonise Bin Laden and turn him from a nobody to the Robin Hood of the Islamic jihadist movement.'

The US bombing only served to antagonise the Taliban and suddenly Mullah Omar needed Osama Bin Laden more than Bin Laden needed Omar. So when Prince Turki returned to Afghanistan the following month to collect Bin Laden, he found a dramatically different Omar – stubborn, sweating and very angry. Over an extravagant lunch at his house, the Taliban leader said, 'How can you ask for the arrest of such a worthy man like Bin Laden, the leader of the fight against the infidels?' Usually a quiet, diffident, almost pious man, the irritated Saudi intelligence chief replied by lecturing Omar about his ingratitude to his former benefactors. In the middle of this tirade, the Taliban leader took a water jug from an attendant and emptied it over his head. 'I nearly lost my temper,' he shouted at an astonished prince. 'Now I am calm, I will ask you a question and then you can leave. How long has the royalty of Saudi Arabia been the hired help of the Americans?'[45]

Lunch went uneaten and Prince Turki walked out with a parting comment: 'You will regret this decision and you will make the Afghan people pay for it.' The visit was cut short and a second private jet – brought specially to fly Bin Laden back to the Kingdom – returned to Riyadh empty. Shortly afterwards, Bin Laden pledged his allegiance to Mullah Omar and recognised him formally as 'amir ul momineen' (leader of the faithful).[46]

Bin Laden knew that it was dependence on America that underpinned the royal family's very existence. His strategy was to destabilise and destroy that relationship. That was why, of the 19 hijackers he selected for the 9/11 operation, 15 of them were Saudis, rather than Egyptians, Syrians or Lebanese. The intention was to make the Kingdom an enemy in the hearts and minds of many Americans and drive a wedge between the two governing elites.

It is remarkable that the relationship has remained intact, if severely weakened. The fact that the vast majority of the 9/11 hijackers were Saudis and allegedly backed by Saudi cash should have torn it apart, or at least ripped it. Populist reaction in the streets of New York City was understandably angry. 'Take their gas and kick some ass', read one street sign. 'Invade Saudi and make it a self-service gas pump', declared another.

The Saudis were embarrassed and appalled. For Prince Saud, the foreign minister, it was 'a shock beyond belief for us. I always describe it as suddenly you wake up one day and you find your child is a mass murderer.'[47] But other senior princes were in denial and claimed it was a Zionist conspiracy. A few days afterwards, Prince Salman, the powerful governor of Riyadh Province, told Robert Jordan, 'This has to have been a Zionist plot. Saudis are not like this. Frankly, Saudis by themselves are not capable of launching a plot this sophisticated which requires this kind of training and technical capacity.'[48] The equally influential Prince Naif, minister of the interior, agreed and was still blaming Israeli intelligence a full year after 9/11.

But in the White House the reaction was virtually 'business as usual'. Two days after 9/11, President Bush was smoking cigars with Prince Bandar in the White House and assuring the Saudi royals of 'their eternal friendship'. Despite evidence that Saudi intelligence initially refused to share information about the 9/11 hijackers with US agencies, Bush said he was 'very pleased with the Kingdom's contributions to the war on terror'.

Despite the tragic magnitude of 9/11, the Bush administration was for some time reluctant to cooperate with any inquiry. When the Senate Intelligence Committee investigated arguably the most important event in US history, they were stonewalled and obstructed. 'The more we pressed for information, the more resistant the White House became to giving it,' said Senator Bob Graham, the Committee's Democratic chairman. 'This behaviour bore all the hallmarks of a cover-up. We had discovered . . . a terrorist support network that, at least at one point, went through the Saudi embassy, and a fundraising network that went through the Saudi royal family. And the more discoveries we made, the more the administration's obstructionism intensified.'[49]

Eventually, Senator Graham's eagerly awaited report was released. But the public were in for a shock: the 27-page section which dealt with Saudi financial links to US-based Al-Qaeda terrorists was a sea of nearly text-free blank spaces. It had been classified by the White House and withheld for 'national security reasons'. Despite protests, President Bush refused to relent, claiming that it would harm ongoing intelligence-gathering operations. Senator Graham, who reread the censored material, countered that the information was 'potentially politically embarrassing' and 'it was as if the President's loyalty lay more with Saudi Arabia than with America's safety.'[50]

The US State Department was not far behind the White House in its appeasement approach to the House of Saud in the aftermath of 9/11. It downplayed the Kingdom's appalling human-rights abuses, its lack of democratic freedoms, absence of a free press and denial of women's basic rights – all key justifications for the US overthrow of the fundamentalist Taliban regime in Afghanistan. Even the moderate Secretary of State Colin Powell said that concerns about terror should not lead the US 'to the point where we rupture relations with a country that has been a good friend for many years'.[51]

So, why – in its ruthless pursuit of the 9/11 murderers and their supporters – has the Bush administration been so unwilling to confront the House of Saud? Oil remains a significant reason, with 14.5 per cent of daily US oil imported from Saudi, which also retains 25 per cent of global reserves. America also needed the Prince Sultan military base and its Combined Air Operations Centre along with Saudi influence on other Gulf states for the invasion of Iraq. 'The US–Saudi relationship was not primarily about oil, which we can buy from anywhere and which they have to sell to some place to keep their system going,' said Walter Slocombe. 'It was about our mutual dependency for security. The Saudis are very good judges of their own self-interest. They recognised that, at the end of the day, they were dependent on us for military defence – against Iran or Iraq. At the same time we needed the Saudis because we needed access to bases if our military were to operate with reasonable efficiency in the region. Without their political support, we probably would not get access to others in the region, which was essential, and also, without their more active consent, we could not get access to Saudi bases themselves, which were extremely helpful, though not absolutely essential.'

There is also a more subtle, insidious reason. It is what Robert Baer calls 'a consent of silence, or, more politely, deference' for the Kingdom.[52] This was acknowledged by Dr Ghazi Al-Gosaibi, Saudi ambassador in the UK from 1992 until 2002. In his book *The Gulf Crisis* he showed how America deployed this 'extreme sensitivity':

> Three years before the [1991] Gulf crisis, King Fahd strongly criticised the American ambassador [Alexander Horan Hume] in the presence of Philip Habib, the envoy of President Reagan. The US State Department immediately recalled the ambassador and replaced him. It is doubtful whether an urbanised Arab country would dare to treat the American ambassador as the Bedouin country did.[53]

One of Alexander Horan Hume's successors, Chas Freeman, now chairman of Projects International, which has several commercial clients in the Middle East, has shown similar deference. In a deposition on behalf of Prince Sultan, the defence minister who was at the time being sued by families of the 9/11 victims for allegedly sponsoring Al-Qaeda via Islamic charities, Freeman said that 'the Kingdom would certainly be deeply insulted' by an adverse ruling in the US courts. He added that adjudication of the claims showed such 'disrespect' for Saudi sovereignty that it was tantamount to the use of a military force against its borders or what he called a *causa belli*.

In response, Jeane Kirkpatrick, former US permanent representative at the UN and member of President Reagan's Cabinet and NSC, criticised Freeman for arguing, in effect, that Saudi sovereignty overrode the rule of law. 'The most troubling aspect of Ambassador Freeman's declaration is the notion . . . that US courts should disregard the judgements of the Congress and the decision of the President to bring the rule of law to bear in combating terrorism.' In her deposition, Kirkpatrick concluded that Freeman 'showed inadequate concern for the rights of an American citizen caught in the grips of the Saudi justice system. Regretfully, I observe in his current affidavit the same tendency to view human rights of Americans as subordinate to the smooth functioning of diplomacy.'

The House of Saud is also protected by fast money swirling around the US capital. According to Robert Baer:

> Any Washington bureaucrat with a room-temperature IQ knows that if he stays on the right side of the Kingdom, some way or another he will be able to finagle his way in to feed at the Saudi trough. There is hardly a living former assistant secretary of state for the Near East, CIA director, White House staffer, or member of Congress who has not ended up on the Saudi payroll . . . With this kind of money out there, of course Washington bureaucrats don't have the backbone to take on Saudi Arabia.[54]

The House of Saud has been spending heavily on K Street, the address of many of Washington DC's lobbyists and think tanks. Most former US ambassadors in Riyadh are retained by law firms, public relations firms and foreign policy centres funded by the royal family. The most notable and ironic of these is James Baker, former secretary of state under President George H. Bush, whose law firm Baker Botts represents the senior Saudi princes who have been accused of backing the 9/11 hijackers. This influence-peddling was acknowledged by Prince Bandar, Saudi ambassador in Washington DC. 'If the reputation then builds that the Saudis take care of their friends when they leave office, you would be surprised how much better friends you have who are just coming into office,' he said during an interview with PBS a month after 9/11.

Prince Bandar remains a pivotal figure in Saudi–US relations. He is not just the ambassador. As a son of Prince Sultan, the defence minister, and a favourite nephew of King Fahd, he has been given licence to negotiate many of the multi-billion arms deals. 'He [Bandar] was like a son to King Fahd,' said Freeman. 'It was a mutual-admiration affair and I think Fahd entrusted him with an enormous amount of responsibility at an early age and was not disappointed.'

Flamboyant, confident and articulate, Prince Bandar is a generous host at his estate in Mclean, Virginia. There is no doubt that US–Saudi relations are much cooler since 9/11, but he retains direct access to the Oval Office and has privileged status. Bandar was shown the secret military plans to invade Iraq in advance and is the only foreign diplomat to have a security detail assigned to him by the State Department.

This is in spite of the fact that Chas Freeman argues that the unique closeness between the two nations no longer exists. 'There was a special relationship that constituted a deal and I think it's gone and is no longer upheld by either party,' he said. 'The deal was a very simple, unadorned exchange of American provision of external security for the Kingdom in return for preferential access to energy.' The former US ambassador says that the deal broke down gradually during the 1990s when the US became less of a protector and more of a security liability as an attractive target for Islamic terrorists in Saudi. The threat to the Kingdom was now internal rather than external. The collapse of the Soviet Union also focused more attention on the US-backed Israel and its treatment of Palestinians, which induced more tension.

Meanwhile, UK–Saudi relations remain warm. Unlike the US,

Britain has not been a participant in Israeli depredations in the occupied territories by subsidising the regime and supplying it with guns that kill Palestinians. 'Their [Saudis'] sense of betrayal by the Americans is much more bitter than whatever they felt towards the British over Iraq,' said Chas Freeman. 'Also, the British have been firm but polite at managing the visa and entry procedures of Arab visitors into the UK. London remains the cultural capital of the Arab world and the centre of intellectual life. It is where their great newspapers are published and where people go to enjoy their freedom.'

However, while the US retains military acquisitorial ambitions in the Gulf, their axis with Saudi will always be strong. Mindful of this role, the House of Saud still exerts power and the Bush administration remains sensitive to its proclivities. In 2002, Crown Prince Abdullah was flying to see President Bush at his ranch in Crawford, Texas. During the journey the pilot of the aircraft was spoken to by a female air traffic controller, so the Federal Aviation Authority replaced the woman so the Saudi could speak with a man.

While the Bush regime has treated the House of Saud like a mischievous younger brother with a poor choice of friends, Al-Qaeda realised that the ruling family was now politically vulnerable. Since 9/11 it has instigated a series of bombings in Riyadh, many of which were blamed on innocent Westerners. After all, it was the House of Saud that defiled and defamed Islam by allowing the American infidels to park their tanks on the holy turf. And it was the royal family who sacrificed Islam for money and corrupt arms deals and wasted the billions of oil revenues on a sleazy and hypocritical lifestyle. As one Saudi diplomat memorably said after 9/11: 'What shocks me most is why they hit America and not us.'

FIVE

A ROYAL PERCENTAGE

'If you tell me that building this whole country, and in spending $350 billion out of $400 billion that we misused or got corrupted with $50 billion, I'll tell you, "Yes, so what?" But I'll take that any time . . . We did not invent corruption, nor did those dissidents, who are so genius, discover it. This has happened since Adam and Eve. It is human nature. You know what? I would be offended if I thought we had a monopoly over corruption.'

Prince Bandar Bin Sultan, Saudi ambassador to the United States,
Frontline, PBS, September 2001

Late one Sunday night in the summer of 2004, Prince Bandar Bin Sultan, the powerful Saudi ambassador to the United States, telephoned a senior executive of Wachovia Bank at his home. The usually unflappable diplomat had a problem: his embassy had more than $10 million in cashier's cheques and no bank in which to deposit them. Three months earlier its long-time bank, Riggs Bank, had dropped the Saudis as a client after embassy officials could not satisfactorily explain large wire transfers overseas by Prince Bandar. Millions of dollars in cheques were then stashed in safety deposit boxes at Riggs Bank branches. But the embassy had no local bank to deposit them in. 'Would you be interested in our business?' asked the anxious ambassador.

The Wachovia executive was aware of the Saudi's predicament because Riggs Bank had been fined $25 million for violating anti-money-laundering laws in its embassy division. He also knew that regulators had uncovered improprieties in 150 Saudi embassy accounts at Riggs. The Bank had failed to file 'suspicious-activity reports' for huge withdrawals of cash – $1 million at a time – and 'unusual transactions' by Prince Bandar, according to the Office of the Currency Comptroller. Minutes of a Riggs Bank meeting on 7 April 2003 showed that the Saudi ambassador requested '$2 million in cash for travelling expenses'. This was denied, so Bandar promptly transferred the funds to another bank.[1]

But there was worse: an FBI and US Treasury investigation had identified more than $27 million in other 'suspicious transactions', including hundreds of thousands of dollars paid to Muslim charities, clerics and Saudi students who were being scrutinised for possible links to terrorist activity. Prosecutors found no evidence that the Saudi withdrawals were criminal in nature, but the transactions were sufficiently suspicious to warrant being reported by Riggs Bank auditors to the US Treasury.[2]

Even in Washington DC, where deference to the Saudi royal family appears to have an infinite capacity, banks could not risk falling foul of the strict anti-money-laundering laws. And former embassy clients of Riggs were proving 'toxic'. For Wachovia, the embassy accounts were relatively small, but the Bank executive took advice – it did not take long – and politely declined Prince Bandar's offer. The ambassador's search for a new bank went on.

One of the 'suspicious-activity reports' revealed a bigger issue that has belittled and besmirched the House of Saud and helped Al-

Qaeda: corruption. The document stated that, in 2003, $17.4 million was transferred from the Saudi Defence Ministry account to an individual in Saudi Arabia identified as the coordinator of 'home improvements/construction' for Prince Bandar. The funds were to build a new palace for the ambassador. As he already owned seven properties around the world, notably a $30 million village estate in Glympton, Oxfordshire, and a $36 million 32-room mansion in Aspen, Colorado, it was difficult to know why he needed another home. But the real issue was that the money came from a government account. 'This is corruption beyond the pale,' commented Ali Ahmed, a prominent Saudi dissident.[3]

For decades the royal family's raiding of state funds for personal use did not generate intense hostility among the Saudi people. The Kingdom's founder, Abdul Aziz, handed out cash and gold coins to princes and potential political rivals to secure their loyalty. Until the 1970s the amounts of money were generally small and pay-offs were accepted in the House of Saud as long as everyone received a slice of the action. There was almost a cultural acquiescence within Saudi society.[4] That changed with the oil boom. Suddenly there was an opportunity to cash in as droves of Western contractors flew into Riyadh to capitalise on Saudi's riches. But instead of a diverse distribution of the wealth, a small number of royal princes secured the largest portion for their private use.

The Saudis claim that this greed only occurred when Westerners arrived bearing gifts. 'For a bribe to be received, someone has to pay it,' said one academic. And as one Saudi economist told an American journalist: 'If there's a corruption problem in Saudi Arabia, it's because you taught us how.'[5] Prince Bandar was almost brazenly upbeat in his approach. He told the PBS *Frontline* programme that between 1971 and 2001 the royal family had spent nearly $400 billion to develop the Kingdom. 'If you tell me that building this whole country, and in spending $350 billion out of $400 billion that we misused or got corrupted with $50 billion, I'll tell you, "Yes, so what?" But I'll take that any time . . . We did not invent corruption, nor did those dissidents, who are so genius, discover it. This has happened since Adam and Eve. It is human nature. You know what? I would be offended if I thought we had a monopoly over corruption.'[6]

For the dissidents and Islamic insurgents, the origin of bribery is irrelevant. It is a grievance which has given them increasing political currency and populist appeal. 'If a poor guy steals a chicken to feed his starving family, then they cut off his hand. But if a prince steals billions, it's OK,' observed the Saudi former diplomat Mohammed Al-Khilewi.[7] The corruption is now so pervasive that it would make Saddam Hussein jealous. Oil revenues are currently pouring in at an estimated $50 billion a year. In theory, that's about $6,700 for every working Saudi. But the income distribution does not work that way. Some of it is used to maintain a fast-growing population of Muslim activists, many of whom are young and unemployed. But most of the wealth is concentrated in the royal family – an estimated 6,000 princes with another 20,000 of their relatives and offspring. 'Some members of the Saudi royal family see the country as though it was their private property,' said Mohammed Al-Khilewi. 'Saudi Arabia is the only family-owned business with membership in the United Nations.'[8]

At the helm of this bounty sits King Fahd, an ailing and fading figurehead since his near-fatal stroke on 29 November 1995. During his 23-year reign he has acquired a private fortune of $20 billion, according to *Forbes* magazine. Most of it is invested in property. For the summer the King owns a 100-room whitewashed palace in Marbella, Spain. Known as 'The Cottage', it is modelled on the White House but is four times its size and is used more by his extended family and his 3,000-strong entourage. When they visit the palace they spend an average of $5 million a day in the local stores, so much so that shopkeepers want to name a street after the King. Built in the 1970s, it was renovated at a cost of $10 million. There is also a separate palace for Prince Salman, his brother, and landing strips for three helicopters, a sports centre, a mosque and some lesser villas for guests and their families. But King Fahd is rarely seen in Marbella. During one rare outing in late August 2002, the tired-looking King, accompanied by 30 women in full-length dark robes, was observed being pushed in his wheelchair up the gangplank of his $50 million royal yacht, the 234-ft *Al-Diriyah*, for an afternoon cruise in the bay. He also possesses a 482-ft boat called *Prince Abdul Aziz* – until 2004, the largest in the world. It resembles a small passenger liner and acts as a heliport.[9]

Across the Pyrenees, King Fahd owns the vast Château de l'Aurore in Golfe-Juan on the French Riviera with fabulous views of the Mediterranean. But in recent years he has spent more time at his Swiss retreat at Collonge-Bellerive, just outside Geneva, Switzerland, because of his deteriorating health. Fitted out with 1,000 phone lines, the estate contains garages for 300 Mercedes and 100 Rolls-Royces for his entourage. From there he receives treatment by his American doctors while his private jet – a Boeing 747, containing a sauna, a banquet room and dominated by gold fixtures – is on standby at Geneva airport. In Saudi Arabia there are another seven palaces, notably the enormous $2.5 billion Al-Yamamah Palace complex in Riyadh, which took four years to build.

The King's worldwide property portfolio is owned by two anonymous secretive Liechtenstein trusts called the Asturion Foundation and Norista Foundation. Asturion has been used by the Saudi ruler since the mid-1970s to shelter his money abroad. It constitutes a legal entity that holds bank accounts of which King Fahd is the beneficiary, according to documents passed to *Der Spiegel* magazine. It is not known how much money the foundation holds, but one of its registered assets is Kenstead Hall, a mock-Tudor mansion on Bishop's Avenue, Hampstead – known as north London's 'Billionaire's Row'.

King Fahd's trusts are run by a Liechtenstein lawyer called Dr Herbert Batliner, whose clients have included the son of former Nigerian President General Sani Abacha and the pardoned fugitive US oil trader Marc Rich. He was also approached by the partner of an Ecuadorian drug baron to set up a trust, but the US confiscated the cash. Dr Batliner, now worth an estimated $400 million, set up these foundations when money-laundering was not illegal in Liechtenstein. 'He had been given assurances that the money was of a legal source,' said Robert Wallner, Liechtenstein's chief prosecutor.

'I'm not a Father Confessor who has to ask his clients if they have obeyed the laws of their homelands,' Dr Batliner once remarked.[10]

These trusts could, in the future, come under regulatory scrutiny because Western banks may refuse to accept deposits from senior Saudi royals like King Fahd – just as Riggs Bank dropped the Saudi embassy account in Washington DC. This is due to new guidelines drawn up to identify 'politically exposed' wealthy individuals whose assets could be confiscated. Banks, particularly in Switzerland, are increasingly wary of accepting new business from rulers of controversial countries, according to *The Guardian*. 'Some banks take the view that we will not have anything to do with members of the Saudi royal family,' said a source close to the Wolfsberg group – an alliance of 12 major banks which has been convened to counter money-laundering.[11]

Their concern follows the embarrassment of some banks being forced to trace and pay back vast fortunes plundered by notorious former dictators like Ferdinand Marcos in the Philippines, Joseph Mobutu in Zaire and General Sani Abacha in Nigeria. 'Accepting and managing funds from corrupt, politically exposed persons will severely damage the bank's own reputation, even if the illegal origin of the assets is difficult to prove,' the Basel Committee on Banking Supervision warned in 2001. 'The bank may be subject to costly information requests and seizure orders from law enforcement.'

If the major Western banks join Riggs and Wachovia in Washington DC and reject Saudi money, it would be a major blow to the House of Saud, who value their international reputation. In November 2001, the family spent £5 million on newspaper advertisements portraying King Fahd as a benevolent paternal figure watching over his kingdom: 'For two decades he has been the quiet symbol of stability and diplomacy,' stated the text. In fact, the stroke in 1995 almost incapacitated the King, who is nearly brain-dead, and his condition produced a prolonged period of political internecine warfare inside the family.

The King's frailty was self-evident a month later when his bowels gave way in his swimming pool during physical therapy in front of his family.[12] He has survived some life-threatening brain spasms and with round-the-clock medical treatment he can sit in a chair and open his eyes, and is occasionally wheeled out for ceremonial events. But he spends most of his days watching cartoons on television, occasionally babbling about his past and present sexual exploits. The last event he can remember in any detail is the Iraqi invasion of Kuwait in 1990 and he often asks for the whereabouts of his long-deceased parents.

As soon as news broke of his stroke, the distant sirens of convoys, private jets and helicopters could be heard descending on the hospital. The first at his bedside was his fourth and favourite wife Jawhara and his extravagantly spoiled son Azouzi. The next to arrive were his full brothers, Princes Sultan, Naif and Salman – the most powerful in the Kingdom apart from Crown Prince Abdullah. They were neurotic about keeping the King clinically alive and could be heard frantically calling doctors all over the world. This was not entirely due to any high regard for their brother: in his later life he had become lazy and a womaniser and over the past 20 years developed embarrassing gambling and drinking habits.[13] No, their priority was to prevent Abdullah, their 79-year-old half-brother, from becoming King. For he made little secret that he planned to cut back on corruption and their royal perks.

Crown Prince Abdullah has always been an aberration in the House of Saud. He represents the Bedouin, conservative, tribal interests in the Kingdom. His mother was from the Shammar tribe, traditional rivals of the Al-Saud clan. Very much the authentic Arab, it was typical that Abdullah was out in the desert when King Fahd suffered his stroke. A superstitious and emotional man, he hates flying and likes to travel by road where possible – usually in a Rolls-Royce with 001 number plates or a customised tour bus.[14] He prefers a simple, relatively frugal lifestyle and his favourite pastime is eating – during one banquet he devoured almost a whole lamb. He once paid his favourite chef $50,000 to fly to Riyadh and cook him his favourite meal, which turned out to be a tuna fish salad, rare mushrooms and hamburgers. But he is not extravagant or corrupt and has turned his back on the palatial luxuries of Riyadh and Jeddah and the bright lights and temptations of Western cities. His rare concession to modernity is the bank of 33 television sets in his office so he can monitor all available satellite channels at once. And his only real indulgence is the breeding of the world's finest Arabian thoroughbred horses at his modest ranch. He owns about 120 mares and 8 stallions in Europe and the United States.

Politically, Crown Prince Abdullah is the traditional Islamic Arab nationalist, a stance at odds with the pro-American policy of King Fahd and his brothers. Before the King's stroke, he had limited power and was seldom consulted. In the late 1980s he was obsessed with the Iranian regime and investigated ways of overthrowing it, based on a fear and dislike of Persia rather than religious prejudice. But when he became the de facto ruler of Saudi in 1995 he developed a shrewd, pragmatic approach and personally brokered a reconciliation with the Iranians.

Among the Saudi public, Abdullah is immensely popular and viewed as straight-talking and honest, particularly compared with his conspicuously avaricious brothers. He used to have a severe stutter, which was an impediment in speaking to his subjects, who regard the poetic use of language as the mark of a true sheikh. For years he rarely spoke on Saudi television until he overcame the problem. A chain-smoker of Vantage cigarettes, he is reputedly semi-literate and does not speak any foreign languages. He prefers to speak Bedouin, with its odd turn of phrase and aphorisms, much to the annoyance of Prince Sultan, the defence minister, who craves the respect and patronage of Western governments. But, despite being occasionally impetuous, he has been an astute and strategic chief executive of Saudi Arabia without ever undercutting King Fahd or reversing his decisions. Crucially, he retains a real power-base as commander of the National Guard, who steadfastly remain loyal to the Crown Prince.[15]

Abdullah makes no secret that he intends to end royal corruption, which was escalating in the mid-1990s despite the Kingdom running up multi-billion budget deficits and national debt. 'The boom is over and will not return. All of us must get used to a different lifestyle,' he said in a thinly veiled jibe at his brothers. For the House of Saud is very much a family enterprise. Every prince receives an allowance, which varies, but can run as high as $270,000 a month for the 24 remaining sons of King Abdul Aziz. They also receive free air travel anywhere in the world and treat Saudi Arabian Airlines like a private service. Nor do they pay for any utilities and telephones. But the big money comes when they exploit their status to cash in from government contracts.

'I think that it is expected that commissions will be taken by officials who are involved in decision-making about government procurement,' said Chas Freeman, who often still meets Crown Prince Abdullah and senior princes. 'It's one of the issues the Crown Prince has been particularly agitated about . . . I think it's endemic and built into the system.'

In 2001, Seymour Hersh of *The New Yorker* obtained details of electronic intercepts of conversations between members of the Saudi royal family as recorded by the US National Security Agency. In the intercepts, which dated from 1994 to 2001, the princes openly talked about cheating the state and even argued about what was an 'acceptable percentage to take'.[16]

The royal fears about Abdullah stamping out corruption were realised in November 1996, a year after the King's stroke. The Crown Prince complained about the billions of dollars that were being diverted by royal family members from a huge state-financed project to renovate the mosque in Mecca. One intercept showed how he urged the princes to get their 'expenses' (i.e. pay-offs) under control.

A few months later he blocked a series of real-estate deals by a prince, enraging other members of the royal family.[17]

Seizing land and property is a major source of ill-gotten gains. As urban development has expanded, the demand for a good location has increased dramatically, pushing up the value of real-estate. Deep public resentment has built up over groups of princes who grab a huge swath of derelict land, register it in their name and then sell it off plot by plot for homes at prices most families can scarcely afford. Another scam is for a prince to order a court to condemn a valuable property or location in the name of the state and then persuade the King to award ownership to him. Senior princes are masters at sequestrating government property for free for themselves and then selling it back to the state – sometimes within a day. Three times Riyadh Zoo has been seized by different princes and each time it was bought back by the administration.

Cafés, restaurants and shops are also vulnerable. 'A prince would walk into a restaurant, see that it was doing well, and then write out a cheque to buy the place which was usually well below the market price,' recalled former CIA officer Robert Baer. 'There was nothing the owner could do. If he resisted, he would end up in jail.'[18] This has alienated the traditional merchant classes, so Abdullah tried to introduce reform and stamp out these practices. But a little-noticed decree is that land and property ownership remains under the control of the Ministry of Local Affairs, which is run by a member of the royal family.

Another money-making operation is to become the legally required Saudi partner of foreign corporations doing business in the construction and service industries in the Kingdom. All major multinational companies have royal business agents who negotiate and procure their government contracts and then collect a percentage of the profits and/or a commission. Much to the alarm of other senior royals, in 1997 Abdullah issued a decree declaring that his sons would not be permitted to go into partnership with foreign corporations working in the Kingdom.[19]

The royal percentage-takers are constantly on the prowl, with King Fahd's sons being the most avaricious. But a direct cut of the sacrosanct oil revenues is reserved for only the most senior princes and even then they only get a small percentage of total production. There are plenty of alternative ruses. One is to simply borrow money from a private bank and refuse to pay it back. This occurred regularly between the late 1970s and mid-1990s when senior House of Saud members borrowed billions of dollars from the controversial National Commercial Bank, managed by Khaled Bin Mahfouz. None of them paid interest and most of the loans were not paid back. This included a ten billion riyal (£1.3 billion) loan to Prince Sultan. Khaled Bin Mahfouz became the royal banker and when King Fahd travelled he was always on hand to provide the cash in Samsonite suitcases (he once boasted of carrying $5 billion during one trip to America). But these royal non-performing loans ruined the National Commercial Bank, which did not even have accounts for three years. Eventually, in 1998, after a long period of chaos, it was bailed out by the Saudi government and now thrives under new management.

If Crown Prince Abdullah succeeds in his anti-corruption crusade, he will need to deal with senior members of his own family. The former insider Mohammed Al-Khilewi, who took 13,000 incriminating government documents with him when he resigned in 1994, says the princes even exploit Islam for financial gain. One of his most damaging revelations is that Saudi diplomats deposit official funds in New York bank accounts, notably the contribution to the United Nations, and then delay their distribution while diverting the interest into their own private accounts. Al-Khilewi is in a position to know because for two years he was first secretary of the Saudi Arabian mission to the United Nations in New York City.[20]

The endemic nature of corruption was discovered by Chas Freeman. After the 1991 Gulf war, a group of mostly Shia Iraqi refugees who had been involved in the rebellion against Saddam Hussein in the south were disarmed and interned by American forces. Knowing that if they were returned to Iraq they would be instantly executed, Freeman persuaded the Saudis to accommodate the refugees. It was not easy because there is no love lost between the Saudi Sunnis and Iraqi Shias. It was like talking devout Irish Catholics into taking in hard-line Protestants. But the Saudis agreed and they built an effective and modern refugee facility in Rafa, in northern Saudi Arabia.

As part of the construction, the Saudis needed a lot of field-grade telephone wire. The US were dismantling their military presence in Europe and removing equipment, so they had the material and shipped it to the Kingdom on an expedited basis. The Saudis installed it and the American government sent them an invoice for the cost of the wire. Two days later the Saudi official telephoned the US military officer who presented the bill and said, 'There is a problem with your invoice.'

'What's the problem?' asked the officer.

'This is only 10 per cent of what we pay under the Al-Yamamah [arms contract – literally meaning 'dove of peace'] commission arrangement.'

'Well, this is what it costs. This is the international price.'

'Well, couldn't you alter the invoice? We'll pay you the higher price.'

'No, this is what it costs.'

On this occasion the Saudi official did not receive his customary kickback. But it was indicative of the almost institutional nature of the problem.

The deep pockets of the royal family are filled mainly from commissions from buying billions of dollars of arms from the West. The Saudi government spends more per capita than any other country in the world – an estimated 35 per cent of its revenue is set aside for the armed forces. In 2001 the Kingdom's defence spending increased by 50.8 per cent after a reduction in previous years, according to US Defence Department figures. That year the US government's Foreign Military Sales programme delivered $2.03

billion of weapons to Saudi and its arms companies exported another $1.02 billion. That equipment excludes Saudi's external defence, because American F-15 combat air patrols over the Gulf take care of that.

Despite all that weaponry, Saudi Arabia has not fought a war since the 1930s and has not contributed in any of the Arab–Israeli wars since 1948. When Iraq was poised to invade in 1990, the royal family needed the US cavalry to rescue them because it could not defend the narrow border it shares with Kuwait. This begs the questions: where does all the defence money go and why are the armed forces so inadequate? A major factor is the heavy dependence on US military protection. Vast amounts are also spent on personal protection for the royal family, notably the National Guard, which must be the most expensive bodyguard service in the world. But equally, many defence contracts are devised purely to generate commissions for the senior princes, and so the use and quality control of the hardware becomes superfluous.

The US government has banned their companies from paying bribes to secure contracts by passing the Foreign Corrupt Practices Act. But insiders say this has been circumvented. 'Saudi corruption in the United States is extraordinary,' said Mohammed Al-Khilewi. 'No commercial or military deal with Saudi Arabia goes through without some Saudi official taking a commission, whatever the law states. The Saudis are brazenly breaking American law. Examine closely the terms of agreement and you will see that the costs are always at least twice the fair market price. Most royal family members take five per cent of any deal but some princes take more.'[21]

As we have seen, the Saudi ambassador effectively admitted this during a PBS television interview. He estimated that of the approximate $400 billion spent on developing the Kingdom since the early 1970s, about $50 billion was lost to corruption. 'Using that ratio as a guide,' calculated Robert Baer, 'perhaps $12.5 billion of the $100 billion in armaments purchased from the US has been kicked back to the Saudi royal family in bribes – about $800 million a year.'[22]

The required commissions are secured by ingenious schemes, notably through the 'offset programme', which means that part of the contract must be invested in the country's infrastructure. 'Look carefully at the deals and you will see that the Saudi government demands that about 35 per cent of all major contracts be "offset" – that is, 35 per cent must be steered back to the Saudi economy,' said Al-Khilewi. 'The foreign companies don't care where the 35 per cent goes as long as they get their 65 per cent. The Saudi royal family members consider this 35 per cent to be their personal commission. They set up phoney companies with a large number of ghost employees. I personally know a prince who bought a building for $300,000, then rented it for $7 million a year to a Western company for seven years.'[23]

From the West's point of view, selling arms and paving the way with inducements is not just profitable for its defence industry, it cements their strategic, oil-for-security relationship. As the major contracts are negotiated on a government-to-government basis and the funds are administered by the US and UK defence ministries, ministers and officials are all too aware of the under-the-table deals.

Some princes are more notorious than others. Take Prince Khaled Bin Sultan, son of Prince Sultan, who has been the defence minister since 1963. His involvement in the arms bazaar started in 1977 when Raytheon, the giant US defence manufacturer, supplied Hawk missiles to Saudi for $2 billion. At the time, Prince Khaled was a 28-year-old army major. But after that deal a joint venture, Raytheon Middle East Systems, was set up, with Prince Khaled as chairman and a 51 per cent controlling shareholder. 'Khaled later [in 1986] became head of Active Air Defence, which was split off from the army to form a separate command,' the Prince's former aviation manager from 1976 until 1992 told me. 'He could now sell missiles to himself.'

Like his father, Prince Khaled was now in the cockpit to make big money. During the 1991 Gulf War, Prince Khaled, by then joint supreme commander of the allied forces, leased his own private jet, a

A TORTURED CONFESSION

Following seven weeks of torture and solitary confinement in a Riyadh interrogation centre and jail, British anaesthetic technician Sandy Mitchell confesses to two car-bombings on 5 February 2001. His wife and three-year-old son were also repeatedly threatened before he made this statement on Saudi TV. (© EPA/EMPICS)

RECOGNITION

Sandy Mitchell receives an award from Dr Mohammed Mofti, director of medical affairs of the Saudi Interior Ministry, for his work as an anaesthetic technician at the Saudi Security Forces hospital in October 2000. Two months later he was arrested after two terrorist car bombs exploded in the Saudi capital. (courtesy of Sandy Mitchell)

AT THE HIGHEST LEVEL

The foreign secretary Jack Straw listens to his Saudi counterpart, Prince Saud, address the conference 'Two Kingdoms: Facing the Challenges Ahead' in London in 2002. Although they had several meetings about the British detainees being tortured in Saudi jails, it was the terrorist bombings in the Kingdom that persuaded the Saudis to negotiate their release. (© PA/EMPICS)

JUST GOOD FRIENDS

King Fahd greets Tony Blair during his visit to Riyadh on 31 October 2001. The trip was controversial because it occurred so soon after 9/11, when evidence was already emerging about Saudi financing of international terrorism. The Kingdom 'is a good and dependable friend to the civilised world . . . not just on a trade and commercial level, but at a political level,' said Blair. (© PA/EMPICS)

ROYAL FORTUNE

Prince Charles with Prince Khaled Al-Faisal, eldest son of the late King Faisal, at their joint exhibition of 'Paintings and Patronage' in Riyadh in February 2001. During this visit the Prince of Wales raised the plight of the imprisoned British men privately with the royal family but was politely ignored. (© EPA/EMPICS)

CHIEF OF INTELLIGENCE

Prince Naif bin Abdul Aziz, the interior minister and arguably the second most powerful member of the House of Saud. He controls the mabaheth, the secret police, and oversees the mutawwa, the religious police.
(© EPA/EMPICS)

DEATH SENTENCE

This is known as 'Chop Chop' square in Riyadh, where public executions take place. Between 1980 and 2003, 1,409 beheadings have occurred here. Most of the victims are foreign workers, the poor and women.
(© EPA/EMPICS)

ARMS AND THE MAN

Sir Richard Evans, chairman of BAE Systems until 2004, denying claims that BAE paid a total of £60 million to prominent Saudis to secure multi-billion-pound defence contracts. 'We are not in the business of making payments to members of any government,' he told a session of the Commons Defence Select Committee. (© PA/EMPICS)

HOSTAGE TO OIL

One of the world's largest oil storage facilities, on the east coast of Saudi Arabia, near the Persian Gulf city of Dhahran. A terrorist attack on this area would be devastating for the global economy, because Saudi controls 25 per cent of the world's oil reserves. (© EPA/EMPICS)

AL-QAEDA BOMBING ON SAUDI SOIL

Part of the wreckage caused by an Al-Qaeda suicide bomb which killed 35 people and injured 200 in Riyadh in May 2003. The target was a compound that housed employees of the Vinnell Corporation, the US security company that trained the Saudi National Guard, which protects the royal family. (Rafael Maldonado)

INSIDE JOB

It was over this wall that some of the Al-Qaeda operatives escaped after they bombed the Vinnell housing compound. Former Vinnell employees say that Saudi National Guard officers gave the terrorists vital inside information. It was after this atrocity that the Saudi government finally admitted that such car-bombings were carried out by insurgents and not by Western expatriates. (© Rafael Maldonado)

AN AILING MONARCH

King Fahd (centre), aged 80, has been confined to a wheelchair since his severe stroke in 1995, and is only nominally involved in state affairs. Every summer he escapes the intense heat of his Kingdom and retreats to his Swiss estate at Collonge-Bellerive or his Spanish palace in Marbella. (© EPA/EMPICS)

WEALTH UNLIMITED

Until 2004, King Fahd's 120-metre long $80 million private yacht, the *Prince Abdul Aziz*, was the largest in the world. It resembles a small passenger liner and has a heliport. King Fahd has accumulated a private fortune of $20 billion since he became ruler. (© DPA/EMPICS)

PRINCE OF HOPE

Crown Prince Abdullah bin Abdul Aziz, the most powerful member of the House of Saud. He is the only serious advocate for political reform and has made himself unpopular in the royal family by trying to clean up royal corruption. (© ABACA/EMPICS)

Boeing 727, to the American and Saudi forces – a blatant act of benefiting from the war. His joint venture operation, Raytheon Middle East Systems, was also awarded all the major service, support, logistic and equipment contracts for the allies, according to the Prince's aviation manager and invoices seen by the author. His company was the sole supplier of every meal and drop of water for some 750,000 soldiers and ancillary staff over 7 months. 'The allegation is that he and some others made a fair amount of money from the war,' said Chas Freeman. 'I don't know whether that's true or not, not having seen his accounts. But if it is, I would say that in Saudi Arabia it's not unusual.'

After the war Prince Khaled was asked to resign as commander of the Saudi armed forces (in his memoirs General Schwarzkopf claimed that he was only chosen for his royal blood and the authority to write cheques). But, flush with hundreds of millions, the Prince invested in real-estate. He bought the Elbow Beach hotel in Bermuda for $70 million after a week-long holiday there. In 1990 he secretly paid $14.38 million for an ocean-to-lake estate at 9110 South Ocean Boulevard, Palm Beach, Florida, from Wilson and Toni Lucom. At first the couple did not know it was Saudi cash, because the named buyer was an offshore company called Ocean Bay Holdings Ltd, based in the Bahamas. It was only when Prince Khaled tried to build a three-floor, 147-room, 53,000-square-foot mansion that his identity emerged. Faced with opposition from the town planners, he then tried to divide the land into 9 lots, but its value dropped and he sold it for $10.6 million. At a dinner party in Palm Beach afterwards, Wilson Lucom said that Prince Khaled bought his estate because the royals believed they might be overthrown and so needed safe havens.

Back home the former general became a media mogul: in November 1995 he bought *Al-Hayat*, the influential and slavishly pro-government Saudi newspaper, and *Al-Wasat*, the political weekly published in London. Just to exert control, the Prince bought 15 per cent of the Saudi advertising agency Tihama for $11.73 million. He also owns a satellite channel on Arabsat which broadcasts throughout the Middle East.

As Prince Khaled's wealth grew, so did his entourage. By 1990 his Boeing 727 was too small and was replaced by a luxurious VIP 707 jet with a price-tag of $30 million. Khaled commissioned his aviation manager to install state-of-the-art facilities and the best possible quality fixtures with a capacity to carry 50 people on a routine flight. 'I want to be able to enjoy the aircraft until 2025,' said the Prince. He wanted innovations, so a miniature digital camera was fitted to the co-pilot's eyebrow window which enabled a passenger to look forward along the aircraft's flight path. Sitting in the back of the aircraft, Khaled was able to steer the camera using a joystick. A secret hidden compartment by the quilted leather-padded headboard of his bed was also installed to hold his security and protection equipment.

All of this James Bond-style gadgetry was, of course, not cheap and the final bill was $33.5 million. Despite being given advance estimates, Prince Khaled refused to pay his aviation manager, Captain Tom Friedrich, and the contractors. An angry and bemused Friedrich was then forced out of Kalair USA, the company which owned the aircraft, after being offered only $80,000 of the $400,000 due to him.

However, Friedrich fought back and sued. Three aviation executives swore affidavits stating that the renovation and design work was 'above the normal expertise of a chief pilot', according to documents filed at the San Antonio district court. In April 1992, Friedrich secured a court order for the 707 jet to be grounded until he was paid. Suddenly, on 22 May 1992, without warning, agents for Wafic Said, the Syrian business manager for Prince Khaled and vice-president of Kalair, flew the aircraft out of San Antonio to Florida, leaving Friedrich high and dry. Once again the pilot obtained a sequestration order for when it arrived in Florida and this time the aircraft stayed put. Kalair USA then proposed an 'expedited trial' if Friedrich dissolved his sequestration order.

Friedrich agreed but then a month later Kalair breached the

agreement. On 11 June 1992, an agent for Wafic Said told him that he would be sued 'for damaging Kalair's good name' unless he backed down. This was rather odd because Kalair did not have a public reputation – it was purely the corporate vehicle for the ownership of the jet. But the company did provide an insight into how senior Saudi princes structured their business affairs. Kalair USA was owned by Kalair Panama which, in turn, was owned by Waseet Saudi Arabia which is part of a trust called the Barada Settlement, listed as a Wafic Said trust in Luxemburg.

The dispute then turned nasty. As financial controller of Kalair, Wafic Said entrusted George Kanaan, a Lebanese-American who worked directly for Prince Khaled as his private banker, to resolve the dispute. A meeting was arranged at the offices of Linklater and Paines, the Prince's solicitors in London. At 7.30 p.m. on 14 September 1992, Friedrich, his wife Kate and his daughter Laura, who also worked for Kalair, gathered in the conference room with Charles Pettit, lawyer for Prince Khaled, and George Kanaan, who told them that he was also acting for the Prince.

When Friedrich outlined his case and asked to be paid, Kanaan scoffed loudly. Then, when his wife Kate said they were considering legal action, the private banker became 'very angry, hostile and menacing', according to a sworn affidavit by Laura that Friedrich later filed in a criminal court. 'If you take this matter up in the States, we will crush your family with the Prince's $50 billion cheque book,' he shouted. 'You will lose everything and you will be finished. If you take it to court, you will have more pain and suffering than you could possibly imagine.'

Laura was outraged by the tone of Kanaan's outburst. 'I was shocked by the underlying insinuations of possible violence towards my family,' she later stated. And so she sought a clarification of his remarks. 'You have already caused us to lose everything but our lives,' she told Prince Khaled's banker. 'Do you mean that we will lose our lives?' Kanaan just stared at Laura Friedrich very angrily and did not dissent or say a word.

As far as the Friedrich family were concerned, the remarks by Prince Khaled's banker constituted a death threat. An official complaint was lodged with the San Antonio police department, but no charges were filed and the civil legal dispute was never resolved.

As Prince Khaled is the ultimate beneficiary of assets via a web of shell companies and trusts in impenetrable locations, he has usually escaped official scrutiny. The exception was when the US Internal Revenue Service (IRS) investigated allegations that Litton Industries Inc., a US defence electronics supplier, paid a $47 million commission to Prince Khaled and wrote off the payments as business deductions. The alleged bribes enabled Litton to win a $1.7 billion contract to build an integrated radar air-defence system for Saudi Arabia. Construction began in 1979 and the scheme was completed in 1993.

The IRS inquiry was based on documents and claims by Stephen Reddy, a lawyer and former manager of Litton Industries Inc.'s housing programme in Saudi. He claims that he was sacked because he raised concerns about the improper payments to Prince Khaled and filed a lawsuit against his former employer. Reddy stated that Prince Khaled and Saudi government officials received between $47 million and $183 million in commissions by manipulating a contract to build houses for the Litton workers living in Saudi Arabia during installation of the radar equipment.

The pay-offs were finessed and facilitated by Litton issuing a $214 million sub-contract to a company controlled by Wafic Said, the Prince's 'personal business agent', for housing construction. This was one of those infamous offset deals. Wafic Said's company then assigned that sub-contract to TAG Systems, registered in Liechtenstein and ultimately controlled by Prince Khaled. TAG Systems in turn sub-contracted the business to a German firm to build the houses for a mere $99 million. The $115 million excess, according to Reddy, was then disbursed to the sub-contractors: one of them being TAG Systems, whose ultimate beneficiary was Prince Khaled, who pocketed $47 million. He also sold land and houses to

Litton at inflated prices. 'Everybody at Litton knew Prince Khaled was in charge of TAG,' said Reddy. 'The Prince made every decision on the job and said that he personally negotiated the broad outlines of the Litton air-defence contract.'[24]

In his lawsuit, Reddy claimed that the excess payments received by TAG Systems represented a 'formal kickback arrangement' struck between Litton and Prince Khaled in the late 1970s. But his case was dismissed by the Circuit of Appeal in California in 1990 and the following year the Supreme Court refused to review it. Reddy reluctantly withdrew his suit in 1994 at the request of the Justice Department after the statute of limitations had expired.

The IRS investigation went beyond the preliminary stage after federal agents raided the Litton Industries head office and took away 1,000 documents. Prince Khaled, through his lawyers, Christy and Viener, denied that he held any 'legal or beneficial interest' in TAG Systems. Litton also denied the allegations, specifically that it had purchased land from the Prince. But Steve Kantor, a former sub-contracts administrator in Litton's Saudi Arabian housing programme, said he attended several meetings where Reddy raised ethical concerns about the company's dealings with TAG Systems. 'He was ignored. I believed him,' recalled Kantor.[25]

Now retired from the military, the 56-year-old Prince spends most of his time travelling in Europe. When in London he stays in the Presidential suite of the Carlton Tower in Knightsbridge, while his entourage occupy at least one floor of the hotel, or he rents a house on The Boltons, an exclusive street in Kensington. In the Mediterranean he cruises on his 219-ft yacht, *The Golden Shadow*. But he remains close to Western weapons manufacturers eager – as always – to sell to Saudi. For many years he was a shareholder in United Technologies Inc., Westland Helicopters and Thomson-CSF.

His father, 80-year-old Prince Sultan Bin Abdul Aziz, the defence minister and the next in line to the throne after Crown Prince Abdullah, has also been accused of corruption. Former CIA officer Robert Baer claims that the defence minister has benefited from a litany of dubious deals: from huge, illicit commissions on the Al-Yamamah arms contract with the UK to covering up shady property deals. In 1995 the minister for rural affairs, Mohammed Al-Shaykh, bravely tried to block the seizure of some valuable land by one of Prince Sultan's sons. 'The only land the royal family had not reached to grab was the moon,' said the minister. Prince Sultan went ballistic and the minister was sacked. According to Baer: 'He [Prince Sultan] did not care so much about his son being out of some money, but he could see how far [Prince] Abdullah intended to take his [anti-corruption] reforms. One day it was his son, the next day it would be him . . . Sultan was absolutely right about being in Abdullah's sights. For the Crown Prince, the crooked property deals were a small piece of the tapestry of corruption. The off-budget deals were the bigger pieces, bankrupting the country, and no one was more up to his ears than Prince Sultan.'[26]

A measure of Prince Sultan's venality is that a fellow member of the House of Saud was driven to publicly indict him: an almost unprecedented event. On 21 May 2003, a nephew of King Fahd, Prince Sultan Bin Turki, alleged that his namesake was 'the oldest and most corrupt' minister in the world while 'his army is in a weak state never seen in history'. In a statement to United Press International, the Prince said that his aim was 'to highlight the prevailing corruption in the Saudi armed forces under the command of the Defence Ministry'.

The maverick Prince called on the government to investigate embezzlement in the $25 billion Strategic Storage Programme, designed to supply Saudi armed forces with jet fuel in case an invading country occupies the oil refineries. Supervised and promoted by the defence minister, the project has been dogged by waste and fraud and in 2001 Prince Abdullah ordered substantial cutbacks. 'All Western and Saudi military and civilian experts, including Aramco, say there is no need for such a programme, because it was not in harmony with Saudi's oil technology, its geography or defence strategy,' said Prince Sultan Bin Turki. 'What has been stolen from the programme could have been enough to build a strong army with hundreds of thousands of fighters and secure a million jobs.'

For the House of Saud, endemic corruption is not only part of their family heritage but also a price worth paying for the massive modernisation of the Kingdom since the early 1980s. It bears repeating that Prince Bandar admitted as much when he said that 'if we got corrupted by $50 billion out of $400 billion, yes, so what?' This cost–benefit justification for royal bribery, however, is difficult to sustain because of the sheer extent of the costs – overpriced contracts, budget deficits, national debt, disgruntlement among ordinary Saudis and the merchant classes.

But there is a more chilling consequence – a substantial political dividend for Al-Qaeda. In their rhetoric, Osama Bin Laden and radical clerics constantly declare that not only has the royal family allowed the infidel Americans to occupy the holy sites, but has also stolen the oil wealth. They call on Muslims to 'stop history's biggest robbery of the wealth of existing and future generations'. It was the ultimate betrayal and a seductive message to young, unemployed Saudi Muslims. This was highlighted by a report by business risk analysts Dun and Bradstreet on Saudi in 2004 which stated that 'factors that have heightened political risk include the corruption of the royal family and abuses of power'.

For British governments and companies, bribing Saudi royal princes and officials – or facilitation payments as they prefer to term it – is how business has always been done in the Middle East. It was not until 2002 that corrupting a foreign official was criminalised. Declassified government documents show how the British government not only knew about the bribery but in some cases authorised it. In the late 1970s an army chief in London was asked by the British ambassador in Venezuela whether the government was prepared to countenance corruption. In a despatch marked 'secret', the Ministry of Defence official replied:

I am completely mystified by just what your problem is . . .
People who deal with the arms trade, even if they are sitting
in a government office, day by day carry out transactions
knowing at some point bribery is involved. Obviously I and
my colleagues in this office do not ourselves engage in it, but
we believe that various people who are somewhere along the
train of our transactions do. They do not tell us what they are
doing and we do not inquire. We are interested in the end
result.[27]

For Britain, the House of Saud is an invaluable ally for selling
weapons, buying cheap, dependable oil and securing support for
access to strategic military bases in the Gulf. There are, of course,
sacrifices to make and prices to pay. And so, in early 2003, when
British expatriates were languishing in a Saudi jail after being
tortured into confessing to terrorist bombings they could not have
committed, how would the government act when the families
pleaded for a more robust, proactive strategy?

SIX

THE DEAL

'You look remarkably well for someone who has been tortured.'
Jack Straw, foreign secretary, to Ron Jones, August 2001

Reclining slightly backwards on the leather chesterfield sofa with his arm stretched along the back, Jack Straw seemed very relaxed. It was 3 p.m. on 18 February 2003, and the relatives had finally been granted an audience with the foreign secretary. It was two years and two months since their loved ones had been imprisoned, tortured and sentenced to death. 'You have my personal assurance that we are doing everything possible to resolve this matter with the Saudi government and secure all the men's release as soon as possible,' he told them.

But the families were not easily convinced. Before the meeting, Margaret Dunn, Sandy's sister, and Yvonne Wardle, Les Walker's daughter, were told that each family would only be given five to six minutes with Straw. 'He's very busy, you know,' said an official. Margaret and Yvonne decided to see him together so they would have double the time and not duplicate each other's questions. As they walked into the grand reception room, dominated by wood panelling, high ceilings and sparkling polished tables, the two women could almost feel the power at the cabinet minister's disposal. Sitting across from a large marble fireplace, Margaret was facing Straw, who was accompanied by three Foreign Office civil servants. She was desperate to exploit the valuable if limited time.

'This is a matter of the highest priority for us,' he said. 'We are trying to resolve it at the highest level.'

But Margaret, blunt as ever, wanted specifics. *The Guardian* had referred to new evidence in government reports about the case which had been kept secret. 'What was this proof?' asked Margaret. The foreign secretary declined to answer.

'Newspapers are not factual, you know,' was his only comment.

With the clock ticking, Margaret fired in the questions: 'How close are we to the pardons that the lawyers and the Foreign Office have been promising?'

'We won't know how close we are until they are released,' replied Straw.

For Margaret and Yvonne, this was an unsatisfactory and bizarre response and from that moment an increasingly uncomfortable foreign secretary dodged and weaved the questions. They felt that they were not getting straight answers and instead, in true *Yes, Minister* fashion, Straw was using twenty words when five would have sufficed. 'Every time I asked a direct question he changed the subject,' recalled Margaret. 'He was trying to use up the five to six minutes without disclosing any information. At one stage he was sounding off at length about a human-rights case but it was in a different country in completely unrelated circumstances.' This infuriated Margaret and so she started interrupting him like a Radio 4 *Today* presenter, but it was not a successful ploy.

On several occasions the Foreign Office official Gail Jenkinson, who sat there with a sympathetic but anguished expression on her face, tried to conclude the meeting. But the two women refused to get up and continued to ask questions. Straw's only commitment was that he was trying to get some of the men released on health grounds and then the other detainees would follow. 'I can only begin to imagine how distressing the situation must be for you and your family,' he said and praised them for dealing with the situation with dignity.

'With respect, you cannot begin to imagine what we are feeling or how difficult it is for us or the men,' replied Margaret. 'I don't want sympathy. I just want to get the men home.'

There was one unguarded moment. Straw said that if the conflict in Iraq proceeded, then the Saudis might use that moment to release the men, because media attention would be on the Gulf and not on any embarrassing disclosures and critical remarks about the House of Saud.

'Spoken like a true New Labour spin doctor!' thought Margaret.

And that was it. The foreign secretary rose from his chair and they shook hands. 'Well, that was a waste of time, money and energy,' Margaret said to Gail Jenkinson, as they left the meeting together. 'He just wouldn't or couldn't give straight answers. I wanted to be convinced so much. But if he cannot convince me that this is important to the government, how could I expect him to convince the Saudis?'

'I am sorry you feel like that but we are doing everything we can,' replied Jenkinson.

'I am sorry, but that's not good enough. I want to meet Tony Blair.'

'He will not be able to say anything different from Jack Straw.'

Walking through the historic corridors of the Foreign Office, Margaret thought, 'Maybe they are doing more than they are saying.' But it was over two years and no progress had been made. She had been assured that Sandy would not go to trial without lawyers. But not only was he sentenced to death in a Saudi court, the British embassy was not informed and did not even know until five months after it happened! The promised retrial never occurred. The government's strategy was self-evidently not working.

Outside the main entrance on King Charles Street, journalists and camera crews were waiting, so the relatives were hastily escorted out by a side door and they left by the back exit of the Foreign Office.

On returning home, Margaret felt deflated and disillusioned. She did not believe that everything was being done and meanwhile Sandy's physical and mental health was rapidly deteriorating. Six days after the Foreign Office meeting, she wrote to Straw:

> We were extremely disappointed that you could offer us no insight into when this [their release] was actually going to happen. I am at a loss to understand why Sandy is still being held in Al-Hiar prison two years and three months later without any details of how or when the situation is going to be resolved.

In response, Straw offered little encouragement. 'You have my personal assurance that our resolve to secure Sandy's and all the men's release as soon as possible has not weakened in the slightest,' he replied. 'We will continue to do all we can.'

Perhaps Margaret was being unreasonable, naive and too harsh in her criticism of the Foreign Office. For a second opinion she spoke to Ron Jones, a Scottish tax adviser, who had been arrested on 15 March 2001 after being injured when a bomb exploded in a dustbin as he was standing outside a bookshop in Riyadh. While lying in his hospital bed with shrapnel wounds and blast burns, he was taken by police guards to the interrogation centre. For the next six weeks, he was beaten daily with a pickaxe handle until he confessed to being part of a 'CIA-backed' bombing campaign. 'The pain was excruciating,' he recalled. 'They said they knew that I had planted the bomb and if I didn't admit it they would torture me until I confessed. I had to write 80 pages and every time I got my "lines" wrong they would beat the hell out of me. They put me blindfolded in a swivel chair and spun me round, singing, and then whacked me each time the chair went round.'[1] He was also subjected to sleep deprivation, psychological duress and given sedative drugs without his knowledge.

Like Sandy, Ron Jones was taken to Al-Hiar prison 'to recover'. Eventually, the authorities admitted that he was innocent and he was released, but only if he signed a statement which denied that he had been tortured and promised not to talk publicly about his treatment. 'I just had to say that I made a false confession because I couldn't stand being in solitary confinement,' he said. 'I also had to apologise to the King and the Saudi people for lying.'[2]

After being forced to stay in Saudi for another three months, Ron Jones returned to the UK. But he had a nervous breakdown and evaluations by Dr Nathaniel Cary, a forensic pathologist at Guy's hospital in London, commissioned by the Foreign Office, concluded that he had been tortured. Nothing was done with the reports and so he decided to take legal action against the Saudis. At first, Cherie Booth QC, the prime minister's wife and human-rights specialist, seemed keen to act as his lawyer. 'I will try to help but I will need to know what territory you are talking about,' she replied in an email. After being told it was Saudi Arabia and that her husband knew about the case, Cherie Booth stopped responding to his emails.

In August 2001, Jones and his wife Sandra met Straw privately at the Foreign Office, but were shocked by his attitude. The foreign secretary was all smiles and sympathy but appeared intent on keeping him quiet and playing down his traumatic experience. 'You look remarkably well for someone who has been tortured,' he said. Jones was stunned, almost lost for words. But his wife was not so reticent. Furious at his insensitivity, she tore into Straw. It was in stark contrast to the previous foreign secretary, Robin Cook, who had travelled down to their home town in Crawley, Sussex, for a private meeting and was more attuned to their concerns, which were about justice as well as welfare.

Jones was scathing about the Foreign Office. 'We should not let them put guilt trips on us about speaking out,' he told Margaret. 'They can do more than what they are already doing. They should be pressing the Saudis to release the men unconditionally. They know about the torture, but they don't have the courage to come out and say it.'

But the government line remained rigid. 'We are indeed in constant contact with the Saudi authorities,' Tony Blair told the House of Commons. 'The best way to approach the matter is not in a public manner but to act behind the scenes, so that we can ensure that we do the very best for Mr Mitchell in these circumstances. I assure my honourable friend that we will continue to do so.'[3]

Seasoned diplomats, however, are dismissive of such rhetoric. 'Based on 20 years as a diplomat, let me tell you that when governments tell you that they cannot speak out in public but are firm in private, they are lying,' said Craig Murray, the former British ambassador to Uzbekistan from 2002 until 2004 who was sacked after speaking out against human-rights abuses. 'If they will not say it in public, they won't say it in private. And even if they do say something in private, the host government will understand from the fact that it is not said in public that this is a formal protest which has no kind of serious intent behind it.'[4]

The government's strategy was limited merely to Sandy's and the other prisoners' health and welfare and no pressure was being applied on the Saudi regime to secure their release. This was confirmed by Baroness Scotland, the Foreign Office minister, in a letter to an MP after his constituent, Dr Stephen Goldby, complained about 'the lack of action by HMG to protect the rights of British subjects abroad':

> The role of the FCO when British nationals are detained overseas is essentially a welfare one. We cannot demand their release. We must respect the Saudi system of law as we would expect them to respect ours. [You are] concerned that the detainees have been held for a considerable time without charge. The Saudi justice system works in a different way to our own . . . You will understand that we cannot intervene in the judicial process of another country.[5]

Behind the scenes, however, opinion was deeply divided. 'When the detainees were first arrested, the Foreign Office drew up a long list of potential retaliatory measures that they could take in order to pressurise the Kingdom to give them up,' said Simon Henderson, head of Saudi Strategies, a UK-based business and political consultancy. 'They knew they were innocent of causing the explosions. This list was whittled down during internal Foreign Office discussions, principally by the Middle East department. Those who know Saudi Arabia most and who have served there try to preserve the British–Saudi relationship in the idealised form in which they like to depict it. But the fact is that, when it comes down to it, the Foreign Office is scared of Saudi Arabia, so we end up with the same result: that we go softly-softly with the Kingdom and they get away with what in this case could be murder.'[6]

The list of measures was contained in a top-secret Cabinet Office report which was compiled in the spring of 2001, about six months after Sandy was arrested. Based on MI6 intelligence, the document described how the Britons were assaulted and threatened and included unflattering comments about Prince Naif as a protagonist of torture and an anti-Western Islamic conservative. The highly classified dossier provoked a fierce debate inside Whitehall between officials who wanted the government to go public and adopt a firmer approach with the Saudi regime and those who warned that would damage Britain's relations with a key ally.[7]

The argument was won by those who pointed out that Saudi Arabia controlled the world's largest oil reserves and played a crucial strategic role in influencing other friendly Gulf states. To annoy Saudi Arabia, said the report, would risk turning neighbouring Kuwait against us. Then there are the commercial factors: the ongoing selling of weapons, notably through the Al-Yamamah contract, which keeps BAE Systems prosperous. 'If Saudi Arabia produced bananas instead of oil,' said one former British ambassador, 'our attitude to their appalling human-rights record would be totally different.'

The document, which was seen by the prime minister, was used to justify the inaction of the Foreign Office and kept secret until its contents were disclosed by *The Guardian* a year after it was circulated. But the authors know of at least two consular officials at the embassy in Riyadh who were unhappy about the absence of more robust tactics. One secretly advised the wife of Ron Jones to bombard the Saudi ambassador in London and Prince Charles with letters and an attached photograph. He had accurately predicted that Sandy and the detainees would be found guilty and it would take years before they would be released. He was so angry about the supine embassy approach that he was removed. On being offered a position in Nicosia, Cyprus, he refused and demanded Beijing. If the Foreign Office refused, he insisted, then he would 'reveal all' about their 'disgraceful dealings' with the Saudis. He was posted to Beijing in a senior position. The other consul remained in Riyadh and privately suggested to Margaret that she should go public.

Despite exasperated protests by the families, the Foreign Office stuck stubbornly to its softly-softly covert diplomatic approach. 'Under no circumstances were we to talk publicly about it to anybody, even within our circle of friends,' recalled Yvonne Wardle. 'We were supposed to keep it as quiet as possible and let the Foreign Office do their job . . . I felt blackmailed by them almost, because they said to me that if I did speak out it would be to the detriment of my dad.'[8]

At times it was as if the relatives harboured national-security secrets. On 29 January 2003, the same day that Blair, Straw and Prince Saud met at No. 10 to discuss Iraq, Margaret spoke to Gail Jenkinson about talking to the press. 'If you must do it,' said Jenkinson, 'you must be very careful. Don't be critical of the Saudis. It's really important that the reporters understand that we will not talk about anything except the men's health.'

Margaret agreed and asked what the strategy was.

'We do want to solve it,' she replied. 'We just don't know how or when.'

Margaret enquired how the impending Iraq war would affect their situation.

'It will possibly have an impact, but hey, millions of lives are at stake here, not just five or six.'

That comment angered Margaret, and Jenkinson later apologised. It was a moment of contrition for an official trapped by the obligation of implementing government policy.

Suddenly there was dramatic news. Six days before the Iraq war, on 12 March 2003, five of the relatives received phone calls from the Foreign Office with the news they had longed to hear: the men were coming home 'within weeks'. That afternoon Gail Jenkinson told Margaret that she was finalising the exit plans and her local police would drive her to Heathrow for the reunion. The families would greet the detainees in the VIP lounge of the airport away from reporters. 'The men will be traumatised,' said Jenkinson. 'The last thing they will need is a crowd of journalists and TV cameramen pushing and shouting, trying to get pictures of them with their families.'

Mary Martini, whose former husband, James Cottle, was incarcerated with the others, received a similar phone call. 'They told us that they would be released imminently,' she recalled. 'We should be ready at a few hours' notice and to keep our phones on 24/7.'[9]

The lawyers confirmed the breakthrough five days later and said they were just waiting for Crown Prince Abdullah to formally endorse the release. 'We have struck a deal,' said Hejailan, calling from Beirut. 'There will be no admission of guilt but a statement will be issued that the men will be released based on their request for clemency. This is totally confidential. Do not repeat it to anyone.'

Margaret and the relatives were ecstatic. They made contingency plans and packed their bags for when the phone call came at short notice and the police car would arrive. 'Every time a car came into the drive, day or night, I would jump up,' recalled Margaret. 'Every time the phone rang I would run to it.' But as the days went by, the doubts crept in.

'I know nothing about this,' said Ken Neill from the embassy in Riyadh. 'I do hope that someone in the UK is not pulling a nasty trick on you.'

A week after the official call about the release, it was apparent that it was a false dawn. The phone call from the police or the Foreign Office never came. The families were bitterly disappointed and very angry. 'I rang up to ask about that conversation [concerning the release],' recalled Yvonne Wardle. 'I was told that I misunderstood what they had said to me, which is the way the Foreign Office deals with these things. So I questioned the other family members who had been told the same thing and we quickly realised that we could not have all misunderstood the same conversation.'[10]

Infuriated and frustrated, the relatives believed the Foreign Office had 'played an unimaginably cruel trick' on them: by raising hopes of release, the government had deceived them into 'keeping quiet' and 'not rocking the boat'. They claimed that Blair and Straw were anxious not to antagonise the Saudis in the run-up to the invasion of Iraq. The Kingdom's influence with the Gulf states was crucial: the US needed to launch their bombing campaign from that region, and the last thing they needed was public criticism of the House of Saud from impassioned British citizens.

The families were now increasingly desperate as the Iraq war preoccupied the Foreign Office. They simply did not believe the promises. 'Words are cheap,' said Margaret. On 17 April 2003, they released an open letter which attacked the administration for abandoning the plight of their menfolk, who were 'left to rot'. 'The men, victims of an abysmally unfair legal system, are in despair that their own government is sacrificing them for global politics and oil interests,' stated the letter. 'Truth does not prevail in the Foreign Office. We have been told a lot of fairy tales . . . Why does Tony Blair tell us of the torture chambers in Iraq? What about the torture chambers in Saudi?'

Meanwhile, Sandy's health remained a concern. When asked about any repercussions of his heart problems, he quickly said 'fine' but, according to Margaret, it sounded as if he was reading from a script. In a second call, on 13 April 2003, he was very depressed and had not seen his lawyers for seven weeks. 'They are not telling me the truth,' he said and sounded like he was losing trust in them and the government.

Despite the criticism, the Foreign Office stubbornly stuck to its policy of not upsetting the House of Saud. This was reinforced at the highest level. When Mary Martini met Jack Straw, he warned her of the dangers of speaking out. 'Quiet diplomacy is best,' said the foreign secretary. 'If you make a fuss, you will back the Saudis into a corner.'[11]

But, by the spring of 2003, this 'quiet diplomacy' was hushed to the point of silence. For the previous two years Margaret had been doubtful about whether ministers really were negotiating or merely asking for legal representation and consular access – both of which were denied for several months anyway. They suspected that quiet diplomacy was a ruse for limited action. 'If we are not careful, the words "confidential dialogue" can become a smokescreen or camouflage to hide behind,' declared Labour MP John Lyons in the Commons. 'It could be another way of saying "Actually we are not doing much". I am not accusing the minister of that, but I would like him to say a little about what that "confidential dialogue" includes.'[12]

The minister refused. But Margaret was read summaries of official reports of meetings between British and Saudi ministers which did provide a rare insight into their approach. During meetings with Prince Saud Al-Faisal, the Kingdom's foreign minister, Tony Blair and Jack Straw certainly raised the illegal prevention of access to consuls and lawyers. Quietly spoken and genteel, Prince Saud has been the foreign minister since 1975. He was educated at Princeton University and is rather stuffy, but he is a respected diplomat and retains some autonomy in decision-making. On 26 June 2001, he told Straw and Blair that he would pass on their concerns to Prince Naif, but 'the judicial process must run its course'.

Later, on 1 November 2001, Blair discussed the cases with Crown Prince Abdullah in Riyadh, who listened attentively but did not comment. The de facto king can be prickly and intemperate at times, notably with defence secretary Geoff Hoon, but his working relationship with Baroness Symons of Vernham Dean, the Foreign Office minister for international trade and development, who has an engaging, disarming manner, was more productive, despite her gender. During a meeting with her on 12 June 2002, Abdullah promised that the situation 'would come to a satisfactory end as quickly as possible' and implied that they would be pardoned.

And on 6 September 2002, while Straw was meeting the Saudi foreign minister at 10 Downing Street about the Middle East peace process, Blair came into the room for a 30-minute meeting and the detainees were discussed. Prince Saud said that Crown Prince Abdullah's earlier promise would be upheld.

By the following month, even Straw was losing patience. On 12 October 2002, the Al-Qaeda bombing in Bali prevented the foreign secretary from meeting Prince Saud. But that afternoon he telephoned the Prince and was more forthright. He said the government was losing patience and the case 'could cast a shadow' over UK–Saudi relations. 'OK, I'll see what I can do,' replied the Saudi foreign minister.

However, 'words are cheap', as Margaret often commented, and endless private 'reassurances', 'fruitful discussions' and 'making all the right noises' again only reminded her of the TV series *Yes, Minister* rather than convincing her that real progress was being made.

There was also a contrast in diplomatic styles. As the former Saudi ambassador in London, Dr Ghazi Al-Gosaibi, explained: 'The customary Saudi manner is: behind the scenes, quietly, calmly, at a measured pace and leaving no time for what cannot be settled immediately.'[13] But even on the most basic, minimal issue of consular access, the Saudis imperiously ignored Blair and Straw for eight months and when it was granted, it was never regular and unconditional.

As one British embassy official in Riyadh commented: 'The Saudis just do whatever they like regardless and we do nothing to stop them.' It was clear from the Foreign Office reports that ministers were raising the case, but there was no negotiation, lateral thinking or pressure being applied.

In public, cabinet ministers were giving the impression that their commercial, strategic and oil interests in Saudi were a bigger priority, despite 9/11, than the Kingdom's funding of terrorism and torture of innocent British citizens. On 1 November 2001, Blair arrived in Riyadh to a warm welcome and the sound of a marching band. 'Saudi Arabia is a good and dependable friend to the civilised world,' he declared. 'I wish to emphasise how strong that relationship is, not just on a trade and commercial level, but at a political level . . . Saudi Arabia has been a key partner of the UK and I have no doubt at all that the relationship will become even stronger still.'

But when asked by Eleanor Goodman, political editor of *Channel 4 News*, about the fate of the Britons who had by then been in prison for nearly a year, he was less decisive. 'This is an issue of course that can be touched upon but I do not think it is sensible to go into it in public,' replied Blair.

'Prime Minister, are you gathering intelligence about the brutes who did this?'

'I don't want to be coy, Eleanor, but we never discuss intelligence issues.'

Ministers only commented publicly when they were forced to in the Commons. On 3 June 2003, a debate was secured by John Pugh, the Liberal Democrat MP for Southport, who accused the Foreign Office of being too timid about the plight of the detainees. 'If it is true that careless talk can cost lives,' he said, 'it is also true that lack of plain speaking can, too. One could ponder whether, if there had been a more open dialogue about the case and more public concern about the possible terrorist dimension, lives could have been saved.'[14]

But Bill Rammell, the Foreign Office minister who replied for the government, did not appear well prepared, perhaps an indication of how seriously it was being taken. When asked questions by MPs, Gail Jenkinson, who was sitting directly behind him, discreetly passed notes to the minister, according to Margaret, who was in the Commons chamber. She noticed at least 14 notes being handed over.

Clearly briefed not to upset the House of Saud even on the torture issue, Rammell told the Commons, 'Saudi Arabia has shown a greater willingness to engage with the international community on human-rights issues. Saudi Arabia has submitted its first report to the UN Committee Against Torture since it ratified the convention in 1997. In May 2002, that committee asked Saudi Arabia about its use of flogging and amputation by judicial and administrative authorities, the powers of the religious police and prolonged pre-trial incommunicado detention . . . We respect the Saudi wish for a legal system based on sharia law, but we are worried about the system's willingness to comply with all international standards. We are encouraged by the Saudi government's ratification of some of the UN human-rights treaties.'[15]

After the debate, Margaret asked Jenkinson about the discreet written briefings. She smiled. 'Who do you think writes all the speeches?' she replied sarcastically. 'They are too busy to do such mundane things.'

A curious feature of the Foreign Office line was that it appeared anxious to deny that the UK's commercial and military dealings with Saudi were more important than human rights – without being asked. 'Some people accuse the Foreign Office of putting our trading and defence relationships with Saudi Arabia before the welfare of the men detained,' Mike O'Brien, the Foreign Office minister for trade and investment, later told the Commons. 'It is worth putting on record that our trading relationship will not prevent us from actively taking up the case of those men with the Saudi government.'[16]

But some MPs were privately dismissive. 'To say that Mike O'Brien was grovelling to the Saudis is putting it mildly,' John Pugh wrote in an email to one relative at 5 p.m. after that debate. 'Having listened to O'Brien today, I am convinced that Foreign Office pressure on the Saudis is a contradiction in terms.'

A Labour MP close to the Foreign Office told the authors, 'There were commercial interests that influenced their approach to the prisoners. There were potential arms contracts that were being discussed. I was told that this was an issue.'

At first the relatives did believe the government. But as time dragged on and some consular officials secretly confided in them, they were convinced that the arms deals and the Saudis' strategic military value took priority. This finally erupted in early January 2003, when Baroness Symons travelled to Saudi Arabia to address a trade conference and announce new business plans and investment schemes in the Kingdom. Mary Martini, whose former husband James Cottle is the father of her three children and was facing 18 years in jail, saw it as an ideal opportunity to pressure the Saudi royal family. But the Foreign Office would only say the meeting 'might' happen. 'Every effort is being made to obtain a call for Baroness Symons on Crown Prince Abdullah to talk about the detainees,' stated a letter to Mary Martini.

An enraged Mary went public. 'Our government is letting these men rot in jail while drumming up more business with the Saudis,' she told the *Glasgow Sunday Herald*. 'It's an insult and disgusting. Something must give, or do we wait until someone dies? It's all about money . . . I'm sick to death with the inaction and seeing Tony Blair hobnobbing with the Saudi royals.'[17]

Mary's worst fears were realised by the trip. Before she left London, Baroness Symons discussed her agenda with Blair. Their main policy areas were: promoting British investment and commercial expertise, particularly in the energy sector, encouraging Saudi to join the World Trade Organisation and persuading the Kingdom to support US–UK efforts to counter the global threat of Saddam Hussein. 'Make these points as clearly and strongly as you can,' said the prime minister.

The British embassy in Riyadh left no one in any doubt about the agenda. On 18 January 2003, the first evening of her visit, British businessmen and their wives were invited to attend a reception and meet Baroness Symons in the Embassy Hall. British–Saudi commercial relations was the priority. 'The minister hopes to hear direct from British businesspeople in the market about the current market climate and prospects and what Trade Partners UK [which helps British exporters] can/should do to promote British commercial interests here,' said the invitation.

The next day Baroness Symons addressed the Chamber of Commerce of the Eastern Province, home to Saudi Aramco and renowned for its agriculture and the world's largest oasis at Al-Ahsa. 'Saudi Arabia is by far the UK's largest trading and investment partner in the Middle East. It is in the region of $3.5 billion annually,' she told the gathering. The speech was presented as a message from Tony Blair, who wanted to emphasise 'how greatly he and Britain values a strong relationship with Saudi Arabia'. She then announced some trade initiatives, but most of her speech was about Iraq and 'the threat from weapons of mass destruction'.

Baroness Symons did speak privately to Crown Prince Abdullah during the visit about the detainees, but returned to the UK empty-handed. The families were now convinced that trade was more important to the government than human rights. But Jack Straw denied it. 'We have a very large British presence in Saudi Arabia,' he said. 'But if you are asking me if it is because of these links that we have adopted this approach to representing the interests of these detainees, the answer is no.'[18]

The foreign secretary's colleague, Peter Hain, now leader of the Commons, was characteristically more candid when he was cross-examined by the Foreign Affairs Select Committee in 1999. At the time, Hain was the Foreign Office minister responsible for Saudi Arabia and he admitted that he had not 'publicly said anything' about human-rights abuses since he took office. When asked if Britain's policy was dictated by business interests, he replied, 'There is always a balance to be struck,' and that the government had to determine 'how we can best achieve better human rights in any particular country'.[19]

The 'balance' between protecting human rights and promoting commercial enterprise has always been uneven in British policy towards Saudi Arabia. The prize of oil and arms exports is paramount despite protests by some distinguished politicians. 'Why do we support reactionary, selfish and corrupt governments in the Middle East instead of leaders who have the interests of their people at heart?' said Stafford Cripps, chancellor of the exchequer during the Labour government of 1945–51.[20]

Propping up the House of Saud has been the prerogative ever since. Declassified documents obtained by Mark Curtis, author of *Web of Deceit*, show that the strategy has been to defend the Gulf elites against external attack but also to 'counter hostile influence and propaganda within the countries themselves'. Training their military and police helps in 'maintaining internal security'. Britain's current commitment to the region is so great that, according to the Ministry of Defence, 'all of the [Gulf] countries have an expectation that we would assist them in times of crisis'. The military officers of all six states in the Gulf Cooperation Council – Bahrain, Kuwait, Oman, Qatar, Saudi Arabia and the United Arab Emirates – are trained in the UK. Britain, alongside the US, provides 'internal security training' and 'military skills' to the Saudi Arabian National Guard (SANG), the 75,000-strong force that protects the royal family from social unrest and coups d'état. Almost every year since the Al-Qaeda bombing in Khobar Towers on 25 June 1996 a British team has been deployed to the Kingdom to provide expertise in other areas such as anti-terrorism.[21]

The underlying commercial motivation was disclosed by former SAS officer Sir Peter de la Billiere, the commander of the British forces during the 1991 Gulf War. In his personal account of the conflict, he recalls Prince Khaled Bin Sultan, commander of the Saudi army, anxiously telling him of the importance of the House of Saud remaining in power. Sir Peter reflected:

I fully understood the Prince's difficulties and sympathised with him, but my understanding attitude was not entirely altruistic. As we, the British, had backed the system of sheikhly rule ever since our own withdrawal from the Gulf in the early 1970s and seen it prosper, we were keen that it should continue. Saudi Arabia was an old and proven friend of ours, and has deployed its immense oil wealth in a benign and thoughtful way with the result that standards of living had become very high. It was thus very much in our interests that the country and its regime should remain stable after the war.[22]

The priority of lucrative arms contracts over human rights was crudely exposed during the government's treatment of Dr Mohammed Al-Masari, a radical Islamic Saudi dissident and physicist based in London. In 1995 Dr Al-Masari jointly led a spirited organisation, the Committee for the Defence of Legitimate Rights (DLR), which bombarded his exiled homeland with faxes accusing the Saudi royal family of human-rights abuses and corruption and called for its demise. The faxes must have been effective because the Saudi royals complained bitterly to the Conservative government and to defence manufacturers Vickers and British Aerospace. Vickers, which was at the time bidding for a huge Saudi order for up to 200 Challenger 2 tanks, warned the Ministry of Defence that Dr Al-Masari's activities posed a threat to British–Saudi trade.

The government responded by tasking MI5 to investigate the political dissident. His phone was tapped. But when the Ministry of Defence put pressure on the Security Service to place Dr Al-Masari under full-time surveillance and officially classify him as a security risk, the request was refused. MI5 replied that he was stirring up hostility against the Saudi royal family and British expatriates in the Kingdom, but he was not a terrorist or a threat to the defence of the realm.

The rebuff did not stop John Major, then prime minister, who was under pressure to appease the irate Saudis. In the summer of 1995 Major personally asked Sir Andrew Green, then undersecretary for the Middle East, to find a way to expel the opposition activist. 'I was trying to remove Islamic extremists like Masari from Britain,' recalled Sir Andrew. 'But, because of our asylum laws, I found I was unable to do so, despite having the support of the prime minister. This man Masari was seriously damaging British relations with Saudi Arabia, but my own staff could do nothing and my people in Riyadh were expressing concern about the weakness of our controls.'[23]

Frustrated by the law, Sir Andrew worked closely with MI6. On 6 September 1995, he telephoned Sir Colin Chandler, then chief executive of Vickers, and told him that Britain had passed intelligence on Saddam Hussein to Saudi Arabia to pacify its anger at Dr Al-Masari's campaign. 'This has earned us many plaudits,' said the Foreign Office official, according to a memo by Sir Colin, later leaked to *The Guardian*.[24]

Sir Andrew, later the British ambassador in Riyadh, personified the cosy relationship between the arms manufacturers and the Foreign Office. Since April 1994, he had been a non-executive director of a Vickers subsidiary – Vickers Defence Systems. He had joined the company unpaid as part of a government scheme to give senior civil servants business experience.

The leaked memo also referred to 'direct Saudi intervention' against the dissident and attempts to 'stifle him personally'. One intelligence operation involved the planned murder of the dissident. 'In the mid-1990s [a Saudi minister] was behind at least two attempts on the life of Mohammed Al-Masari,' said Robert Baer. 'Surely that ought to be reason enough for Al-Masari to join others in taking up arms against Al-Saud.'[25]

Baer discovered the plot from a Jordanian intelligence official who had knowledge of the incidents. In 1995 the CIA was tipped off by Jordanian intelligence that one of its undercover assets, a Palestinian extremist, had been contracted by the Saudis to assassinate Dr Al-

Masari. This was confirmed by another US intelligence official who later told *Newsweek*: 'There's no question that the Jordanians told us about the [murder] contract. What especially upset US officials is that this was the second time that [he] was believed to have attempted to assassinate Al-Masari. He had been previously warned not to do so a year earlier and was now doing so again . . . We never accused him or confronted him directly. This was embarrassing to the Saudis and we are not in the business of embarrassing the Saudis.'[26]

The murder plots were aborted. But the Conservative government still targeted the campaigner. In January 1996, the Home Office sought to deport Dr Al-Masari to the tiny Caribbean island of Dominica. This was abandoned after protests by human-rights groups and Al-Masari remains in the UK. The experience only intensified his revolutionary fervour against the House of Saud and he grew closer to Al-Qaeda's way of thinking. Later that year Sir Andrew Green became the ambassador in Riyadh and now campaigns against British asylum laws. The House of Saud continues to hound Dr Al-Masari: in 2004, a policeman was jailed for corruptly accepting money from a Saudi diplomat to spy on Al-Masari by illegally tapping into the police national computer.[27]

The targeting of Dr Al-Masari reflected Western priorities: defence contracts and appeasing the Saudis first, defending democracy and human rights second. As Michael Howard, home secretary at the time, acknowledged: 'If there are two ways in which we can comply with our international obligations [on human rights] – one of which damages our national interest and the prospects of jobs in Britain and one which does not – we are perfectly entitled to choose the way which does not damage our interests.'[28]

The Labour government elected in 1997 sang perfectly in tune with that philosophy. 'Arms sales were one of Tony Blair's blind spots and he was strongly supported by Jack Straw,' said former cabinet minister Clare Short. 'They considered it their duty to promote British arms sales whenever possible.'[29] Despite the ethical foreign policy which Robin Cook had tried to implement, New Labour continued to supply weapons to countries of which it disapproved. Top of the list is Saudi Arabia. In 2003 the UK exported £189.3 million of hardware to the Kingdom.

The major British beneficiary is BAE Systems, which receives £2 billion a year from the ongoing Al-Yamamah contract with the Kingdom, which was originally negotiated in 1985. From his first day in office, Blair went out of his way to help BAE Systems and acted as its unofficial travelling salesman. The company chairman, Sir Richard Evans, was one of the very few businessmen whose regular requests to see the prime minister were always granted. 'Whenever he [Evans] heard of a problem he would be on the phone to No. 10 and it would get sorted,' said a Downing Street aide.[30] This was confirmed by Robin Cook, foreign secretary from 1997 until 2001, who recorded in his diary:

> In my time I came to learn that the chairman of British Aerospace appeared to have the key to the garden door to No. 10. Certainly I never once knew No. 10 to come up with any decisions that would be incommoding [disadvantageous] to British Aerospace, even when they came bitterly to regret the public consequences.[31]

BAE Systems made a conscious effort to cultivate the government. In 1998 the company donated £5,000 or more to the Labour Party under the umbrella scheme of sponsorship and in 2000 handed over another minimum of £5,000 plus £12 million as sponsors of the Mind Zone of the Millennium Dome. Since 1997 it has sponsored meetings at Party conferences and retained Labour peer Lord Taylor of Blackburn as a paid consultant. BAE also flies cabinet ministers around in the company helicopter and chairman's private jet and distributes free tickets to Labour MPs for sporting and cultural events like the Opera House in Covent Garden.

In 1998 BAE acquired GEC Marconi for £7.7 billion and there

was an immediate protest that this would restrict competition in the industry and concentrate too much power in one company. The director-general for fair trading, John Bridgeman, agreed and recommended that the deal be referred to the Competition Commission. But Stephen Byers, then trade and industry secretary, overruled his decision and allowed BAE to gobble up GEC Marconi without an inquiry. Sir Richard Evans was sitting on the government's Competitiveness Advisory Group and Competition Council and the company's referral could have resulted in him declaring a conflict of interest.

The prime minister certainly has a soft spot for the arms manufacturer. In January 2000 he even interrupted a family holiday in the Seychelles to act as a salesman for BAE. South Africa announced that it would buy £4 billion in military equipment from European companies and invited bids. Despite being on vacation, Blair led a delegation to South Africa and 'batted for Britain'. The result was that BAE won the major prize by selling their Hawk aircraft in a £1.6 billion deal. But it was heavily criticised because of South Africa's high poverty levels and resulted in a major corruption inquiry, which cleared South African government officials and BAE of wrongdoing.

Blair has often clashed with his own ministers after they objected to some of BAE's contracts. In February 2000, the government granted export licences to the firm to supply spare parts for Zimbabwe's antiquated Hawk aircraft. Robin Cook, then foreign secretary, and other ministers opposed the decision because the Hawk was being used by Zimbabwe during predatory raids in the Democratic Republic of Congo. But Cook and the others were overruled by the prime minister. It was only when President Mugabe's warmongering operations became so outrageous that the licences were rescinded. Blair also repeatedly pressed India to buy 60 Hawk jets worth £1 billion despite the real risk of war with the nuclear-armed Pakistan.

The following year, cabinet warfare broke out over BAE's

application for a licence to export a £28 million long-range military radar system to Tanzania. As one of the poorest countries in the world, senior ministers argued that Tanzania did not need this expensive project. 'It was very difficult to believe that the contract had been agreed without corruption and it was causing great concern to the World Bank,' said Clare Short, then international development secretary, who strongly opposed the licence. 'The proposal was in clear breach of a revised EU code negotiated by Robin Cook to honour a 1997 manifesto promise to tighten controls on arms exports.'[32]

In cabinet, Short argued that the project was 'dubious and damaging' and a breach of their own policy on weapons sales. She secured the backing of the chancellor Gordon Brown, foreign secretary Robin Cook and trade and industry secretary Patricia Hewitt. But No. 10 were not supportive. 'Then Robin Cook was replaced by Jack Straw and I could not persuade the prime minister, even in a case like this, to take a stand against British Aerospace,' recalled Short. 'Blair was immovable, despite my strong support from the World Bank and the Treasury.'[33]

After strong lobbying and Blair's resolute backing, BAE prevailed and Tanzania spent the £28 million on the military radar system, although a second phase was not commissioned. An inquiry by the International Civil Aviation Organisation later concluded that Tanzania could have bought a suitable system for 25 per cent of the price it paid to BAE. 'The whole episode left a very nasty taste about the behaviour of British Aerospace and the unbalanced attitude of the prime minister towards arms sales,' reflected Short.[34]

For BAE Systems, the Al-Yamamah deal has always been the most crucial to its fortunes and contributes 20 per cent of its profits. It was originally conceived in the early 1980s when President Reagan tried to sell some F-15s, a strike aircraft, to Saudi. The Israeli lobby, through Congress, vetoed the deal, so BAE promoted their Tornado, a more advanced and menacing aircraft but more expensive than the rival French Mirage 2000. Conscious that the Saudi princes were easily intimidated and neurotic about threats from neighbouring states, the Ministry of Defence argued that the offensive Tornado would be an effective deterrent.

The Saudis agreed and, in May 1985, Prince Bandar, the ambassador in Washington and a favoured confidant of King Fahd, flew to London and negotiated directly and privately with Margaret Thatcher. It was a government-to-government contract which was agreed on 26 September 1985. But the negotiations then embarked on a mysterious course. Two days before the contract was initialled, Britain's chief of air staff was told that the Saudis were buying not just 48 Tornados but an extra 24 planes for 'an air-defence role'. And just for good measure, they also ordered 30 Hawk trainer aircraft from BAE. A deal of already awesome proportions had ballooned into something colossal and unprecedented. It was Britain's biggest-ever arms contract, worth a total of £15 billion.[35]

The Saudis paid for Al-Yamamah in oil. But it was not a pure barter arrangement – the equivalent of exchanging two goats for a pig. Some 600,000 barrels of oil a day were sold to BP and Shell, who refined it and sold it on the open market. The proceeds were then paid on a monthly basis to a special Ministry of Defence trust bank account in London with BAE as the custodian and the Saudis as the beneficiary. The account was then drawn on by BAE as the aircraft were delivered. 'This, in effect, was a general slush fund for the Saudi Ministry of Defence,' said Chas Freeman. 'They could debit anything they wanted against this account and BAE would do the procurement. It was not subject to public scrutiny in either country. And it was not part of the Saudi defence budget . . . The fact is that if you have an essentially limitless trust fund that you can buy anything you want from with no one the wiser, no matter how honest or patriotic your initial instincts might be, the temptation for abuse is large.'

Al-Yamamah was a huge commission-generating machine. A large proportion of BAE's hardware and spare parts were sold at a high premium – or a 'friendship price' as the Saudis like to call it –

and the difference was distributed in pay-offs in various tranches to Saudi defence officials, intermediaries and, according to Freeman, 'members of the royal family'.

Former CIA officer Robert Baer claimed: 'Most of the commissions went to Prince Sultan [defence minister], his family and a legion of middlemen.' Numerous sources calculate the commissions accounted for at least 30 per cent of the contract.

As the prime contractor, BAE was not only supplying Saudi with offensive fighter aircraft but was virtually running its air force. It was also exempt from export licensing by the British government, which meant that there were no restrictions on the deployment of the weapons. But it was not a one-off deal. Al-Yamamah allowed for upgrades of hardware, spare parts, support equipment and building of air force and naval bases and, in 1988, another 72 Tornados were purchased. The total price was now £20 billion.

The Al-Yamamah contract needed constant nurturing, because it was flexible and renewable with opportunities for fresh pickings. Each year the Saudis decided how much of their order would be delivered and hence controlled the revenue stream. And the key figure in these decisions was Prince Turki Bin Nasser, head of the Saudi royal air force and son-in-law of Prince Sultan. A qualified fighter pilot, he holds the title of major-general and has run and overseen Al-Yamamah since its inception.

Desperate to retain the business, BAE Systems set up a secret slush fund to keep Prince Turki and prominent Saudis happy and indebted to the company. In 1988, soon after Al-Yamamah 2 was signed, BAE hired Tony Winship, a dapper, smooth-talking former RAF wing-commander. He had a special value: he was a long-standing close friend of Prince Turki and they had flown together in the Middle East. Winship moved into a lavish apartment at the Carlton Tower hotel, Belgravia, a favourite meeting place for Saudis and a long way from BAE's HQ, and set up an office to run the operation. He had been authorised by BAE executives to pay for anything that Prince Turki, his family and demanding entourage desired: houses, sports cars, accommodation in luxury hotels, yachts, cash, prostitutes, gambling trips, trips in private jets, medical bills, unlimited restaurant meals and gifts.

Winship hired Peter Gardiner, managing director of Travellers World Ltd, a travel agency, as an intermediary to channel the payments to Prince Turki. Between 1989 and 2002, the head of the Saudi air force received a total of £17 million and a further £43 million went to other influential Saudis, according to documents obtained by *The Guardian*, which first disclosed the BAE slush fund. Gardiner would pay the bills and advance money to Prince Turki and friends and then invoice Winship. Every month he took a large briefcase crammed full of receipts and invoices to see Winship at the Carlton Tower for an audit meeting. The wing-commander always stressed the need for confidentiality and he would consolidate all the bills into one invoice for BAE to avoid a paper-trail. 'He wanted to keep it very private, very secret,' recalled Gardiner. 'He didn't want prying eyes looking at any of these transactions.'[36]

Back at BAE's head office these single-sheet invoices were handed to Steve Mogford, the executive in charge of the Al-Yamamah project. Mogford would authorise them by scribbling in the corner: 'OK to pay', according to documents obtained by the BBC's *Money Programme*. In 1995 alone, Mogford, who reported directly to chief executive Sir Richard Evans, personally signed off invoices for over £3 million for the Saudi slush fund.

From his office in St Albans, Hertfordshire, Gardiner organised the breathtakingly extravagant lifestyle of Prince Turki, his associates and his chief aide, Brigadier General Nasser Al-Abaykan, the defence attaché at the London embassy. In 1995 a cargo plane was hired at a cost of £165,000 just to carry Prince Turki's shopping across the Atlantic. A fax from DAS Aviation Services to Prince Turki stated:

> Personal and confidential . . . I organised a DC8-63 series
> aircraft to take one Rolls-Royce and crates of furniture from

Los Angeles to Dhahran . . . Today I spoke with Tony
Winship and he advised me you would like to bring two cars
back from Saudi Arabia to Los Angeles.[37]

Travelling with the customary entourage, Prince Turki's hotel visits
were indulgent, even by Arab standards. The air force chief often
stayed at the Royal Lancaster hotel in London. Accompanied by at
least two valets and a butler, he would also have associates, so
Gardiner would book an entire floor. For 4 to 5 nights, the bill was
£70,000 – paid for by BAE Systems, who would also pick up the tab
for lavish holidays. In August 1998, a party of 50 Saudi princes and
princesses checked into a floor of suites at the Kahala Mandarin
Oriental hotel in Oahu, Hawaii. Under the shadow of Diamond
Head, the island's volcano, the group enjoyed one of the world's best
hotels. They then hired a fleet of cars and over the next few days flew
in a private Boeing 707 to Maui, another Hawaiian island, to stay at
the Grand Wailea hotel. The total cost of the trip was £250,000 –
again covered by BAE Systems.[38]

Meanwhile, Al-Yamamah was in trouble. By early 1996 it was an
intolerable burden on Saudi finances. The Kingdom was struggling
to top up the defence budget from oil revenues and BAE even had
to borrow $400 million to keep the contract solvent. Exasperated by
the huge commissions raked off by his family, Crown Prince
Abdullah tried to cancel Al-Yamamah during a cabinet meeting on
5 September 1996. But Prince Sultan successfully argued that the
Kingdom was too dependent on British equipment to change. The
following year the defence minister was pressing the Saudi
International Bank to come up with $473 million just to keep the
arms deal afloat.[39]

For BAE, the Saudi contract has been fundamental to its
existence. In 1998, out of an order book which increased to £28.1
billion, 11 per cent was accounted for 'by Al-Yamamah and training
services'. So when Tony Blair came to power, the company had Saudi
business worth some £3 billion, and the original order was still in

progress. In 1998 BAE delivered the last batch of Tornados and received 400,000 barrels of oil a day plus an estimated £1 billion top-up payment which, typically, did not arrive until January 1999. To this day the contract brings in revenue as a service contract to maintain the Tornados and Hawks and BAE employs 5,000 people in Saudi for that very purpose.[40]

Mindful of the unstable and unpredictable state of Al-Yamamah, BAE increased the cash-flow to Prince Turki. A fund that was paying out £300,000 a year in 1990 was by the late 1990s distributing an annual £3 million. This included paying off the Prince's American Express bill, which averaged at £100,000. Gardiner, who transferred the money at BAE's insistence, did not ask questions. 'I knew that Al-Yamamah was a huge contract and this was just part of it,' he recalled.[41]

Large cash deposits were also moved into Prince Turki's Bank of America account in Los Angeles, where he had acquired a Beverly Hills mansion. In July 2000, an email to Travellers World stated: 'Tony [Winship] has requested that we pay to T1's [Prince Turki's] private LAX bank account the sum of $132,030.' Three months later, there was a flurry of speculation that Al-Yamamah might be expanded and Prince Turki flew to London to see Geoff Hoon. On 10 October 2000, a 'further $66,000' was paid into the Prince's Los Angeles account.

On his arrival, the head of the Saudi air force moved into the Royal Lancaster hotel with his entourage for several days. The total bill came in at £80,285.44 plus £2,200 in tips – paid for by BAE. During his stay, on 12 October 2000, Prince Turki visited Hoon at his office in Whitehall and they discussed the Al-Yamamah project and the Middle East. He delivered a message from his father-in-law, the defence minister Prince Sultan, and introduced his successor as head of Al-Yamamah within the royal family. Hoon responded by thanking Prince Turki for his 'work in support of the Al-Yamamah programme which has brought benefits for both nations over many years'.[42] The Prince celebrated by spending a few days at Champneys, the health farm in Tring, Hertfordshire, at BAE's expense – £30,327.19.

Despite owning houses in Barcelona, Riyadh, Dhahran, Beverly Hills and Sussex Square, near Hyde Park, Prince Turki felt the need to stay at the most luxurious hotels at BAE's expense – Maxim's in Paris (£62,000), Carlton Tower (£49,000), Caesar's Palace (£46,000) and New York Plaza (£240,000).

But on 14 February 2002, the BAE slush fund was confronted with possible closure when it became illegal under the new Anti-Terrorism Act for private companies to pay foreign government officials. After taking legal advice, Peter Gardiner realised that this form of cosying up to Prince Turki would need to stop. 'We could not continue because I or the other directors of the company would be liable to penalties or jail,' he said.[43]

Gardiner informed Tony Winship, the employee in charge of the fund, that he would be resigning because of the new law. He was shocked by the wing-commander's response. 'Winship indicated to us that he had heard from BAE that they were looking for new ways round this,' said Gardiner. 'It would take some time to put a new system in operation but a lot of effort was being put into it . . . He said, "Don't worry, it will continue. It is too important to give up."'[44] At least one hotel bill for the Saudi minister was paid after the new Act came into power.

Documents obtained by *The Guardian* indicate that Sir Richard Evans, BAE chairman, may have been privy to the discussions about continuing the fund. On 13 March 2002, a month after the bill was passed, Winship telephoned Stuart Fordyce, finance director of Travellers World, and said that he just had 'a very positive meeting' with Sir Richard. He said that the BAE boss was 'very supportive and reinforced the message already given to you by Prince Turki'. Three weeks later, on 8 April 2002, a meeting took place between Sir Richard and Prince Turki. This was referred to in a letter by lawyers for Travellers World which stated: 'I am advised that BAE intend to continue paying for the Prince Turki Bin Nasser programme.'[45]

Sir Richard Evans, who had been involved in Al-Yamamah for nearly 20 years as BAE's assistant marketing director for Saudi Arabia in the mid-1980s and was now chairman, appeared unperturbed by the serious nature of the allegations. After Peter Gardiner blew the whistle and made thousands of documents available to *The Guardian* and the authorities, the Ministry of Defence police and the Serious Fraud Office launched investigations. Sir Richard was then summoned to give evidence to the Commons Select Committee on Defence. When asked if BAE had made payments to members of the Saudi royal family, he replied: 'Well, I think that business practices have been changing over a period of time. I can certainly assure you that we, and I believe most companies, are not in the business of making payments to members of any government. This is not a question of people passing, as you suggest, large sums of money to employees of governments. It is just not the way that business is done.'[46]

It was a baffling denial, given the prodigious amount of documents which proved that BAE did pay an employee of a government – Prince Turki. Even the company has not denied the slush-fund allegations, merely maintaining: 'We rigorously obey all the laws of the UK.' There is no suggestion that Sir Richard, now retired, or BAE broke the law, but Sir Richard may be recalled to give evidence to the committee. His former colleague Tony Winship remains at BAE and is still at the Carlton Tower hotel. Meanwhile, his old friend Prince Turki is spending more time in Saudi Arabia as environment minister. The Prince will have to survive with his five homes, Boeing business-jet and yacht. The days of spending £15,000 a night of BAE's money on trips abroad are gone, although ironically he has made inquiries about buying a luxury hotel on the continent.

The House of Saud reacted with characteristic aggression to the allegations. Highly sensitive to public shame and damaging publicity, Saudi defence officials warned the British government in October 2004 that it would receive no further contracts if the royal family is embarrassed by the investigations into the BAE slush fund.[47]

The threat was made at a sensitive time because the company was in discussions to extend Al-Yamamah. Known as the 'Saudi Sustainment Programme', the talks focused on upgrading the Tornados with modernised avionics and missile systems and extending the service contracts to the armed forces. The Saudi royal air force has been considering the retirement of some of the aircraft to pay for refitting and updating the rest of the fleet. BAE was also trying to sell its Eurofighter Typhoon combat aircraft. The new orders would be worth an estimated £4.4 billion.[48]

The value placed by the Labour government on these arms sales was shown when it secretly authorised the Export Credit Guarantee Department (ECGD) to insure BAE's contracts in the Kingdom. Under the arrangement, disclosed by *The Guardian*, the government will pay BAE the value of the order if the brittle Saudi regime collapses and the successor refuses to meet its obligations. These commitments were signed on 1 September 2003, by the ECGD, part of the DTI, with the backing of defence secretary Geoff Hoon. An analysis of ECGD accounts revealed that in each year between 2001 and 2004 the government provided BAE with more than £1 billion of cover for its Saudi deals. That figure appears in the accounts under an obscure heading: 'Other insurance.'[49]

As the House of Saud's foundations have been increasingly unstable because of terrorist bombings since 9/11, the guarantee appears to be a risky venture. 'It seems very unwise for us to pledge our money on what seems to be an increasingly shaky regime,' said Peter Kilfoyle, the former Labour defence minister. 'This seems to be a triumph of optimism over reality.'[50] The Ministry of Defence declined to comment about the covert nature of the ECGD cover for BAE: 'Everything to do with Al-Yamamah is confidential.'

While negotiations were renewed to secure more arms contracts from the Kingdom, Sandy Mitchell was still languishing in jail. The prospects were as gloomy as ever. The false hope of release in March 2003 was a bitter and emotionally draining experience for Margaret.

Distributing the open letter and sending emails to senior politicians was done in desperation and hope rather than expectation. On the Foreign Office's own admission, it had no policy apart from 'quiet diplomacy at the highest level'.

Some optimism was built up by a series of meetings between Jack Straw and Crown Prince Abdullah, Prince Saud, the foreign minister and Prince Turki Al-Faisal, the ambassador to the UK, on 15 April 2003, in Riyadh. But the discussions, held at Al-Yamamah Palace, focused almost exclusively on war-ravaged Iraq and the Palestinian problem. The report from the Foreign Office indicated that the plight of Sandy and other detainees was only briefly mentioned. Straw was unable to make any progress, and returned to London with not even a vague timetable for the men's release. 'We all have to look at the bigger picture,' Rachel Ingham, a Foreign Office official told Margaret.

Ten days later, on 28 April 2003, Margaret rang Gail Jenkinson at the Foreign Office. She told Gail Jenkinson that she felt the situation was desperate, with little hope and no progress: Straw had come back from Riyadh with no timescale or positive development. Ever devoted to the party line, Jenkinson replied that 'everything was looking positive'.

Increasingly frustrated, Margaret had been listening to this for over two years. 'But we have no timescale,' she said angrily. 'Isn't it time we think again about possible new strategies?'

'What is the alternative?' replied an equally irritated Jenkinson. 'We cannot change our strategy. What else can we do, Margaret? Publicly speak out against the Saudis? Withdraw diplomatic links? That will not work and it won't happen. And if we did any of those things, then you definitely won't get Sandy back. This is the only solution. If there was any real alternative, don't you think we would have tried it by now? This way is working but you won't see that until it has actually worked and they are home.'

'Yes, but the bottom line is that they are still there and there is no sign that this is going to end,' said Margaret.

'I understand,' said Jenkinson. But before she could continue Margaret put the phone down. She was too upset to continue the conversation. The burden of secrecy imposed by the Foreign Office had taken its toll on her. Knowing that one public criticism of the Saudis could, according to the government, result in her brother's death, she felt a huge and stressful responsibility. It was as though she held Sandy's life in her hands. But now there appeared to be no solution or strategy coming from the Foreign Office. How was this nightmare going to end, she asked herself.

SEVEN

RELEASED BY AL-QAEDA

'Allah loves not the shouting of evil words, except by one who has been wronged. For they have the right to public redress.'

The Qur'ān

11.15 p.m., Monday, 12 May 2003. Nine Al-Qaeda suicide bombers, dressed in traditional Arab costume and armed with automatic weapons and grenades, are hunched inside a grey American sedan as it drives slowly towards the iron gate of the guardhouse. Their target is a compound in Riyadh that houses 900 expatriates, including 300 Americans employed by the Vinnell Corporation to train and advise the Saudi Arabian National Guard, which protects the royal family. After passing a sign on the high perimeter wall that warns 'Visitors must be escorted', the terrorists jump from the car and immediately open fire, killing two Saudi guards who are equipped only with an unloaded 50 mm machine gun atop a truck. Taken by surprise, an

American security trainer, and recently converted Muslim, is also shot dead. The car then attempts to ram the gate but gets stuck. Unfazed, the bombers walk through the pedestrian entrance and, apparently knowing where the switches are, push the button that opens the sliding metal gate to the complex.

Within seconds, a Dodge Ram utility truck, packed with explosives, is speeding through and drives towards the cluster of three four-storey apartment blocks. Shooting from the back of the lorry and throwing grenades along the way, the bombers scream in Arabic: 'We are entering the compound. We are right next to the enemies of Allah.' They drive directly to High-Rise 1, the most populated block which houses 50 military unit and tactical trainers, and park at the precise point for maximum impact. The attackers then shout repeatedly: 'Allahu Akbar [God is great]' and a few seconds later the bomb is detonated by the driver. The explosion, estimated to be a 400-lb Semtex bomb, is devastating. The front of High-Rise 1 is destroyed and concrete, glass and sleeping inhabitants are hurled in all directions. The blast destroys several offices and housing units and is felt several kilometres away, shattering windows in the neighbourhoods.

One victim that night is Felix Acevedo, a 31-year-old Vinnell security officer and former military policeman. As soon as he hears the gunfire from his bedroom on the fourth floor, he knows that worse is to come. He runs down the corridor, turning off the lights on the way, and shouts at two colleagues, Nelson Lopez and German Diaz, 'Let's get out of here fast.' As they run down the stairs, they see from the window the terrorists lurking outside with rifles and a truck with a large box on the back. Lopez grabs his knife and they make it to the lobby. But it is too late. Suddenly, a flash of light blinds them and they instantly know it is a bomb. They crouch down to protect themselves. But the force of the blast is too strong and glass and concrete fly everywhere, amplified by a terrible crescendo of noise. Diaz dies almost instantly from deep lacerations, Lopez sustains major injuries to his face and Felix's ear is practically blown off, left hanging by a small piece of flesh. Both his legs are broken and he has glass and concrete deeply embedded all over his back, shoulders and throughout the right side of his body.

Bleeding profusely and unconscious, Felix is taken to the emergency room at the King Fahd hospital. His condition is critical and deteriorating rapidly. Due to blood loss and trauma there is no time to take him to the operating room, so the surgeon immediately cuts open his abdomen to release the pressure. It is another five days before it is closed again and his ear is sewn back on. His condition is so serious that he requires 94 units of blood and blood products. He also has surgery for the removal of a large foreign body, which turns out to be a bone from another victim who had been hit. For the first few days, his face is so swollen and cut that he is unrecognisable and branded an 'unknown'. This is a traumatic period for his parents, who have not been contacted and naturally fear the worst. Eventually his colleagues recognise him and he is taken off the ventilator. It is not until 17 July 2003, two months after the bombing, that he is released from hospital.

Felix is lucky to be alive. The Vinnell compound is the primary target, but is just one of three bombings that shake Riyadh that traumatic Monday night. Five minutes earlier, two other housing complexes, containing a mix of Arabs and Americans, were also attacked. In the hospital all hell has broken loose. By 11.55 p.m., the ER is full of wounded people, many sitting in chairs covered in concrete dust and blood, shivering and reeking of smoke. Some have pieces of glass embedded in their face. One needs his scalp sewn back on. In the wards, the victims are all in shock and this frightens even the most experienced nurses, who try to reassure them. The Vinnell Corporation representative repeatedly asks impatiently when 'my guys' will be discharged and is told: 'Just back off.' The Saudi staff are deeply embarrassed that such an atrocity could happen in their homeland. The total death toll is 35, including 7 Americans, and an estimated 200 are injured. It has been the most devastating terrorist assault since 9/11.

The next morning the sound of gunfire can still be heard but it is leftover ammunition catching fire and exploding. As the stench of cordite still lingers heavily in the air and the streets are littered with glass and concrete from the decrepit buildings, Vinnell employees discuss the atrocity. The bombing operation was implemented in barely three minutes, with clockwork precision. As US military officials later acknowledged, it was a sophisticated, coordinated assault based on meticulous intelligence. But was it an inside job? Several Vinnell employees whom the authors have interviewed believe that Al-Qaeda were secretly assisted with inside information from members of the Saudi Arabian National Guard (SANG). They also claim that security at the gate was extraordinarily negligent and the Saudis received clear, repeated and detailed warnings which should have resulted in measures that could have saved lives.

The survivors of the atrocity were shocked. But the targeting of Vinnell, a subsidiary of US defence giant Northrop Grumman, was no accident. Since 1975 the corporation has been training SANG in the use of weapons, tactics, logistics, battle operations and physical security. Closely aligned with the US government and intelligence agencies, Vinnell has plenty of political clout and is the embodiment of the hated American presence in the Kingdom. During the 1991 Gulf War, company employees were seen fighting alongside Saudi troops. Its current contract, worth $831 million, was negotiated in 1998.

For the Saudi royal family, the Al-Qaeda bombing should not have been a surprise because they were repeatedly warned that Islamic terrorists were targeting softer, less secure targets in Riyadh. But Prince Naif chose to ignore the danger signs or went into denial. Three weeks before the attack, Robert Jordan, the US ambassador in Riyadh, received intelligence reports that Al-Qaeda were 'in the final phases of planning attacks against Western interests in Saudi Arabia'. He immediately told the Saudi authorities and sent them three letters asking them to provide more armed security at US installations and housing compounds. He also pleaded with Vinnell to upgrade their security.[1]

On 1 May 2003, ten days before the bombing, the US State Department announced there were 'strong indications' of an attack. This was based mostly on intercepted satellite phone calls, emails and 'intelligence traffic' showing contact between Osama Bin Laden's son, Saad, and an Al-Qaeda cell in Riyadh. The state of alert was heightened and the threat level raised from 'yellow' to 'orange'. Five days later a huge weapons cache was discovered by police at an Al-Qaeda safe house in Riyadh. It later emerged, according to the *Washington Post*, that the arms had been sold by SANG members to the terrorists.[2]

Ambassador Jordan's warnings were ignored. Security was not improved or even modified. 'The security measures were virtually non-existent,' said Lt-Colonel Rafael Maldonado, a former Vinnell military instructor who was injured during the bombing. 'There were only two to four Saudi guards stationed at one compound corner with only 9 mm guns. There was a 50-calibre machine gun mounted on a Styer wheeled vehicle but it was unloaded because the gun did not have a belt to connect the ammunition box to the machine-gun feeder. Observation was useless because there were no night-vision devices to detect any attack until it was too late. There were no metal detectors, no closed-circuit TV to monitor access and record activities, no wire barriers above the security walls to prevent unauthorised entry, no weapons checks and no bomb-detection dogs. And Saudi nationals not working at Vinnell were not checked on entry.'

SANG could have stationed a platoon as a quick-reaction force in the event of an attack. But the guards deployed at the Vinnell compound were not allowed to carry weapons. And so Al-Qaeda were confronted with SANG guards without loaded weapons and a machine gun with no ammunition! 'It would have been a blood bath if the terrorists performed a sweep of the area to kill at will, because most of us were outside our buildings in the open and the fires lit up the area,' recalled Maldonado. 'We were pulling bodies from the rubble of the other housing units. All we had were rocks, sticks and knives as our only line of defence.'

The absence of security leads many former Vinnell employees to believe that Al-Qaeda received inside help from some SANG members. They point to the discovery of a detailed map of the compound in the trunk of the sedan left behind after the bombing. They also found an improvised ladder near the gate consisting of a 55-gallon drum, 6 concrete blocks stacked on top and several shoe markings made by people clearly rushing to escape. 'There is no doubt that this compound was too big and complex for the bomb to be detonated without inside help,' said Maldonado.

More significantly, shortly after 9 a.m. on the day of the bombing, Maldonado noticed several vehicles lining up outside his office and none of his Saudi co-workers were present. Outside he encountered a Vinnell adviser who was very upset. He told Maldonado that a SANG commander had suddenly decided to leave the compound and perform night manoeuvres with 50 Vinnell trainers. 'I don't understand why they are doing it,' he said angrily. 'I don't know why they are going into the field for just one night.' Maldonado was also puzzled and even more curious when he drove past the local mosque at noon and noticed far fewer pairs of sandals outside the door than usual.

Former Vinnell employees believe that removing 50 of the 70 trainers on a pointless expedition 40 miles away was deliberate, leaving the compound defenceless on that fatal night. 'There is no doubt that we were set up,' recalled Maldonado. 'All those trainers taught tactics and gunnery to the SANG. They were essential to the programme. I think that someone in the upper echelons of SANG knew what was going to happen in advance and tipped off the project manager. It was not until the early morning of the next day that a company of armed SANG soldiers showed up and they then left shortly before noon for prayers.'

Ambassador Jordan, who had regularly warned Vinnell and the Saudi royals for weeks before the attack, was livid and outraged. He was particularly upset by the loss of seven American lives. The next day, 13 May 2003, Jordan and Colin Powell, US secretary of state, visited Crown Prince Abdullah for a private meeting. Looking stunned and 'white as a ghost', Abdullah was absolutely shaken to the core by the bombing. If he had been in a state of denial about Al-Qaeda, it ended that morning.[3]

A few days later the Crown Prince met George Tenet, then director of the CIA, in Riyadh. Tenet was blunt in his assessment. 'Unless you act quickly, Al-Qaeda are going to kill you, murder your family and launch the next stage of terrorist attacks against the United States from the Saudi homeland,' he told the startled Prince. 'I gave him a plan of action,' recalled the former director. 'This good man – and I believe he is a good man – took me up on the challenge.'[4]

The response of other prominent Saudis was limited in substance and qualified in methodology. Prince Naif denounced the terrorists and called for public assistance in capturing 19 suspects. Their names and photographs were published in the press. The embassy in London declared that the Kingdom 'condemns all forms of terrorism', but added that it 'strives to show that combating terrorism is not an attempt to subjugate the world to the requirements and considerations of a particular civilisation. Efforts to combat terrorism must be free of double standards and international law should be applied equally and without discrimination.'

Islamic reaction showed how Al-Qaeda has retained support inside Saudi. Three prominent clerics issued a statement claiming that the accused were not terrorists but 'pious and devout' men and 'the flower of the mujahideen'. They claimed that the Saudi authorities, acting on US orders, were using the suicide bombers as a pretext for persecuting fighters who have 'participated in the jihad against the malevolent Crusaders' and 'distinguished themselves with courage and heroism'. The clerics called on the population to disobey the request for help and warned that any assistance to the police would constitute aid to the US in its war against Islam. Responding to the call, 33 activist clerics lobbied the government and attacked the reformists for abandoning jihad.

Within two weeks the Saudi Interior Ministry announced that the alleged mastermind of the bombing had been traced. On 27 May 2003, Ali Abdul Rahman Al-Ghamdi, a leading Al-Qaeda operative and 29-year-old economics graduate, and three associates were arrested after leaving an internet cafe in Madinah. Their car was stopped at a checkpoint by security officers. Al-Ghamdi gave himself up willingly and without a struggle.

The Riyadh attack produced a complete sea-change in the Saudis' attitude towards internal security. After years of inactivity and negligence, they were now forced to take it seriously. A joint intelligence taskforce was set up in which Americans and Saudi officials sat shoulder to shoulder reading the same material off the same computer screen based in a secret location in the Kingdom. This intelligence has been used to penetrate Al-Qaeda cells and, in January 2004, a further eight Al-Qaeda activists were captured in Switzerland in connection with the Riyadh bombing and charged with providing 'logistical support to a criminal organisation'.

The events of 12 May 2003 were a seismic shock and woke the authorities from their complacent slumber. 'Let me be honest: 9/11 meant nothing in Saudi Arabia,' said Mshari Al-Thaydi, a young Saudi writer. 'Some didn't believe that any Saudis were involved in it. Others thought it was a conspiracy or was deserved because of America's support for Israel . . . 12 May was our 9/11. Since then, Saudis have had to recognise that Al-Qaeda is not a fantasy. It is here.'[5]

The epic, almost theatrical, scale of the atrocity also had an impact on the Saudi authorities' attitude towards the Western detainees. The House of Saud could no longer sustain the myth that all these car-bombings were perpetrated by Scottish tax accountants and hospital workers from West Yorkshire. It was now more difficult for Prince Naif to insist that Sandy Mitchell and friends were terrorists hired as undercover MI6 agents by the British embassy.

Inside Al-Hiar prison the activities of Prince Naif's secret police had not changed. In early May 2003, Ibrahim and Khaled visited Sandy and, to his shock, told him that the decision to execute him had been confirmed. As most of the guards and the governor were telling him that he was innocent, Sandy was not sure whether to believe his tormentors. But it was quite possible that the Interior Ministry would try to bury their mistakes rather than expose them, he thought.

'I am innocent and you know it,' he replied.

'Make another statement saying that you are guilty and repentant and I promise that you will get a pardon,' said Khaled.

'You can take my head but you will pay for it with your souls, because you know we are innocent.'

That sent Ibrahim into a frenzy of shouting and ranting that he would die in prison unless he confessed again. But Sandy, no longer in chains and stronger physically, was not intimidated this time. Frustrated and noticeably less confident, Ibrahim eventually called the guards and the prisoner was sent back to his cell.

When Sandy heard about the bombing in Riyadh from the guards, he was encouraged because it further proved that Al-Qaeda not Westerners were the culprits. On the afternoon of 12 May 2003, before the bombing, a meeting between Blair, Straw and Prince Saud at No. 10 was described as 'very positive' by Gail Jenkinson. Although she had heard this all before, Margaret was cautiously optimistic.

'The clemency letters have to be updated and presented to Prince Saud by our ambassador,' said Jenkinson. 'We need to strike while the iron is hot.'

But Margaret was still wary. 'I hope this is not another false dawn. I don't know if I could cope with that,' she thought as she put the phone down.

Three days later Margaret finally broke her silence on the BBC Scotland *Frontline* programme. She was highly critical of the Foreign Office. 'I was told this was a priority and I believed them,' she said.

'For two-and-a-half years I have said nothing and waited for the Foreign Office to do their job. I am certain that this is not a high priority any more and Sandy is going to die.'[6]

It now looked as though Al-Qaeda – ironically and grimly – could be doing the Foreign Office's job and acting as the catalyst for Sandy's release. On the morning of 20 May 2003, Gary Powell, an anti-terrorist officer at Scotland Yard who liaised with Sandy's family, called Margaret. He said that the Saudis had requested British assistance and expertise to investigate the attack and a team from Scotland Yard had been flown to Riyadh immediately. 'I have spoken to the guys and people are openly talking about the release of the men,' he said.

The next day Prince Turki Al-Faisal strongly hinted that the men would be released. At first he defended the arrest and prosecution. 'These people were not randomly picked in order to blame them for something that had taken place, for the sake of blaming them,' he told BBC Radio 4's *World At One* programme. 'These people were tried, convicted, evidence was presented in court against them and they were sentenced.' But he added, 'Our concern is that not only is justice done for the victims of the crimes that took place, but also to keep the relationship between the two countries on a friendly basis and not allow anything to interfere with that. The legal system in Saudi Arabia allows for clemency and all of these considerations are being worked out between your government and mine.'

After the stark, apocalyptic warning by CIA director George Tenet, Crown Prince Abdullah was now taking a more proactive role. On 1 June 2003 he discussed the case with Tony Blair at the G8 trade summit in Evian, France. The prime minister asked when the men would be released. 'I can reassure you that it will be resolved soon,' replied Abdullah. But he declined to outline a specific timetable and there was only a vague understanding agreed between the two leaders. To avoid the Saudis' notorious habit of procrastination and diplomatic obfuscation, Blair wrote a letter to the Crown Prince to confirm their consensus. 'He has asked for a written assurance [about the release],' said a Foreign Office official. 'No one really expects anything back in writing, but it reduces the scope for [Saudi] wriggling.'

The Crown Prince's remark appeared to be more than polite diplomatic language. The day after Blair's letter was delivered to Prince Abdullah, Margaret met Gail Jenkinson in the Commons and for the first time discussed the logistics of Sandy's release. But she was in for yet another surprise when she asked what would actually happen: 'Would the embassy know when they are being released?'

'Ken Neill will have to buy the airline tickets, so they would know,' replied Jenkinson. 'The men will be expected to sign an "intent to pay" form which means they will need to repay the cost of the fares.'

Margaret was stunned. 'Well, there is no money.'

'It will not need to be repaid straight away.'

'My brother has been arrested, tortured, been to hell and back and put in a cell in solitary confinement for two-and-a-half years. Do you mean to say that we are now expected to pay for the privilege of flying him home?'

'You cannot expect the government to stand the cost.'

'Hell will freeze over,' she replied angrily. 'It is absolutely ridiculous.'

Margaret then asked about specialist medical and psychiatric treatment, given the extreme physical and psychological abuse the men had suffered. 'I would go and see your GP,' said Jenkinson. 'If there is a problem, then we will see if we can help.'

An incensed Margaret left the Commons and had a drink with Ron Jones. She then told John Lyons, Labour MP for Strathkelvin and Bearsden, who was campaigning on Sandy's behalf, that the Foreign Office had refused to pay the air fare. Shocked by the government's attitude, Lyons raised the issue two weeks later in the Commons: 'I put on record that I am horrified that the Foreign Office should take that stand. It is crass and insensitive. It displays the sensitivity of a torturer. I cannot believe that it has made that decision. This should not be a consideration at this stage.'[7]

Clearly embarrassed, the government appeared to back off. During the same debate, Mike O'Brien, the Foreign Office minister for trade and investment, replied to Lyons's criticism: 'In such cases, the Foreign Office can, if required, make funds available to British nationals and their families. We shall consider their ability to pay. The loan is usually made available so that British nationals do not have to worry about funding tickets immediately and can return to the UK as quickly as possible. However, I take my honourable friend's point and we may have the opportunity to talk about the matter later.'[8]

The minister's public response was, in fact, ambiguous, so Margaret wrote to James Watt, head of the Foreign Office's consular division, asking for clarification and explaining that she could not afford the ticket. In private, their position was more firm, and they confirmed their refusal to pay the air fare: 'We presume from previous experience that the Saudi authorities will ask the embassy to arrange for tickets on the men's behalf. In this case, we could make a loan available for ticket purchase to the UK, subject to an undertaking to repay.'

The main concern during the summer was that throughout July and August most of the Saudi royal family departs for their palaces and mansions in Spain, Switzerland and the south of France and the Kingdom grinds to a halt. Despite all the positive noises and nuances, the wheels of justice were grinding slowly. At 9.50 p.m. on 13 June 2003, the families were jolted again with an abrupt turn of events. Ron Jones's wife, Sandra, discovered on the internet that Sir Derek Plumbly, the British ambassador in Riyadh who had worked so diligently on Sandy's behalf, was being posted to Cairo in three months' time.

Margaret was devastated. She viewed Sir Derek as the only diplomat who had made Sandy's case a priority. Very upset, at 10.20 the following morning she called Jenkinson. 'Why didn't you tell us?'

'I didn't think it was important,' she replied. 'A new ambassador is not that critical. They move about all the time.'

'But you told us that Sir Derek had a good working relationship with the Crown Prince and various princes. It will take some time for a new ambassador to get to know the case and build up that relationship again.'

The Foreign Official again said that the ambassador's role was not that critical, because they are posted around so much.

'But you told me previously that relationships are VERY important to the Saudis, which is why you keep sending Baroness Symons, because she gets on so well with Crown Prince Abdullah.'

Silence on the end of the phone. Jenkinson did not reply and said that she did not know when the men were being released. Margaret ended the phone call, very disappointed and angry.

To Jenkinson's credit, she called back later that afternoon and apologised for not informing her about Sir Derek's departure. 'No one realised how strongly you and the families felt about it,' she said.

But Margaret was unforgiving – she had always asked about personnel changes. 'Not good enough,' she wrote in her diary.

Characteristically, Sir Derek postponed his departure as ambassador until he secured Sandy's release. The most encouraging sign came on 9 July 2003, during a meeting between Prince Turki Al-Faisal and a delegation of six MPs at the Saudi embassy. Led by John Lyons, they represented all the British detainees still incarcerated. Prince Turki, an affable and quietly spoken ambassador, was playing an increasingly influential role. For just over an hour he listened attentively as each MP outlined their constituent's case for clemency and handed over letters on behalf of the families. 'Their detention is a major obstacle to good relations between the United Kingdom and your country,' said Lyons.

The Prince did not acknowledge their innocence but indicated that the men would be released. 'We are keen to resolve this as soon as possible,' he said and added that he would be talking to King Fahd about the matter very soon. The MPs left the embassy cautiously optimistic.

A few months earlier Prince Turki would not even have agreed to meet the MPs. Clearly, the Saudis were conceding ground and would use the clemency plea as their public justification for releasing the men. The real reason, of course, was the Al-Qaeda bombing in Riyadh. Even Margaret, ever the sceptical realist, thought the end could be in sight.

After so many false alarms, Margaret needed reassurance from someone she could trust. At 4.45 p.m. on Monday, 4 August 2003, she telephoned Sir Derek Plumbly on his mobile in Riyadh. 'The end is very close now,' he said wearily. 'Every obstacle has been cleared now. I would rather not give you a specific date because I fear I may be proved wrong, but we are very near.'

Two days later, on 6 August, Sir Derek flew to Cairo to take up his new posting and within hours the men were officially pardoned. That same afternoon, incredibly, there was a last-minute hitch. At 1.40 p.m., just as Margaret was leaving her house to go back to work, the phone rang. It was Gail Jenkinson. 'Can we give assurances to the Saudis that you will not speak to the press?' she asked.

'Say whatever it takes,' she replied.

At 4.25 p.m. Margaret spoke to Hejailan, Sandy's lawyer, about the final arrangements. He said the men would be home on Friday and he had hired a doctor and two bodyguards to accompany them on the flight. Once the papers were signed, it was closure. But to the bitter end, secrecy was a prerogative. 'Please do not say a word to anyone,' said Hejailan. 'It is important that the media are not there [at the airport]. That is a condition of the release.'

The Saudi obsession with secrecy was more intense than usual because they were anxious not to reveal a major reason for the release: a covert deal whereby the Americans agreed to transfer Saudis from Guantanamo Bay in exchange for the release of the Britons. Citing US military and British diplomatic sources, the *New York Times* claimed that five Saudi members of Al-Qaeda were flown from Guantanamo on 14 May 2003, two days after the bombing, and in return King Fahd granted clemency to the Britons. Until then senior princes were using the detainees as a bargaining tool. 'The Saudis kept making the excuse about us [the US and UK] having the Saudis at Guantanamo,' said a US State Department official.

Another US source said: 'This presented itself as a way for the United States to help its friends, both the Brits and the Saudis. It's what diplomacy is all about.'

It was the Saudis' idea and they were effectively using Sandy, Bill and Les as hostages.[9]

Meanwhile, Margaret was still not convinced about their release because of distressing false alarms in the past. The next morning, Thursday, 7 August, she was working on a petition to give to the Saudi ambassador in London, when Hejailan called again. 'The men are definitely coming home, either late tonight or tomorrow morning,' he said.

'Thank you, Sheik Salah,' she replied in a flat, emotionless tone of voice. 'That is great news.'

The lawyer must have thought that she had developed deafness or had gone mad because he kept repeating the news.

'Yes, I heard you, thank you. Don't worry, I won't tell anyone,' she said calmly. There was no way she was going to get excited yet.

It was only when Gail Jenkinson called to confirm that she knew it was true. 'It is not a done deal until they are actually in the air, but they should be arriving on the early morning flight tomorrow,' she said. 'We don't want the press to get hold of this until they are flying. Please wait until I call you in the morning before you leave for Heathrow.'

Margaret put the phone down and started to shake. She did not know whether to laugh or cry. She called Noi, Sandy's wife, and gave her the good news. 'Are you sure Sandy is really coming home?' she asked warily.

Meanwhile, Sandy was spending his last day inside Al-Hiar prison. When Colonel Said told him about his release, the guards appeared as happy as the prisoners. After showering, Sandy changed into some clothes brought by his lawyers and began dreaming about his return. But when the Colonel came into his cell again later that night, he had a troubled look on his face. 'There is a problem,' he said. 'Bill [Sampson] is refusing to get dressed and will not cooperate. Would you speak to him?'

It was nearly three years since Sandy had last seen his friend Bill, who was arrested at the same time and tortured with the same brutality. Sandy eagerly agreed. But when he stepped into his cell, he almost threw up. The place was a disgusting mess and the stench of excrement almost knocked him over. Sandy was angry at the conditions that his friend was being held in and his respect for the Colonel rapidly faded. 'If he knew that I was innocent, then he must have known Bill was equally a victim, so why he did he allow such barbaric conditions to exist?' he thought.

Lying in the corner of the filthy cell, Bill was in terrible shape. He looked like someone who had spent the past three years in Belsen concentration camp during the Second World War – all skin and bones with bloody sores covering his fragile, naked body. The last time Sandy had seen Bill he weighed about 98 kg and now he was reduced to no more than 64 kg. Thankfully, he appeared to have retained his sense of humour. 'Hi, Dinky, what are you doing here?' said Bill, looking up as Sandy walked into the cell.

'We are going home,' said Sandy.

'Fine, I am going like this,' replied Bill. 'They have kept me like this all the time, so I want the world to see what they have done.'

Sandy could see his point, but he also knew that the Saudis would never allow the world to see how they had really treated them. Eventually, Sandy persuaded Bill to shower and dress into some clothes, even though they looked four sizes too big for him.

When Colonel Said walked into the cell, Bill strode up to him and spat in his face. Sandy was concerned that this would jeopardise their release. But when his friend quietly described how they had made his life a constant hell, he was quietly proud of him. He was still fighting back.

On arriving at the airport in Riyadh early on Friday morning, Sandy and Bill were whisked into a private lounge where they were met by an RAF medical team and Ken Neill from the embassy. It was the first time that Sandy had seen the other detainees since his arrest nearly three years earlier. They were all broken men and mere shadows of their former selves, physically and psychologically – nervous, timid, fearful and insular.

When they were escorted onto the Boeing 777, the captain greeted them warmly and shook their hands. 'I am very pleased to be taking you all home,' he said. On the flight home the RAF nurses and doctors, who specialised in looking after hostages and prisoners of war, soon realised from experience what the detainees had suffered. Sandy and the men were relieved that at least some people out there knew they were innocent. For the rest of the flight the men related their own stories of torture, abuse and injustice at the hands of the servants of the House of Saud.

As the Boeing jet was flying across Europe, Margaret was already travelling down to Heathrow with Noi and her son Matthew. As they drove down the motorway, Gail Jenkinson rang on the mobile. 'The plane is on its way. You can set off now,' she said.

'We already are,' replied Margaret and the Foreign Office official laughed.

'I thought as much.'

Even on the long drive south, Margaret still thought the Saudis might detain her brother. 'My biggest fear was that the Saudis wanted to show the outside world how "compassionate" they were by giving the other men a pardon, but then show how strong they were to their own people by executing Sandy,' she recalled. She kept trying not to think about it, but the vision kept recurring. Eventually they arrived at Heathrow airport police station and they met the relatives of the other men in a narrow, grey, dingy room next to the canteen. Everyone was quiet and pensive, lost in their own thoughts. Matthew was getting restless, so Margaret took him outside to watch the planes. But it was such a hot day that it only made him more restless.

The families were then driven to the VIP building. Surrounded by plain-clothed policemen, all looking very serious, it felt like a scene out of an American police TV series. The atmosphere was then lightened when they were greeted enthusiastically by the VIP official whom Margaret had seen on television meeting foreign royalty. 'Welcome to Heathrow,' she said brightly in her cut-glass accent as if they were celebrities or had just won the lottery.

'This is totally bizarre,' thought Margaret.

The families were then ushered into a separate room with several sofas and plenty of space for everyone. In the corner, *Sky News* was breaking the news that the men had landed at Heathrow. As she watched the television, the names of the detainees were running along the bottom of the screen. The only name missing was Sandy's! Noi looked across at Margaret in sheer panic and fear.

'Don't worry,' replied Margaret, who walked over to see Gail Jenkinson standing in the entrance foyer. 'Are you sure he is on the plane?' she asked, her anxieties suddenly flooding back.

Jenkinson looked edgy. 'Margaret, of course he's on the plane,' she replied.

But Margaret was not quite reassured. 'What if they had not let Sandy go at the last minute?' she thought. She felt sick but did not dare show her nerves to Noi.

The television showed a long-range shot of the men disembarking from the aircraft. Margaret could see Bill Sampson, Les Walker, a glimpse of Jimmy Lee, official-looking men but still no sign of Sandy. Everyone was getting excited, but Margaret's heart was pounding and she felt sick again. What was going on? Had he been held back? As the minibus arrived at the VIP building, it was difficult to see the men through the laughing, shouting crowd. And then there he was, the last one into the room. As Sandy struggled through the crowd to the back, greeting old friends on the way, Margaret shouted, 'Are you coming to say hello to us or not?' They hugged but there were no tears. He then embraced Noi tightly and glimpsed his beloved four-year-old son, Matthew, nervously hiding behind his mother and a little shy.

'Look Matthew, it's Daddy,' said Noi. 'He's come home to us.' And within seconds they were laughing and playing on the floor like a couple of kids.

After a few minutes of talking to the other families, Sandy was introduced to Gail Jenkinson. 'You do know that I am innocent,' were his first words to her. Margaret expected her to say what she had told her so many times on the phone: that she did not believe he was guilty. But she just smiled and said that the press were asking for a group photograph and a few words. A statement was hastily prepared, saying how happy they were to be with their families and thanking everyone for their support. The men exchanged telephone numbers and at last Margaret, Noi and Sandy were on their way home. There was no celebration party. They were too exhausted. Just before they went to bed, Sandy was leaving the kitchen. 'Oh, turn out the light, would you?' said Margaret. Sandy reacted with a look of fear and confusion. It was an unsettling reminder of the cell where the lights were never turned off. It was Friday, 8 August 2003 – two years and eight months since his arrest.

After the euphoria of the homecoming, it was not long before reality set in. In a sense Sandy was still being tortured psychologically. He was diagnosed with post-traumatic stress disorder and to this day suffers from panic attacks, memory loss and recurring nightmares of his ordeal. Images of the sheer glee on the faces of those who were torturing him keep coming back to him. 'It is like being an alcoholic,' he said. 'You take one day at a time. I have good days and have weeks where it's OK. But the slightest conflict or stress on a particular day can set me back weeks.' The ordeal of the Saudi inquisition is ever-present. 'I will carry my guilt with me, perhaps for the rest of my life,' he reflected. 'Not for the bombings, but for accusing other innocent men of complicity while under torture in the hope that my Saudi interrogators would stop the pain and leave my wife alone. I knew what they meant when they said, "She is just a Thai so we can do anything we want to her." The closest I can come to explaining my experiences is rape. Although I was not physically raped by them, I endured a mental equivalent which helped them break me alongside the physical torture.'

The top priority was to find him high-quality psychiatric counselling. The Foreign Office recommended a specialist care clinic at the Edenfield Centre on the outskirts of Manchester, about 32 miles from where Sandy lives in Halifax, Yorkshire. It was not exactly convenient or practical but Margaret drove Sandy to the establishment for an appointment. As they arrived, the entrance was down a long wooded lane separate from the hospital. They needed to be buzzed into the building and the reception staff were housed behind a thick Perspex screen. The 'specialist care' turned out to be a secure unit for the victims and perpetrators of violent crime. 'We don't judge people. We are here to help,' explained the social worker. As they walked through the corridors, all they could see were locked doors. It was like a scene out of *One Flew Over the Cuckoo's Nest*.

Sandy looked bewildered and, although the consultant, Dr Holloway, was pleasant and sympathetic, it was obviously completely inappropriate. 'What on earth were the Foreign Office thinking when they suggested this institution?' Margaret thought as they looked around. 'They had nearly three years to prepare for this eventuality and a secure unit miles away is the best they could do.'

A troubled Sandy left with only a prescription for tranquillisers. He hardly spoke on the way home. A furious Margaret called Jenkinson on her return and complained bitterly. Not only would it take two buses and a train just to get there – and Sandy could not negotiate public transport by himself – it was totally unsuitable.

'I am very sorry, but it's the best we could do at such short notice,' she replied.

In fact, Margaret had been discussing the need for specialist care for the men with the Foreign Office for several months. That night, he was very distressed and woke up with terrible screaming fits which woke up everyone in his sister's house.

'Mummy, why is Daddy crying?' asked his four-year-old son, Matthew. 'What's wrong with Daddy?'

Homeless, unemployed and penniless, Sandy was dependent on

the generosity of Margaret and her family. He felt abandoned and betrayed by the government. Fortunately, he instructed Geoffrey Bindman and Partners, the experienced and effective solicitors who specialise in human-rights cases, to consider taking legal action against the Saudis. Apart from compensation, Sandy was equally determined to clear his name and redress the injustice. At first, Bindman suggested that he give the Saudi government the opportunity to redeem themselves and the Foreign Office recommended writing private, respectful letters asking for a meeting with the ambassador. Sandy did so and the Kingdom ignored him. And so, along with Bill Sampson and Les Walker, he began civil proceedings against the individual Saudi persecutors and the Interior Ministry. He was shocked to discover that one of the interrogators who had tortured him brutally almost daily for several months had been promoted by the Interior Ministry in early 2003.

The independent evidence that Sandy was tortured was known to the Foreign Office for some time. In October 2002, a team from the United Nations Commission on Human Rights concluded there was firm evidence that five Britons, including Sandy, were tortured. The UN special rapporteur, Param Cumaraswamy, interviewed the prisoners and stated that their descriptions of abuse were 'consistent'. He also 'found that there have been substantial irregularities in the case that must throw doubt upon the validity of the accused's confessions'. The UN envoy then met Prince Naif and told him that the situation was 'unacceptable' and the men should be released. The Prince replied that the 'judicial process was still not complete'.

After Sandy was released he was examined by the Parker Institute in Denmark, the world's top centre for assessing whether people have been tortured. Referring to Sandy's case, the doctors concluded: 'There is an overall accordance between the presented torture history, the described symptoms and the results of today's examination. The findings are consistent with the alleged torture with a high degree of support.'

Armed with this evidence, Sandy sought to demonstrate both to prospective employers and the law courts that he was innocent and his confession only secured under repeated torture. He required the assistance of the Foreign Office on both counts. As an anaesthetic technician, it was vital to register with a medical agency and the Medical Defence Union (MDU) to apply for jobs. Legally, Sandy had a criminal record and the MDU told him that he needed a letter from the Foreign Office which confirmed his innocence before he could be registered. The document was also crucial evidence for his lawsuit against the Saudi torturers.

At first Sandy believed it would not be a problem. Soon after his release in August 2003, Jack Straw telephoned him and said, 'I am so pleased that you are free. I am at your service. If you need to speak to me, please call Gail any time and I will call you back.' Privately, the foreign secretary told Labour MPs that he knew the men were innocent and had been tortured. But publicly he refused to say so. On 8 September 2003, Geoffrey Bindman formally asked the Foreign Office for the letter declaring their innocence. Baroness Symons replied seven weeks later: 'Under our consular remit, we do not make a judgement about an individual's guilt or innocence. We cannot, therefore, provide a letter exactly as you suggest, but I enclose a sample of a letter we could provide.'

The draft statement did not even hint at Sandy's treatment. Instead, the Foreign Office praised its own role:

> During _____'s detention, the British government made clear publicly our deep concerns about his case. Our concerns, including the lack of transparency in the judicial process, were such that they were raised with the Saudi authorities at the highest levels, including by the prime minister and the foreign secretary. On 8 August 2003, the foreign secretary said that he greatly welcomed the release of the men from custody. He was relieved they had returned to the UK and their families. It had obviously been a difficult time for the men and their relatives.

It is true that the Foreign Office has a policy that it will not publicly criticise the legal procedure of a foreign state or make judgements on cases which have been processed through the courts. But lawyers argue that, in Sandy's case, his conviction was obtained, according to independent experts, by torture and so 'the consular remit' is invalid. As Geoffrey Bindman stated in a letter to Baroness Symons:

> I would be interested to know what authority exists for the surprising proposition that a government cannot express an opinion . . . My clients are innocent and they should not be expected to prove their innocence, least of all by their own government. There is no evidence of guilt against them save for confessions extracted by torture. That torture has been verified by unimpeachable medical evidence . . . What possible constitutional objection can there be to your public acknowledgement of the facts?

He never received a reply.

Observers also argue that if a Briton had been framed, detained and tortured in Iraq, then Tony Blair and Jack Straw would have expressed outrage and publicly denounced the foreign state. Statements would have been made to an angry Commons and ministers would be full of talk of retaliation and sanctions. As *The Independent* pointed out: 'But this is Saudi Arabia, which has a great deal of oil and is officially an ally of Britain, and whose favours and military contracts we seek with obsequious enthusiasm and substantial corruption at the highest levels.'

Eventually, on 21 January 2005, more than a year later and only after pressure from Sandy's lawyers, the Foreign Office suggested a new, expanded version of the letter. It grudgingly accepted that the 'government is not aware of any credible evidence that Mr X was guilty of the crimes of which he was convicted'. The Foreign Office then rather tortuously addressed the issue of torture without confirming what it was saying in private:

Mr X and the other men detained at the same time have alleged they were tortured while in detention. The men's allegations of torture are very detailed . . . The FCO is not in a position conclusively to confirm or deny the men's allegations or torture. However, we note the strength of the evidence they have brought forward and that the Parker Institute has corroborated four of the men's allegations that they were tortured.

Despite ministerial expressions of sympathy and kind words, the Foreign Office was doing virtually nothing to help the tortured men. It did arrange for Sandy to have tests at the Medical Foundation for the Victims of Torture and medical treatment. But it refused to pay his travel costs to go to Manchester for counselling and £150 to renew his wife's immigration status. Within seven weeks of his release, Sandy was desperate and in despair. On 22 September 2003, an enraged Margaret called Gail Jenkinson and said she was taking up Jack Straw's offer of help. 'Sandy is in a state,' she said. 'He is homeless, penniless and in desperate need of help − financially and emotionally. We have been abandoned and no one gives a damn. You have had nearly three years to put everything in place and it's a shambles. It's a disgrace.' Jenkinson replied that the Foreign Office could not do much more, but agreed to pass on the message. The foreign secretary did not call back.

Sandy merely wanted to live a conventional life. 'It's very simple,' he said at the time. 'If our government would say publicly that I am innocent, then I can work again. They will not say what they have told my sister privately − that they believe I am innocent − for political reasons.'

It was only due to the efforts of Alice Mahon, Labour MP for Halifax, that his housing benefit and social security were authorised. 'The difficulty is that the Western governments are still talking about Saudi like it is an ally, but it is a brutal, autocratic regime and should be held to account,' she said.[10]

As for the Saudi royal family, they reacted with arrogance to Sandy's release and legal action. In October 2003, Prince Naif had the effrontery to open a human-rights conference at the King Fahd Cultural Center in Riyadh. In his opening address, he said that human rights were protected by sharia law. 'Islam cemented the principles of justice, peace and harmony 1,400 years ago before any international laws were even thought of,' the Prince told the delegates. When asked afterwards about the torture claims, he replied, 'These are baseless accusations.'[11]

Adel Al-Jubeir, the foreign affairs adviser to Crown Prince Abdullah, still claimed publicly the men were terrorist bombers. When asked about abuse, he replied, 'We deny that. Well, let them be examined by medical doctors.'[12]

Prince Turki Al-Faisal, the Saudi ambassador in London, hoodwinked the Foreign Office and avoided meeting the men and his lawyers to discuss a settlement. On 15 December 2003, Bindman and Partners planned to hold a press conference to launch its legal action against the House of Saud. On advice from the Foreign Office, the law firm postponed it after Prince Turki agreed to a meeting if 'respectful letters' were written to the Crown Prince. The letters were duly written and Prince Turki duly refused to meet Sandy and the detainees. The meeting has never taken place.

The legal sights are now set firmly on the two Saudi torturers: Ibrahim and Khaled. Sandy's lawyers believe that they can be prosecuted by the Criminal Justice Act because they were public officials committing torture in an official capacity and so are covered by the UN Convention Against Torture (which Saudi is a party to). This means that they could be extradited to the UK. Accordingly, Bindman asked Baroness Symons to take appropriate steps to extradite Ibrahim and Khaled. 'The question of whether to commence a prosecution is a matter for the police authorities and the Crown Prosecution Service based on the evidence they have available to them,' she replied.

The Foreign Office appeared anxious to avoid any legal action against the House of Saud and refused to support the men. 'It is a matter for them and their lawyers,' said Baroness Symons loftily. But when Ron Jones, another torture victim, tried to sue the Saudis, the government despatched the Treasury solicitor to the Court of Appeal to uphold the State Immunity Act, which protects foreign regimes from prosecution. That served to help the Saudis.

As Labour MP John Lyons declared in the Commons, 'I am unhappy that we should interfere in a claim against the Saudi government by a person who was tortured and beaten. We should be doing exactly the opposite: we should do everything we can to assist such a claim. We should not stand in the way of it or raise a constitutional hurdle, but should make sure that those who are responsible for torture and beatings are brought to court and that the victim has his day in court to accuse them.'[13]

So far no action has been taken through the criminal system. But on 28 October 2004 there was a major development in response to Ron Jones's case. The Court of Appeal ruled that foreign states like Saudi Arabia should no longer have blanket legal immunity in respect of systematic torture carried out by its officials. As Ibrahim and Khaled have been hiding behind the State Immunity Act, this means that Ron Jones, Sandy, Bill Sampson and Les Walker may yet have redress in the British High Court. 'So far the Saudi government has not accepted responsibility for the actions of their officials,' said Geoffrey Bindman after the judgement. 'It must now do so.'

EIGHT

A HOSTAGE TO SAUDI OIL

'What would you call a Bush energy policy that keeps America dependent on a medieval monarchy with a king who has lost most of his faculties, where there is virtually no transparency about what's happening, where corruption is rampant, where we have asked all Americans to leave and where the education system is so narrow that its own people are decrying it as a factory for extremism? Now that's what I call naive, reckless and dangerous.'

Thomas Friedman, *New York Times*, 3 June 2004

The fire started by accident. Just after 8 a.m. on 11 March 2002, a teenager at the Girls' Intermediate School No. 31 in suburban Mecca, the holiest city of Islam, sneaked back to the stairwell to smoke a cigarette before classes. A hall monitor spotted her on the rubbish-strewn landing at the top of the stairs and she hastily tossed the butt, without extinguishing it, onto a pile of discarded books and papers.

Twenty minutes later the teachers smelt smoke and one shouted 'Fire!' Within seconds, a panic more intense than the raging flames rapidly swept through the four-storey decrepit building which was almost Soviet in its grey shoddiness. As the flames engulfed the corridors, about 750 girls, aged between 13 and 17, poured into the single, narrow stairwell, desperate to avoid the blaze. The stampede collapsed the staircase and the only escape was the front door. But it was locked and the only person with a key was the illiterate male caretaker who had left the building on a menial errand and closed the door.

Suddenly the electricity went off and the screaming, suffocating young girls began to die in the dark. The fire brigade could have forced an entry. But the headmistress required authorisation from a higher male authority to call them. Instead she fled the building and ordered that the door remain locked behind her.

The firefighters and ambulances arrived promptly, but so did members of the mutawwa: the religious police who are, in reality, zealous vigilantes and drawn, like most of Osama Bin Laden's disciples, from the fanatical followers of the Wahhabi creed. They belong to the officially sanctioned Committee for the Promotion of Virtue and Prevention of Vice, overseen by Prince Naif, which implements a narrow interpretation of Islam, enforcing gender segregation and strict dress codes, ensuring businesses close during prayer times and harassing religious minorities. Young and aggressive, they are recognisable because their robes are shorter, their beards are longer and they carry a short stick.

Originally known as the Society for the Propagation of Good and the Abolition of Evil, the mutawwa achieved lasting fame in 1969 for its declaration that the Earth was flat and the US landing on the moon was a lie propagated by international Zionism.[1] They spend most of their time spying on, accosting and beating up women if they miss the prayer-time curfew or if their abaya (black garment) does not cover their entire body or if they are eating in restaurants with a man who is not a relative. A law unto itself, its members are mostly unemployed high-school drop-outs who can be seen prowling the shopping malls in gangs with canes, ready to enforce its rigid version of religious law.

And yet the mutawwa have extraordinary official authority and operate with impunity. They are empowered to detain people for a maximum of 24 hours before delivering them to the police. But many prisoners are held for weeks without officials notifying their families. It was their authority which was imposed that fateful morning as the fire raged. According to eyewitness reports, mutawwa officers argued heatedly with the emergency services and the police, who were desperate to enter the school. The rescuers were warned that there could be no contact with the girls if all of their bodies were not fully covered, because their male relatives were not there to collect them.

Inside, clothing was not on the minds of the hysterical, trapped girls who saw their friends burning to death in front of them. As the firemen and mutawwa argued outside, valuable time was lost and some girls tried to escape. It was like a football-stadium disaster. 'Girls panicked, screaming and pushing each other at the front door. Some girls in front of me were killed as they were squeezed against the door,' said Tahani El-Harethy.

'I pushed forward with the crowd because I was afraid of the fire, but the locked door stood between the girls and life,' said one survivor. 'Some girls jumped from the top of the stairs, but I was overcome by smoke. I only woke up in hospital.'

Another, Aysha Akbar, recalled, 'I tried to run, but my foot got jammed in the cast-iron banisters of the staircase. I fell and the other girls were trying to jump over me but some stepped on me. They broke my leg and ankle.'

Some pupils did escape via a gate but inevitably left their headscarves behind or their full-length black abayas were torn. Others were still in their nightdresses. They were immediately forced back inside the burning building by the mutawwa to cover themselves, according to several eyewitnesses. Some mutawwa even assaulted rescue workers who were trying to save the children.

'Instead of extending a helping hand, they were using their hands to beat us,' said one.[2]

Eventually, after angry exchanges, the regular police subdued the mutawwa leader, confiscated his ID and dragged him away. The door to the school was opened and the fire extinguished. But by that stage it was too late: 15 girls had needlessly died and over 40 were injured with horrific burns. For those left outside – powerless and frustrated – the pain was almost unbearable. On hearing news of the fire, distraught fathers rushed to the school, only to find their daughters already dead, lying on the pavement.[3]

The tragedy that unfolded that morning was relatively small compared with 9/11, but, for a brief moment, it had a profound significance and impact. An unprecedented wave of anti-government protests, the majority of them by women, broke out. Sensing the public mood of outrage and anger at the blind intolerance of the mutawwa, Crown Prince Abdullah realised it was a rare opportunity to clip the wings of the religious establishment. 'I want you to start now to investigate what happened in Mecca,' he wrote in a sharply worded public letter to his brother Prince Sultan. 'The deaths were unacceptable, the work of negligent, incompetent and careless officials.' Predictably, Prince Naif defended the religious police and claimed they were outside the burning school 'to ensure that the girls were not subjected to any kind of mistreatment'.

But Saudi newspapers were allowed to publish at length heart-wrenching eyewitness accounts from the hospital bedside of the survivors which, for the first time, contained implicit criticism of the mutawwa. Suddenly, Saudis were confronted with the stark and grim consequences of religious intolerance. For the victims were ordinary Saudis, not spoiled princesses raised in marble palaces and driven to school in Rolls-Royces. And so it became the catalyst for Crown Prince Abdullah, a very intuitive ruler, to more openly introduce reform and modernisation and reduce corruption.

By Saudi standards, the reforms were significant. The Presidency for Girls Education, controlled by the uncompromising clerics to enforce segregation, was merged with the Ministry of Education. That may appear superficial but it meant that girls could be taught the same curriculum as boys – a major step in such a conservative Islamic society. Prince Abdullah also allowed women to have their own ID cards instead of appearing as mere wards of their husbands. The Wahhabi clerics howled with protest and claimed that it was a licence to prostitution because their ID photographs would be unveiled. But the measure was implemented.

The tragic school fire encapsulates the conflict between the rigid, austere, conservative Wahhabi community represented by Prince Naif and Prince Sultan and the modernising, reforming element led by Crown Prince Abdullah. Since the uprising in 1979, the austere religious establishment has retained enormous power and influence. This was reinforced after the 1991 Gulf War when the hardline clerics agreed not to object to the American infidels occupying the sacred land. That incurred a political debt by the House of Saud which the clergy called in by refusing to concede to any reforms. Women who demanded driving licences were not only denied them, but arrested for demonstrating about the issue.

A pattern from the past was repeated in the 1990s: when confronted with internal dissent from the clerics, the House of Saud made concessions which ensured that the Wahhabi foundation of the regime remained intact. The mutawwa's power was strengthened: beheadings more than tripled from 59 in 1994 to 191 in 1995, not just for murder but for religious crimes like sorcery. Christian activists were jailed, people were ruthlessly flogged for 'moral lapses' and beds were even checked to ensure their owners had risen for morning prayer. 'The wartime economic boom is over,' said one local Saudi in 1996. 'The royal family is under attack, so they let the zealots run loose. The new head of the mutawwa was just given $18 million to train these 3,000 idiots, most of them lower-class rejects from our good schools who cannot get real jobs anywhere else.'[4]

The word 'mutawwa' is respectfully translated as 'deeply devout Muslims', and many of them come from Buraydah, an oasis surrounded by desert for hundreds of miles in all directions. As the journalist Edward Pilkington found when he visited Saudi Arabia: 'The terrain is harsh, pounded by a sun that will push the temperature to an extreme of 50 degrees. The residents – Bedouins whose lives only 50 years ago were entirely dependent on the camel – hold views that match the fierce terrain. For decades the town resisted the introduction of the radio and telegraph as un-Islamic. When the Saudi royal family began educating girls for the first time in the early 1960s, they protested so forcefully that the army was brought in.'[5]

It is a fundamentalist paradise. 'This is the centre of Saudi Arabia,' said the owner of a local farm. 'It is pure here. There is no mixing with other cultures.'

The consequence of such fanaticism is a contempt and hatred for non-Islamic cultures and religions. Today the Imams in mosques across the globe do not disguise their incitement to kill non-believers and many of their themes are endorsed by the Saudi Ministry of Islamic Affairs and distributed as guidance. In one Saudi government text for seventh-graders, available at the mosque in Washington DC, visitors were told: 'Jews are worse than donkeys.' In another government publication gathered from the King Fahd mosque, a sermon by the cleric Sheik Bin Uthaimin is quoted: 'Our doctrine states that if you accept any religion other than Islam, like Judaism or Christianity, which are not acceptable, you become an unbeliever. If you do not repent, you are an apostate and you should be killed because you have denied the Koran.'[6]

In October 2003, shortly before Robert Jordan left Riyadh as the US ambassador, he received a translation of a sermon in the Grand Mosque in Mecca. At first it appeared to be a plea for greater tolerance, condemning violence, intimidation and terrorism. But then the cleric concluded with a rather different message: 'Oh God, please destroy the Jews and the infidels and all those who support them.'[7]

Moderate Muslims argue that the Wahhabis are like a crazed

SAUDI BABYLON

totalitarian sect that has hijacked, distorted and besmirched the good name of Islam. Former CIA director James Woolsey likened the situation to medieval persecution: 'The Wahhabis claim to be acting in the name of religion. But they are only acting in the same way that Torquemada and the Dominicans around him operated in the name of Christianity when they ran the Spanish Inquisition in the late fifteenth and early sixteenth centuries – killing large numbers of Jews, Muslims and other Christians while also stealing their money . . . There are hundreds of millions of good, decent Muslims out there, so this is not a war against Islam. It's a war against people who call themselves Muslims whose views are a counterpart of Torquemada. Indeed, if you took the Spain of Ferdinand and Isabella and the Inquisition and magically moved it into the twenty-first century and discovered 25 per cent of the world's oil underneath it, you would have a [fundamentalist] Christian version of Saudi Arabia.'

This extreme brand of Islam created a totalitarian, police-state mentality which has been accepted by the House of Saud – or certainly not rejected. The establishment clerics were militant in their ideology but loyal to the government and so were allowed to create an environment that enabled the more extreme Wahhabis to flourish. It was almost as if the Taliban or Khmer Rouge had taken over.

For the Wahhabis, intimidation and punishment is integral to the implementation and survival of its creed. Flogging, amputation of limbs and capital punishment is permissible under sharia law. The death penalty applies to anyone proved guilty of 'corruption on earth', which includes a range of offences – from homosexuality to witchcraft to adultery. The judge can exercise discretion, but between 1980 and November 2002, 1,409 executions took place in Saudi Arabia. Most of the victims were foreign workers, the disadvantaged and women. On 24 April 2000, the Associated Press correspondent Anwar Faruqi described the scene at a public beheading:

Policemen clear a public square of traffic and lay out a thick, blue plastic sheet about 16 ft by 16 ft on the asphalt. The condemned, who has been given tranquillisers, is led from a police car dressed in his own clothing. His eyes are covered with cotton pads, bound in plaster and finally covered with a black cloth. Barefoot, with feet shackled and hands cuffed behind his back, the prisoner is led by a police officer to the centre of the sheet and made to kneel. An Interior Ministry official reads out the prisoner's name and crime before a crowd of witnesses.

A soldier hands a long, curved sword to the executioner. He approaches the prisoner from behind and jabs him with the tip of the sword in the back so that the prisoner instinctively raises his head. It usually takes just one swing of the sword to sever the head, often sending it flying about three feet. Paramedics bring the head to a doctor, who uses a gloved hand to stop the fountain of blood spurting from the neck. The doctor sews the head back on, and the body is wrapped in the blue plastic sheet and taken away in an ambulance.[8]

Secret trials, torture, no legal defence after uncorroborated confessions and arbitrary detention without charge are features of the Saudi judicial system. Crimes involving national security are so broadly defined that they encompass all non-violent opposition to the government. The Saudis refuse to allow the UN Human Rights Committee to investigate allegations of systematic torture in the Kingdom. 'Sharia law is derived from the Koran,' a Geneva-based Saudi diplomat told the *New York Times*. 'This law has existed for 1,400 years and the [UN] committee wants to change it. I am sorry, you cannot. It is a question we cannot discuss.'[9]

Concern for human rights in Saudi Arabia ranks very low on the agenda of the US and UK governments. Apart from noting that women face discrimination and the court system is secretive, abuse of human rights is barely mentioned by the UK Foreign Office or in US State Department presentations to Congress about programmes to promote democratic values across the world. Unlike other brutal dictatorships, British and American officials rarely – if ever – publicly criticise Saudi for torture and brutality, even of their own expatriates. This was acknowledged by Chas Freeman, although he denied that Saudi was a special case: 'Human-rights issues are important and deserve attention, but they cannot be the exclusive objective of foreign policy with any foreign country . . . In Saudi Arabia, clearly the issues of energy dependence, Islam and terrorism and also commercial interests in the past all have their weight.'

The dominance of the intolerant Wahhabis created an atmosphere in which Al-Qaeda thrived. As the clerics wailed against the presence of the infidels blaring out from loudspeakers in the 5,000 mosques of Riyadh (in 1960 there were no more than 8), the message was clear: the expatriates are fair game. For the Islamic insurgents, the foreigners were also targets because the House of Saud was dependent on Western expertise for its survival.

After 9/11 Al-Qaeda switched its attention to the Kingdom. By early 2003, Westerners were regularly the targets of random shootings, and minibuses carrying other foreign workers were being sprayed with gunfire. Sticks of dynamite were being found in shopping malls. The looming war with Iraq stoked the fire with ordinary, young Saudis as the sight and sounds of violence against their fellow Arabs on satellite television ignited their emotions.

The triple suicide bombings in Riyadh on 12 May 2003 that killed 35 people, including 9 insurgents and 7 Americans, was the turning point. That was their 9/11 and from that moment the expatriates took security more seriously and their shopping expeditions in Riyadh involved buying razor wire and surveillance equipment rather than designer clothes.

After years of concealing the threat of militant Islam inside the Kingdom and putting innocent Westerners in jail for the bombings, the House of Saud was forced to act. As usual, it turned to America for help. FBI investigators, including specialists in surveillance, flew to Saudi to work more closely with its security forces in their mission to break up terrorist cells. It was a risky and controversial strategy. The FBI is not the most culturally sensitive agency and often has great difficulty dealing with local US states, let alone Arab governments with prickly senses of sovereignty. And their arrival invoked memories of US troops encroaching on the sacred land in 1991. But the FBI and the mabaheth, the Interior Ministry security police, established a modus operandi in terms of access to crime scenes where forensic evidence needs to be examined. Improvements were made and the names and faces of the 26 most-wanted Al-Qaeda terrorists were published on the Internet and in Saudi newspapers. 'We need to bring people from other countries to work with us jointly, whether it be from Indonesia or Pakistan or Saudi Arabia,' FBI director Robert Mueller told the US Council on Foreign Relations.

But there was a major obstacle: Saudi intelligence agencies were heavily infiltrated and riddled with Al-Qaeda agents, to such an extent that their operations were moved into neighbouring Gulf states. Mabaheth, the organisation responsible for countering Al-Qaeda, was itself penetrated by Al-Qaeda, according to an investigation by *The Times*.[10] As of July 2004, their staff was 80 per cent sympathetic to the Islamic insurgents, said a source with first-hand knowledge of the counter-terrorism unit. He pointed to the fact that many of the 26 most-wanted terrorists were former police and military officers from the Interior Ministry. 'To fight Al-Qaeda, they need to start [recruiting] again from scratch,' said the inside source. 'I am not hopeful the Saudis will do so.'[11]

Although the FBI, CIA, MI6 and Scotland Yard's anti-terrorist squad are certainly working much closer with their Saudi counterparts, they still face obstruction and opposition from the clergy and compromised Saudi security forces. The Saudi internal security budget may have topped $7 billion by 2003, with a virtually open-ended capability to spend on any operation. But for the Al-

Qaeda entryism to be purged, all members of mabaheth would need to be dismissed and then vetted for militant sympathies before being rehired.

Senior Saudi princes maintained publicly that they were winning the war against Al-Qaeda. 'Out of six terrorist cells that have been identified in Saudi Arabia, five have been dismantled either through killings or arrests and the sixth one is in the process of being dismantled,' Prince Turki Al-Faisal, the Saudi ambassador in London and former intelligence chief, told *Channel 4 News* in February 2003.

This capacity for denial was demonstrated a mere three months later when the Al-Qaeda suicide bomb struck in Riyadh. On 9 November 2003, terrorists hit another residential compound in the capital and left 17 non-Saudi Arabs dead. On 21 April 2004, a car bomb exploded outside the General Security building in Riyadh, killing at least four and injuring over 148 people. On 1 May 2004, four armed militants attacked the Yanbu Petrochemical company complex. This was the first time an economic target was attacked, heightening fears that the oil sector could be affected. One Saudi and five foreign workers died. And on 30 May 2004, jihadists went on a 25-hour rampage in Al-Khobar, the heartland of the Kingdom's oil production. The terrorists carefully moved between complexes and offices inhabited by Shell, Lukoil and the Arab Petroleum Investment Corporation. They killed nineteen expatriates and three Saudis.

The latter operation against the oil companies was sophisticated and carefully planned. As Thomas Friedman of the *New York Times* pointed out:

> Surely the most chilling aspect of the latest terrorist attack in Saudi Arabia against foreigners was in reports from the scene about how the Saudi militants tried to capture or kill only the non-Muslims, and let Muslims and Arabs go.

The gunmen told the hostages that they were interested in harming only infidels and Westerners. 'Now where would the terrorists have learned such intolerance and discrimination?' asked Friedman. 'Answer: in the Saudi public school system and religious curriculum.'[12]

In November 2004 the Saudi government boasted that it had virtually defeated the indigenous insurgents. But, as the old Arab saying goes, 'denial is not just a river in Egypt', and Saudi leaders were still deluding themselves that Al-Qaeda was a spent force. On 6 December 2004 their illusions were shattered when five Al-Qaeda agents stormed the US consulate in Jeddah – one of the most heavily protected buildings in the Kingdom – by hurling grenades at the gate. A three-hour firefight broke out. Five Saudi consulate employees and four assailants were killed and several more injured. After taking 17 people hostage, the assailants used them as human shields but were eventually overcome.

Saudi officials blamed 'a deviant group' – their euphemism for Al-Qaeda – but the audacity of attacking such a formidable target shook the government. Two weeks later Osama Bin Laden issued a new videotape urging his supporters to overthrow the House of Saud. In a long speech, he called on ordinary Saudis to topple the regime by protesting in the streets in the manner of 'people power' revolutions elsewhere. To head off a bloody 'armed uprising' by disaffected youth, the Saudi elite had to reform, said Bin Laden.

The violence from May 2003 until December 2004, in which over 80 people were killed, showed that Al-Qaeda were carefully targeting oil companies, installations and Westerners. The police have arrested or killed 17 of the 26 most-wanted Islamic militants and an operational planner has fled the country. Their efforts, however, are impeded by influential clerics praising suicide bombers, some Saudi National Guard members providing inside help to the terrorists, the US invasion of Iraq and an education system which preaches religious intolerance and a culture of death.

The militants are all too aware that the House of Saud is

dependent on oil both for its own wealth and lifestyle but also to ensure that America keeps it in power. After the attack on the oil companies in Khobar in June 2004, Al-Qaeda's former leader in Saudi, Abdul Aziz Al-Muqrin, was delighted because the oil price reached its highest level for 21 years. He declared on the Internet that it was 'a new victory' which 'put the Saudi government in a deep crisis'. That is why the top priority is now the security of the oil fields. Former CIA officers Robert Baer and James Woolsey argue that the biggest terrorist threat comes from a fully loaded 747 flying into the desulphurised towers at the oil refineries at Ras Tannurah, a port on the Gulf. With an output of 4.5 million barrels per day, that would remove vast amounts of oil off the market and send the world economy into chaos. The Saudi rulers are nervously sitting on a keg of dynamite – the oil reserves – and, as a former senior US intelligence official described it, 'They're petrified that somebody's going to light the fuse.'[13]

Publicly, the government argues that the risk of serious damage to oil production by a successful attack is very low. 'At any one time, there are up to 30,000 guards protecting the Kingdom's oil infrastructure, while high-technology surveillance and aircraft patrols are regular and anti-aircraft installations defend key locations,' said Nawaf Obaid, a security consultant to the royal family.[14]

Some UK consultants, like Kevin Rosser of Control Risks, believe that Saudi's multiple ports, pipeline and excess capacity will soften the blow. 'The golden goose is not a sitting duck,' he quipped.[15] But the US appears less convinced, as it has secretly stored nearly 700 million barrels in salt caverns along the Texas and Louisiana coastline – enough to last almost three months and, if released, to bring petrol prices down at a stroke.[16]

The 'terror premium' has certainly made Saudi vulnerable as a major oil exporter. Some analysts now argue that the West should no longer be reliant on the Kingdom, because of new alternative markets like Russia and the Caspian Sea, and that Alaskan oil would give the

US 'energy independence'. And they point out that Saudi Arabia accounts for only 8 per cent of US crude oil anyway, with Canada, Venezuela and Mexico being three of the top four suppliers to the US. 'It doesn't matter where we buy the stuff,' said one former senior defence official. If the West reduced its dependence, say US analysts, the political dividend is that it could at last get tough with the Saudis on terrorism, human rights and corruption.

But the geological and commercial reality is that the Kingdom still controls the international oil markets and wields its black gold as a political instrument. The Saudis not only export more oil than anyone else (about 8 millions barrels a day), fully 25 per cent of the world's proven reserves – 262 billion barrels, no less – lie under the sands of Islam's sacred land. Four neighbours – Iran, Iraq, Kuwait and the United Arab Emirates – each have 10 per cent. Russia, Alaska and Nigeria combined cannot match Saudi. Oil is the Kingdom's secret political weapon. Unlike other countries, Saudi retains several million barrels of surplus capacity on hand for emergencies. In May 2004, Aramco, the state-owned oil company, claimed that it can raise its output above 10 million barrels per day 'rapidly'.[17]

This spare capacity gives the Saudis enormous political and economic power, because they can influence oil prices, almost at will, by simply increasing production. Take Saudi surplus out of the game and the market loses its stability and liquidity. By pumping a few extra million barrels a day, Saudi played a major role during both Gulf Wars and the Iraq–Iran war. Then there is the cost of production. The capital expenses for deep-water drilling in the Gulf of Mexico or lifting oil out of the Caspian Sea is an estimated $6 a barrel, while raising a barrel in Saudi costs barely $1.

Russia has been touted as the new oil superpower. But it has only about 20 per cent of the proven reserves on which the House of Saud sits, needs much of its oil for domestic use, has limited ability to expand output in the medium term and its production and marketing costs are much higher than the Middle East. Other pretenders to the throne are Nigeria, Venezuela and Indonesia. But they are unstable regimes with constant security threats and dogged by political unrest.

The reality is that while the US continues to import nearly 25 per cent of its oil from the Kingdom, the West will overlook – or certainly be complacent about – its citizens being tortured, corrupt arms deals and Saudi support for international terrorism. It is a high price to pay. 'It is a situation that I believe gives another country far too much control over America's national security and economy,' said Senator Bob Graham, former chairman of the Senate Intelligence Committee.[18]

However, the Saudis are equally dependent on the United States – and not just for military and security protection. Its oil revenues from the US are the only way of paying for the royal family's profligate, lavish lifestyle and for funding a growing generation of unemployed youth whose main educational qualification appears to be 'Islamic studies'. The Saudis have, in turn, invested billions in the US – from real-estate by Prince Naif to US Treasury bonds to shares in Apple Computers, News Corporation, Citicorp and AOL-Time Warner – and an estimated $500 billion in cash on deposit in US banks.

The princes did withdraw some $150 billion from the US after 9/11 for fear that their assets would be frozen by a punitive Washington. But that still leaves an estimated $450 billion of Saudi holdings in the US economy, according to Raymond Seitz, vice-chairman of the investment bank Lehman Brothers and a former US ambassador in London.[19] 'Inevitably, when you have Saudi Arabia being portrayed as not cooperating fully with the US [after 9/11], some Saudi investors will panic and leave,' said Prince Al-Waleed Bin Talal in November 2002. Al-Waleed is the world's sixth-richest man; he owns the Savoy Hotel in London and is the largest single international investor in New York. 'Inevitably, some funds will be withdrawn and some assets will be liquidated and moved to other regions of the world.'[20] This would cause a major recession in the US economy, which would be a catastrophe for the House of Saud and its indulgent, extravagant princes.

After failing to diversify its economy, Saudi Arabia remains a hostage to the price of oil, which accounts for 75 per cent of government revenue and 90 per cent of foreign exchange earnings. After the boom of the 1980s, oil prices dropped to historic lows between 1997 and 1999 and the Saudi economy floundered: hard-currency reserves declined, government borrowing increased, the trade imbalance widened and real gross domestic product stagnated. But record crude prices in 2000 suddenly turned round its current account and produced a rare surplus of $14.8 billion. By 2004, export oil revenues were $110 billion for the year (up from $61 billion). Such income and high net foreign assets can sustain the Kingdom's high domestic debt and regular budget deficits. As one Reuters correspondent commented: 'To speak of a bankrupt Saudi Arabia is like saying there is no water in the sea.'[21]

However, the Kingdom does face an economic problem with serious political and security implications: high unemployment of between 20 and 25 per cent. Since 1980 Saudi Arabia's population has exploded from 7 million to 26.7 million (including 7 million foreign workers), thanks to one of the highest birth rates in the world of 3.8 per cent and zero family planning. This has been accentuated by income per capita declining from $19,000 in the early 1980s down to about $7,600. As the economy can no longer afford the welfare net that once guaranteed every Saudi a government job and most of the state revenue still feeds the bloated House of Saud, unemployment has hit the Kingdom hard. For the first time the country is confronted with real poverty, an increasing under-class and vast disparities in wealth between the royal family and ordinary people.

With 60 per cent of the male population under the age of 20, this has produced a growing new generation of bored, disillusioned, unemployed young men. Each year 400,000 of them go straight from university to joblessness. They have been educated to participate in a world only if it is first purified by the Wahhabi creed. As they walk aimlessly through the streets of Riyadh and wander into the mosques, whose clerics issue blood-curdling cries of holy war, young Saudis are vulnerable prey to Al-Qaeda. The recruitment pitch is simplistic but clear: the infidel Americans have stolen the oil wealth in league with the greedy, corrupt House of Saud. Islam has been betrayed. The only answer is jihad. 'Young people feel they have no future,' said Abdulhai, a successful Saudi businessman. 'That is why so many turn to drugs and why it is so easy for religious fanatics to recruit young Saudis and brainwash them into becoming Islamic militants.'[22]

This is reinforced by an absence of alternative views. 'In an increasingly open world, rank-and-file Saudis see events through an increasingly narrow lens. Western news is censored and often simply banned,' argues Robert Baer. 'The Saudis have pioneered the use of Internet filters and blocks. Most Saudis are limited to local newspapers and TV like Al-Jazeera, through which Osama Bin Laden has chosen to distribute his communiqués.'[23]

Since 9/11 sporadic brawls and hooliganism by young people have broken out, during which the crowd shout anti-American and royal family slogans. The government has responded with infrastructure schemes which aim to reduce the country's dependence on foreign labour and force private firms to employ Saudis. But many of them are unqualified to work in a modern economy. As Thomas Friedman of the *New York Times* points out:

> Saudi Arabia will be able to thrive only if it can reform its schools to build young people who can innovate and create wealth from their minds – not just their [oil] wells. That means revamping the overcrowded Saudi universities which right now churn out endless graduates in Islamic studies or liberal arts, but too few with the technical skills a modern economy demands. It also means revamping the Saudi legal system to attract foreign investors to create jobs. That means real transparency, rule of law, independent courts and anti-corruption measures. Without those changes, this country

[Saudi] is going to get poorer and poorer, because 40 per cent of the population is under 14 – meaning that the biggest population bulge has not even hit the labour market yet. This could be dynamite.[24]

The reaction of the House of Saud to the crisis is crucial. But it has also been hit by a population surge: the extended royal family – including all the relatives – now stands at 30,000. In the absence of family planning, this will rise to at least 50,000 in 25 years' time. As they show no sign of relinquishing their privileges and perks or supporting such reform, the House of Saud itself will not just be a huge financial burden but also an obstacle to political stability.

The problem for the reformers is that the high oil price has alleviated the government's economic fears and traditionally that means the regime reverts back to its reactionary habits. The heady days of 2002, when people took to the streets in protest and demonstrations swept across the Eastern Province after the school fire, are long gone. In September 2003, a Saudi dissident, Abdul Al-Tayyar, was arrested and jailed after accusing the government of suppression on Al-Jazeera television. In March 2004, a group of reformists were jailed for calling for a constitutional monarchy. By early 2005, three were still waiting trial. In September 2004, the regime banned all state employees from publicly questioning government policy. And the following month it announced that the long-promised local elections would only cover half of the seats, with women entirely excluded. Few people bothered to register to vote, prompting one columnist to lament that there was more interest in the stock market than in the 'historic' election.[25]

The other impediment is that only Crown Prince Abdullah, one of the few members of the ruling elite untainted by corruption, has reformist instincts. He is often blocked by his half-brothers, notably over allowing women the right to drive. These half-brothers, including Prince Naif, Prince Sultan and Prince Salman (Governor of Riyadh), comprise a stubborn, powerful faction which plots to restrain the

Crown Prince's attempts at enlightenment. They are known as the 'Sudairi Seven' after their mother, Hassa Bin Sudairi, who was the favourite wife of the nation's founder, King Abdul Aziz.

By virtue of experience, ability and age, Crown Prince Abdullah is the heir apparent, but the Sudairis have impeded his accession to the throne while allowing him a leading role in governing the country. They are particularly concerned by his plans to clean up sleaze, perks and corruption and since King Fahd's stroke in 1995 there has been a bitter power struggle inside the family. The battle for succession could be highly disruptive and bloody. 'The Saudis are mentally five minutes away from the tent and they will pull their swords and go for each other,' said a former US ambassador to Saudi.[26]

But other sources believe the family has far too much to lose by prolonged infighting and they will close ranks. 'A deal has already been done,' said a political risk analyst. 'Prince Sultan has agreed that Abdullah will succeed but only on the condition that Sultan succeeds the Crown Prince.'

Some insiders believe that certain members of the Sudairi Seven implicitly support the fanatical Islamic clerics in order to derail even the most incremental changes in the Saudi way of life. This is evident by allowing militant sermons to be broadcast on official, government-owned TV stations. Witness Salah Al-Budayyir in 2003: 'Oh Muslims, preserve the sanctity of Islam and protect Muslim society from being undermined by innovations, superstitions, sins and offences. The enemies of religion – including Christians, atheists and Westernised deviants who ride their bandwagon – continue to wage campaigns against the Islamic nation.' He concluded with a prayer to Allah to support Islam and destroy the enemies of religion.

That sermon was a barely concealed attack on political modernisers like Prince Abdullah, who, a few days earlier, had laid down a tough ultimatum for Islamic extremists to surrender or face death. And the fact that the broadcast was sanctioned at the highest level by Prince Naif should not be underestimated.

Despite this rearguard action, Abdullah has powerful backers in Washington DC who view him as a source of stability and moderation. He is also far from alone inside the House of Saud. In November 2003, Prince Talal Bin Abdul Aziz, a full brother of King Fahd, told the *Sunday Times* that his country's autocratic rulers were paying the price of terrorism for failing to implement democratic reforms. A former finance minister who was forced into exile in the early 1960s after campaigning for change, he said there was no justification in Islamic theology for absolute rule. He added that the prophet Mohammed was a democrat and wanted all people to be equal and happy. 'God asked him to consult the people before action,' said the Prince.[27]

Democracy is also regarded in Washington and London as the solution to Saudi's problems. 'You don't get real economic development without democratisation,' said Ned Walker, former US ambassador to Israel and Egypt who was also a senior diplomat in Riyadh. 'For the long-term stability of the governments in the region, we should encourage democratisation, which means that we have to help them build civil societies in the context of their cultures.'[28]

The unfortunate, inconvenient consequence of holding a popular election is that Osama Bin Laden would be the next president of Saudi Arabia. A Saudi intelligence survey taken in mid-October 2001 of educated professional Saudis between the ages of 25 and 41 concluded that 95 per cent of them supported Bin Laden's cause. When asked by the *New York Times*, the Saudi intelligence chief Prince Nawwaf Bin Abdul Aziz confirmed the existence of the survey but declined to comment on the level of support. He said it was due to anti-American hostility based on their unflinching support for Israel.[29] The support for Bin Laden was verified a year later by Dr Ghazi Al-Gosaibi, then the Saudi ambassador in London, who told *The Spectator*: 'Please don't kick the ambassador out for saying this, but if you go around the Muslim world, you will find the vast majority of people will support Osama Bin Laden and this is more tragic than the [9/11] attack itself. Why would such a crime like this find such support, not just on the streets of Riyadh, but on the streets of Turkey, Tunis and London? It comes down to the question of why people hate America.'[30]

The last time there was an authentic democratic election in an Arab state was in Algeria in late 1991. When it became apparent that the fundamentalists would win an overwhelming majority and impose an Islamic constitution, the military intervened. The country was then plunged into a civil war that killed hundreds of thousands of people. Given the level of support for Al-Qaeda, there is every reason to believe that Saudi would suffer the same fate with the US-trained National Guard 'restoring order'.

As the 'wrong side' would win, it is inconceivable that the House of Saud would authorise an election. Moderate concessions, like more consultative councils, or 'majlis', may placate the Kingdom's merchants and middle classes, but the problem of royal corruption, for example, can only be rectified by an independent judiciary and a return to the rule of law. That will involve tough, brave and decisive leadership by Prince Abdullah rather than a tortuously slow road to political accountability.

Equally, Islamic terrorism can only be dealt with at its roots – rather than retribution after the event, when it is too late. Saudi commentators understand that the causes of terror lie in the schools and universities. Dr Khalil Al-Khalili, a lecturer at Riyadh's main Islamic university, teaches 600 students a year and estimates that more than 50 per cent support Bin Laden. 'We want our young people to be the raw material for a better future,' he said. 'But if they are left with no guidance, with no positive way forward, then yes, they will be the raw material for violence.'[31]

The Al-Qaeda operatives carrying out the bombings in Saudi in 2004 have the same mentality and ideology as the extremists who stormed the Grand Mosque in 1979. If you do not advocate their brand of Wahhabi Islam, then you are an infidel and that gives them the theological licence to kill you. The similarities to Stalin and the show trials of the 1930s and Pol Pot and the genocide of the 1970s are chilling. 'If we as a nation decline to look at the root causes, as we have for the past two decades, it will only be a matter of time before another group with the same ideology springs up,' noted the Saudi writer Raid Qusti in 2004. 'Have we helped create these monsters? Our education system, which does not stress tolerance of other faiths – let alone tolerance of followers of other Islamic schools of thought – is one thing that needs to be re-evaluated from top to bottom. Saudi culture itself and the fact that the majority of us do not accept other lifestyles and impose our own on other people is another.'[32]

One Arabic professor at King Saud University, Hamza Qablan Al-Mozainy, even argues there is a 'culture of death in our schools'. He says that some teachers promote discussions on how dead bodies are prepared for burial because that will show whether the deceased led a 'decadent or righteous life'.[33] It was a subtle justification of jihad.

Since 9/11 such criticism of the religious educational establishment has led to a naked power struggle between the Wahhabists and Crown Prince Abdullah. The religious elite claim they are equal partners in a symbiotic pact with the House of Saud which has been the foundation of the Kingdom since its earliest origins. But the Crown Prince counters that they are mere respected advisers. The Saudi political system must somehow evolve, but a profound cultural schizophrenia prevents the ruling powers that be from agreeing on the details of reform and the speed of its implementation. The result is paralysis, with Abdullah quietly trying to modernise but shackled by the powerful clerics and senior princes. 'Don't rush us,' is Prince Bandar's riposte to calls for modernisation.

Then there is the pressure from across the Atlantic Ocean. 'The royal family is stuck between the religious establishment and the rising generation [of disaffected youth] on the one hand and the US on the other,' said Mai Yamani, of the Royal Institute of International Affairs. 'The US is demanding reforms but Abdullah is seen by the Wahhabi religious establishment and the new breed as compromising himself by talking about normalisation of relations with Israel.'[34]

Fearful for its survival, the House of Saud will always run to the willing arms of the Americans, who accept it as a Faustian pact. For the US government has long known about Saudi Babylon. A secret CIA memo, circulated at the State Department and National Security Council and leaked in 2002, noted how the 'culture of royal excess has ruled over the Kingdom with documented human-rights abuses'. The report added that 'democracy has never been part of the equation' and described the House of Saud as an 'anachronism' that is 'inherently fragile' and that there were 'serious concerns about its long-term stability'.

And yet the US government shows no signs of filing for divorce in its high-risk tempestuous marriage to the Saudi royal family. It justifies its oil-for-security deal with the vast needs of its consumer economy for cheap, plentiful and secure petrol. There are also the equally important strategic benefits in deflecting initially Soviet and, more recently, Iraqi geopolitical ambitions. But this arrangement could still end in calamity as Bin Laden remains at large and Al-Qaeda continues to attack Western military and economic targets.

Confronted with this threat, President Bush has refused to explore energy conservation and alternative sources rather than being held hostage by Saudi oil. During his first administration, Vice-President Cheney dismissed those who supported energy preservation and fuel efficiency as naive and dreary do-gooders. One of those advocates, the *New York Times* columnist Thomas Friedman, responded:

> Well, what would you call a Bush energy policy that keeps America dependent on a medieval monarchy with a king who has lost most of his faculties, where there is virtually no transparency about what's happening, where corruption is rampant, where we have asked all Americans to leave and where the education system is so narrow that its own people

are decrying it as a factory for extremism? Now that's what I call naive, reckless and dangerous.[35]

Al-Qaeda has thrived since 9/11 and continues to maim and murder innocent people in Saudi and elsewhere partly because of US and UK foreign policy. The unwillingness of Western governments to publicly criticise the torture, corruption and greed of the House of Saud and the 2003 Iraq war has fuelled support for Islamic militancy. But there is another major, overlooked factor as to why Al-Qaeda has flourished: the detention, torture and framing of Western expatriates has allowed these home-grown Saudi terrorists to operate with impunity in the Kingdom. Perhaps the worst crime and the most corrupt act is that for nearly three years, while Prince Naif and his secret police locked up and tortured innocent men like Sandy Mitchell, the real killers were allowed to roam the streets of Riyadh and set off car bombs. And the Western governments looked the other way.

NOTES AND REFERENCES

CHAPTER ONE: THE SAUDI INQUISITION

1 For a description of Mabatha Interrogation Centre see *Correspondent: Saudi Arabia – State of Denial*, BBC2, 24 November 2002.

2 The use of torture equipment manufactured by British defence companies was first disclosed by *Dispatches: The Torture Trail*, Channel 4, January 1995.

During a House of Commons debate on 21 January 2004, Bill Rammell, the Foreign Office minister, responded to the revelation that the British detainees were tortured with equipment manufactured in Britain. He told Parliament: 'I am sure that all of us shared the horror and revulsion when that fact was revealed . . . In March 1994 an open, individual export licence was granted for the export of shackles to destinations that included Saudi Arabia. In an announcement to Parliament on 28 July 1997 – under a Labour government – known as "The Torture Statement", the then foreign secretary Robin Cook committed the government to taking the necessary measures to prevent the export or transhipment from the UK of leg irons, gang chains and shackles – excluding normal handcuffs – and electric-shock belts designed for the restraint of human beings . . . Saudi Arabia was specifically removed as a destination on the Export Licence on 25 July 1997 . . . All other things being equal, similar equipment could not be exported today.' (House of Commons, *Hansard*: 'Human Rights (Saudi Arabia)', 21 January 2001.)

3 Margarette Driscoll, *Sunday Times*, 7 September 2003.

CHAPTER TWO: CAUGHT IN AL-QAEDA'S WAVE OF TERROR

1 Saïd, p. 219.

2 Interview with Ain Al-Yaqeen, *Saudi News Magazine*, 29 November 2002.

3 Paul Kelso and David Pallister, *The Guardian*, 30 January 2002.

4 *Ibid.*

5 *Frontline Scotland: Riddle in the Sands*, BBC1 Scotland, 3 April 2001.

6 *Dispatches: The Secrets of the Saudi State*, Channel 4, 5 March 2002.

7 Baer, p. 25.

8 Seymour Hersh, *The New Yorker*, 22 October 2001.

9 Brian Whitaker, *The Guardian*, 14 February 2003.

10 *Dispatches: The Secrets of the Saudi State*, Channel 4, 5 March 2002.

11 Before he married Noi, Sandy went out with a girl whom his flatmate was attracted to at the time. Infuriated, his flatmate placed a frozen kipper in Sandy's bed. When Sandy related this tale to his friends at the Empire Club, he was instantly nicknamed Kipper.

12 *Frontline Scotland: Riddle in the Sands*, BBC1 Scotland, 3 April 2001.

13 *Ibid.*

14 Paul Kelso and David Pallister, *The Guardian*, 9 May 2003.

15 *Al-Jazeera* (Arabic Newspaper), 1 October 2002.

16 *Frontline Scotland: Riddle in the Sands*, BBC1 Scotland, 3 April 2001.

17 *Al-Riyadh*, 5 February 2001.

18 Mackey, p. 279.

19 Philip Johnston and Caroline Davies, *Telegraph*, 14 March 2003.

20 Caroline Davies, *Telegraph*, 13 October 2001.

21 *Ibid.*

22 Mackey, p. 270.

CHAPTER THREE: A SECRET DEATH SENTENCE

1 Paul Kelso, *The Guardian*, 28 February 2002.

2 *Ibid.*

3 Mike Hornby, *Liverpool Daily Post*, November 2003.

4 James Lee was an engineer and landlord of the Leg's Arms, an illicit bar on a Westerners-only compound in Riyadh. He was arrested on 28 March 2001. He later appeared on Saudi state television to admit his role in the bombing campaign. He was sentenced to 12 years in jail.

5 *Channel 4 News*, 20 February 2003.

CHAPTER FOUR: SLEEPING WITH THE ENEMY

1 See articles by Irwin Stelzer in the *Sunday Times*, 17 March 2002; 11 August 2002; 8 December 2002; 24 August 2003.

2 Kenneth Pollack, *Foreign Affairs*, July/August 2003.

3 *Ibid.*

4 John R. Bradley, *Washington Times*, 5 February 2004.

5 Gold, pp. 57–8.

6 *Ibid.*

7 *Ibid.*

8 *Storyville: The House of Saud*, BBC3, produced and directed by Jihan El-Tahri, Alegria and Rain Media Productions, 2 September 2004.

9 *Ibid.*

10 Baer, p. 77.

11 *Ibid.*, pp. 77–8.

12 *Ibid.*, p. 79.

13 *Ibid.*

14 *Ibid.*, p. 80.

15 *Storyville: The House of Saud*, BBC3, produced and directed by Jihan El-Tahri, Alegria and Rain Media Productions, 2 September 2004.

16 *Ibid.*

17 *Ibid.*

18 *Ibid.*

19 *Ibid.*

20 Mackey, p. 297.

21 *Storyville: The House of Saud*, BBC3, produced and directed by Jihan El-Tahri, Alegria and Rain Media Productions, 2 September 2004.

22 Richard Brooks, *Sunday Times*, 8 February 2004.

23 *Storyville: The House of Saud*, BBC3, produced and directed by Jihan El-Tahri, Alegria and Rain Media Productions, 2 September 2004.

24 *Ibid.*

25 *Ibid.*

26 Fareed Zakaria, *Sunday Times*, 27 June 2004. Originally published in *Newsweek*.

27 *Storyville: The House of Saud*, BBC3, produced and directed by Jihan El-Tahri, Alegria and Rain Media Productions, 2 September 2004.

28 Dr Saad Al-Fagih, *The Guardian*, 29 January 2002.

29 Report by Council on Foreign Relations, October 2002.

30 John R. Bradley, *Washington Times*, 11 February 2004.

31 *Frontline*, Interview by Lowell Bergman, PBS, September 2001.

32 *Ibid.*

33 *Ibid.*

34 *Ibid.*

35 Steven Pollard, *The Times*, 18 August 2003.

36 Baer, p. 127.

37 Seymour Hersh, *The New Yorker*, 22 October 2001.

38 Daniel Benjamin and Steven Simon, pp. 306–7.

39 *Ibid.*, p. 287.

40 'Intelligence Newsletter, 23 November 1995'. Quoted in Unger, p. 181.

41 *Middle East Quarterly*, Volume 5, Number 3, September 1998.

42 Interview with *Al-Riyadh*, 23 June 2001.

43 *Frontline*, Interview by Lowell Bergman, PBS, September 2001.

44 Roula Khalaf, *Financial Times*, 1 November 2003.

45 Jason Burke, *The Guardian*, 28 October 2001.

46 *Ibid.*

47 Interview on *Breakfast with Frost*, BBC2, 28 February 2005.

48 *Frontline: House of Saud*, PBS, 23 November 2004.

49 Graham, p. 202.

50 *Ibid.*, p. 216.

51 Simon Tisdall, *The Guardian*, 28 November 2002.

52 Baer, p. 15.

53 Dr Al-Gosaibi, p. 111.

54 Baer, p. 44.

CHAPTER FIVE: A ROYAL PERCENTAGE

1 Michael Isikoff, *Newsweek*, 12 April 2004; Nora Boustany and Terence O'Hara, *Washington Post*, 10 June 2004.

2 *Ibid.*

3 Michael Isikoff, *Newsweek*, 12 April 2004.

4 Mackey, p. 212.

5 *Ibid.*, pp. 212–3.

6 *Frontline: House of Saud*, PBS, 23 November 2004.

7 *Middle East Quarterly*, Volume 5, Number 3, September 1998.

8 *Ibid.*

9 James Roumeliotis and Lela Mrakovic, *Yacht Vacations and Charters*, 20 July 2004.

10 David Pallister, Owen Bowcott and Alex Bellos, *The Guardian*, 17 July 2002.

11 *Ibid.*

12 Baer, p. 23.

13 Saïd, p. 55.

14 Scott McLeod, *Time Magazine*, 4 April 2002.

15 Mackey, p. 214.

16 Seymour Hersh, *The New Yorker*, 22 October 2001.

17 *Ibid.*

18 Baer, p. 172.

19 Seymour Hersh, *The New Yorker*, 22 October 2001.

20 *Middle East Quarterly*, Volume 5, Number 3, September 1998.

21 *Ibid.*

22 Baer, p. 154.

23 *Middle East Quarterly*, Volume 5, Number 3, September 1998.

24 *Los Angeles Times*, 3 July 1995; *Los Angeles Times*, 28 March 1996.

25 *Ibid.*

26 Baer, p. 173.

27 Rob Evans and David Leigh, *The Guardian*, 18 February 2005.

CHAPTER SIX: THE DEAL

1 Paul Kelso, *The Guardian*, 31 January 2002; Adam Lusher, *Sunday Telegraph*, 11 May 2003.

2 Adam Lusher, *Sunday Telegraph*, 11 May 2003.

3 House of Commons, *Hansard*, Column 942, 1 May 2002.

4 Lecture at Royal Institute of International Affairs, Chatham House, 8 November 2004.

5 Quoted in David Leigh, *The Guardian*, 1 February 2002.

6 *Left to Rot*, BBC1 Scotland, 13 May 2003.

7 Richard Norton-Taylor and David Pallister, *The Guardian*, 31 January 2002.

8 *Left to Rot*, BBC1 Scotland, 13 May 2003.

9 Neil Mackay, *Glasgow Sunday Herald*, 20 April 2003.

10 *Left to Rot*, BBC1 Scotland, 13 May 2003.

11 *Ibid.*

12 House of Commons, *Hansard*, Column 489, 21 January 2004.

13 Quoted in speech by Sir David Gore-Booth, former British ambassador to Saudi Arabia, to *Le Cercle*, 20 June 2003, Salzburg.

14 House of Commons, *Hansard*, Column 45, 3 June 2003.

15 House of Commons, *Hansard*, Column 138, 18 June 2003.

16 *Ibid.*

17 Neil Mackay, *Glasgow Sunday Herald*, 20 April 2003.

18 *The Today Programme*, BBC Radio 4, 29 April 2002.

19 House of Commons Foreign Affairs Select Committee, First Report, Session 1999–2000, paragraphs 15–16. Quoted in Curtis, p. 259.

20 Curtis, p. 253.

21 *Ibid.*, pp. 256, 261.

22 De la Billiere, p.116. Quoted in Curtis, pp. 253–4.

23 Deborah Orr, *The Independent*, 26 July 2003.

24 *The Guardian*, January 1996.

25 Baer, p. 23.

26 Michael Isikoff and Mark Hosenball, *Newsweek*, 4 May 2003.

27 Sean O'Neill, *The Times*, 5 October 2004.

28 *The Independent*, 6 January 1996.

29 Short, p. 120.

30 Kampfner, p. 170.

31 Cook, diary entry for 19 December 2001, p. 72.

32 Short, p. 119.

33 *Ibid.*

34 *Ibid.*

35 John Newhouse, *The New Yorker*, 9 June 1986.

36 Baer, p. 174.

37 *The Money Programme: Bribing for Britain?*, BBC2, 5 October 2004.

38 David Leigh and Rob Evans, *The Guardian*, 4 May 2004.

39 Robert Winnett and David Leppard, *Sunday Times*, 25 July 2004.

40 Baer, pp. 174–5.

41 Alexander Nicoll, *Financial Times*, 26 February 1999.

42 *The Money Programme: Bribing for Britain?*, BBC2, 5 October 2004.

43 House of Commons, *Hansard*, Column 1346, 24 May 2004.

44 *The Money Programme: Bribing for Britain?*, BBC2, 5 October 2004.

45 *Ibid.*

46 David Leigh and Rob Evans, *The Guardian*, 5 May 2004.

47 House of Commons, Minutes of Evidence taken before Defence Committee, 5 May 2004.

48 Dominic O'Connell, *Sunday Times*, 14 November 2004.

49 Dominic O'Connell, *Sunday Times*, 14 September 2003.

50 Rob Evans and David Leigh, *The Guardian*, 27 November 2003; 14 December 2004.

CHAPTER SEVEN: RELEASED BY AL-QAEDA

1 *Frontline: House of Saud*, PBS, 23 November 2004.

2 Dana Priest and Susan Schmidt, *Washington Post*, 18 May 2003.

3 *Frontline: House of Saud*, PBS, 23 November 2004.

4 Douglas Jehl, *New York Times*, 10 November 2004.

5 Fareed Zakaria, *Sunday Times*, 27 June 2004. Originally published in *Newsweek*.

6 *Left to Rot*, BBC1 Scotland, 13 May 2003.

7 House of Commons, *Hansard*, Column 135, 18 June 2003.

8 *Ibid.*, Column 136.

9 Don Van Natta and Tim Golden, *New York Times*, 4 July 2004.

10 Emma Harris, *Halifax Courier*, 25 November 2003.

11 *Arab News*, 14 October 2003.

12 *The World This Weekend*, Interview, BBC Radio 4, 17 August 2003.

13 House of Commons, *Hansard*, Column 483, 21 January 2004.

CHAPTER EIGHT: A HOSTAGE TO SAUDI OIL

1 Robin Allen, *Financial Times*, 9 November 2002.

2 Paul Harris, Nick Pelham and Martin Bright, *The Observer*, 28 July 2002.

3 Giles Whittell, *The Times*, 14 August 2002; Christopher Dickey and Rod Nordland, *Newsweek*, 15 July 2002.

4 Gold, p. 166.

5 Edward Pilkington, *The Guardian*, 2 July 2002.

6 'Saudi Publications on Hate Ideology', report by The Freedom House, Washington DC, February 2005.

7 *Frontline: House of Saud*, PBS, 23 November 2004.

8 Human Rights Watch, *Human Rights in Saudi Arabia: A Deafening Silence*, December 2001.

9 Robin Allen, *Financial Times*, 9 November 2002.

10 Richard Beeston, Daniel McGrory, Rana Sabbagh-Gargou, *The Times*, 5 July 2004.

11 *Ibid.*

12 Thomas Friedman, *New York Times*, 3 June 2004.

13 Seymour Hersh, *The New Yorker*, 22 October 2001.

14 *Jane's Intelligence Review*, June 2004.

15 *The Economist*, 27 May 2004.

16 Jane Padgham, *London Evening Standard*, 3 June 2004.

17 *The Economist*, 27 May 2004.

18 Graham, p. 106.

19 John Rossant, *Business Week*, 9 September 2002; Robert Kaiser, *Washington Post*, 18 February 2002.

20 Nic Hopkins, *The Times*, 29 November 2002. Prince Al-Waleed's investments as of November 2002 include EuroDisney, Apple Computers, Planet Hollywood, AOL Time Warner, Citigroup, Motorola and News Corporation.

21 Quoted in speech by Sir David Gore-Booth, former British ambassador to Saudi Arabia, to *Le Cercle*, 20 June 2003, Salzburg.

22 Richard Beeston, *The Times*, 18 July 2003.

23 Baer, p. 161.

24 Thomas Friedman, *New York Times*, 20 February 2002.

25 *The Economist*, 9 December 2004.

26 Stuart Wavell, *Sunday Times*, 21 October 2001.

27 Irene Hell and John R. Bradley, *Sunday Times*, 16 November 2003.

28 *National Journal*, 6 October 2001.

29 Elaine Scislino, *New York Times*, 27 January 2002.

30 Boris Johnson, *The Spectator*, 20 September 2002.

31 Edward Pilkington, *The Guardian*, 17 July 2002.

32 *Arab News*, Saudi English-language newspaper column quoted in *New York Times*, 3 June 2004.

33 Al-Watan, quoted in *New York Times*, 3 June 2004.

34 Thomas Friedman, *New York Times*, 3 June 2004.

35 *Ibid.*

BIBLIOGRAPHY

Al-Fagih, Dr Saad, *The Guardian*, 29 January 2002

Al-Gosaibi, Dr Ghazi A., *The Gulf Crisis: An Attempt to Understand*, Columbia University Press, Columbia, 1993

Al-Jazeera (Arabic Newspaper), 1 October 2002

Al-Riyadh, 5 February 2001; 23 June 2001

Al-Yaqeen, Ain, *Saudi News Magazine*, 29 November 2002

Allen, Robin, *Financial Times*, 9 November 2002

Arab News, 14 October 2003

Baer, Robert, *Sleeping With the Devil*, Crown Publishers, New York, 2003

Beeston, Richard, *The Times*, 18 July 2003

Beeston, Richard, Daniel McGrory and Rana Sabbagh-Gargou, *The Times*, 5 July 2004

Benjamin, Daniel and Steven Simon, *The Age of Sacred Terror*, Random House, New York, 2002

de la Billiere, Sir Peter, *Storm Command: A Personal Account of the Gulf War*, Harper Collins, London, 1993

Boustany, Nora and Terence O'Hara, *Washington Post*, 10 June 2004

BIBLIOGRAPHY

Bradley, John R., *Washington Times*, 5 February 2004; 11 February 2004

Breakfast with Frost, BBC2, 28 February 2005

Brooks, Richard, *Sunday Times*, 8 February 2004

Burke, Jason, *The Guardian*, 28 October 2001

Channel 4 News, 20 February 2003

Cook, Robin, *The Point of Departure*, Simon and Schuster, London, 2003

Correspondent: Saudi Arabia: State of Denial, BBC2, 24 November 2002

Council on Foreign Relations, Report, October 2002

Curtis, Mark, *Web of Deceit: Britain's Real Role in the World*, Vintage, London, 2003

Davies, Caroline, *The Telegraph*, 13 October 2001

Dickey, Christopher and Rod Nordland, *Newsweek*, 15 July 2002

Dispatches: The Torture Trail, Channel 4, January 1995

Dispatches: The Secrets of the Saudi State, Channel 4, 5 March 2002

Driscoll, Margarette, *Sunday Times*, 7 September 2003

The Economist, 27 May 2004; 9 December 2004

Evans, Rob and David Leigh, *The Guardian*, 27 November 2003; 14 December 2004; 18 February 2005

Fouda, Yosri and Nick Fielding, *Masterminds of Terror*, Mainstream, Edinburgh, 2003

The Freedom House, 'Saudi Publications on Hate Ideology', Washington DC, February 2005

Friedman, Thomas, *New York Times*, 20 February 2002; 3 June 2004

Frontline: House of Saud, PBS, 23 November 2004

Frontline, Prince Bandar, interviewed by Lowell Bergman, PBS, September 2001

Frontline Scotland: Riddle in the Sands, BBC1 Scotland, 3 April 2001

Gold, Dore, *Hatred's Kingdom*, Regenery Publishing, Washington, 2003

Gore-Booth, Sir David, speech to *Le Cercle*, 20 June 2003, Salzburg

Graham, Senator Bob, *Intelligence Matters: The CIA, the FBI, Saudi*

Arabia, and the Failure of America's War on Terror, Random House, New York, 2004

Harris, Emma, *Halifax Courier*, 25 November 2003

Harris, Paul, Nick Pelham and Martin Bright, *The Observer*, 28 July 2002

Hell, Irene and John Bradley, *Sunday Times*, 16 November 2003

Hersh, Seymour, *The New Yorker*, 22 October 2001

Holden, David and Richard Johns, *The House of Saud: The Rise and Rule of the Most Powerful Dynasty in the Arab World*, Holt, Rinehart and Winston, New York, 1981

Hopkins, Nic, *The Times*, 29 November 2002

Hornby, Mike, *Liverpool Daily Post*, November 2003

House of Commons, Foreign Affairs Select Committee, First Report, Session 1999–2000

House of Commons, *Hansard*, 'Human Rights (Saudi Arabia)', 21 January 2004

House of Commons, *Hansard*, Question to the Prime Minister by John Lyons, 1 May 2002

House of Commons, *Hansard*, 'British Prisoners (Saudi Arabia)', 3 June 2003

House of Commons, *Hansard*, 'Mr Sandy Mitchell', 18 June 2003

House of Commons, *Hansard*, 'Human Rights (Saudi Arabia)', 21 January 2004

House of Commons, *Hansard*, Commons Written Answers: Al-Yamamah Contracts, 24 May 2004

House of Commons, Minutes of Evidence taken before Defence Committee, 5 May 2004

Human Rights Watch, *Human Rights in Saudi Arabia: A Deafening Silence*, December 2001

The Independent, 6 January 1996

Isikoff, Michael, *Newsweek*, 12 April 2004

Isikoff, Michael and Mark Hosenball, *Newsweek*, 4 May 2003

Jane's Intelligence Review, June 2004

Jehl, Douglas, *New York Times*, 10 November 2004

Johnson, Boris, *The Spectator*, 20 September 2002

Johnston, Philip and Caroline Davies, *The Telegraph*, 14 March 2003

Kaiser, Robert, *Washington Post*, 18 February 2002

Kampfner, John, *Blair's Wars*, Simon and Schuster, London, 2004

Kelso, Paul, *The Guardian*, 31 January 2002; 28 February 2002

Kelso, Paul and David Pallister, *The Guardian*, 30 January 2002; 9 May 2003

Khalaf, Roula, *Financial Times*, 1 November 2003

Lacey, Robert, *The Kingdom: Arabia and the House of Saud*, Avon Books, New York, 1981

Left to Rot, BBC1 Scotland, 13 May 2003

Leigh, David, *The Guardian*, 1 February 2002

Leigh, David and Rob Evans, *The Guardian*, 4 May 2004; 5 May 2004

Los Angeles Times, 3 July 1995; 28 March 1996

Lusher, Adam, *Sunday Telegraph*, 11 May 2003

Mackay, Neil, *Glasgow Sunday Herald*, 20 April 2003

Mackey, Sandra, *The Saudis: Inside the Desert Kingdom*, Norton, New York, 2002

McLeod, Scott, *Time Magazine*, 4 April 2002

Middle East Quarterly, Volume 5, Number 3, September 1998

The Money Programme: Bribing For Britain?, BBC2, 5 October 2004

Murray, Craig, Lecture at Royal Institute of International Affairs, Chatham House, 8 November 2004

National Journal, 6 October 2001

Newhouse, John, *The New Yorker*, 9 June 1986

New York Times, 3 June 2004

Nicoll, Alexander, *Financial Times*, 26 February 1999

Norton-Taylor, Richard and David Pallister, *The Guardian*, 31 January 2002

O'Connell, Dominic, *Sunday Times*, 14 September 2003; 14 November 2004

O'Neill, Sean, *The Times*, 5 October 2004

Orr, Deborah, *The Independent*, 26 July 2003

Padgham, Jane, *London Evening Standard*, 3 June 2004

Pallister, David, Owen Bowcott and Alex Bellos, *The Guardian*, 17 July 2002

Pilkington, Edward, *The Guardian*, 2 July 2002; 17 July 2002

Pollack, Kenneth, *Foreign Affairs*, July/August 2003

Pollard, Steven, *The Times*, 18 August 2003

Priest, Dana and Susan Schmidt, *Washington Post*, 18 May 2003

Rossant, John, *Business Week*, 9 September 2002

Roumeliotis, James and Lela Mrakovic, *Yacht Vacations and Charters*, 20 July 2004

Saïd, K. Aburish, *The Rise, Corruption and Coming Fall of the House of Saud*, Bloomsbury, London, 1995

Schwartz, Stephen, *The Two Faces of Islam: The House of Saud from Tradition to Terror*, Double Day, New York, 2002

Scislino, Elaine, *New York Times*, 27 January 2002

Short, Clare, *An Honourable Deception? New Labour, Iraq and the Misuse of Power*, Simon and Schuster, London, 2004

Stelzer, Irwin, *Sunday Times*, 17 March 2002; 11 August 2002; 8 December 2002; 24 August 2003

Storyville: The House of Saud, BBC3, produced and directed by Jihan El-Tahri, Alegria and Rain Media Productions, 2 September 2004

Tisdall, Simon, *The Guardian*, 28 November 2002

The Today Programme, BBC Radio 4, 29 April 2002

Unger, Craig, *House of Bush, House of Saud*, Scribner, New York, 2004

Van Natta, Don and Tim Golden, *New York Times*, 4 July 2004

Wavell, Stuart, *Sunday Times*, 21 October 2001

Whitaker, Brian, *The Guardian*, 14 February 2001

Whittell, Giles, *The Times*, 14 August 2002

Winnett, Robert and David Leppard, *Sunday Times*, 25 July 2004

The World This Weekend, BBC Radio 4, 17 August 2003

Zakaria, Fareed, *Sunday Times*, 27 June 2004

INDEX

235

SAUDI BABYLON